RACE *and* DISPLACEMENT

RACE *and* DISPLACEMENT

Nation, Migration, and Identity in the Twenty-First Century

EDITED BY MAHA MAROUAN
AND MERINDA SIMMONS

FOREWORD BY HOUSTON A. BAKER JR.
INTRODUCTION BY PHILIP D. BEIDLER
AFTERWORD BY TRUDIER HARRIS

THE UNIVERSITY OF ALABAMA PRESS
Tuscaloosa

Manufactured in the United States of America

Typeface: Minion and Goudy Old Style

Cover photograph: *The Underground Railroad*, Charles T. Webber, 1893. Cincinnati Art Museum.
Cover design: Michele Myatt-Quinn

∞

The paper on which this book is printed meets the minimum requirements of American National Standard for Information Sciences—Permanence of Paper for Printed Library Materials, ANSI Z39.48-1984.

Library of Congress Cataloging-in-Publication Data

Race and displacement : nation, migration, and identity in the twenty-first century / edited by Maha Marouan and Merinda Simmons ; foreword by Houston A. Baker Jr. ; introduction by Philip D. Beidler ; afterwod by Trudier Harris.
pages cm
ISBN 978-0-8173-1801-7 (trade cloth : alk. paper) — ISBN 978-0-8173-8679-5 (e book) 1. Race relations in literature. 2. Refugees in literature. 3. Culture conflict in literature. 4. Displacement (Psychology) in literature. I. Marouan, Maha, 1975– editor of compilation. II. Simmons, Merinda, 1981– editor of compilation.
PN56.R16R33 2013
809'.933552—dc23

2013013862

Contents

Foreword

Houston A. Baker Jr.

> I sensed, too, that the Southern scheme of oppression was but an appendage of a far vaster and in many respects more ruthless and impersonal commodity-profit machine.
>
> —Richard Wright, "How Bigger Was Born"

> African existence is neither a linear time nor a simple sequence in which each moment effaces, annuls, and replaces those that preceded it, to the point where a single age exists within society. This time is not a series but an *interlocking* of presents, pasts, and futures.
>
> —Achille Mbembe, *On the Postcolony*

The interlocutor in Robert Hayden's "Middle Passage" declares:

> Deep in the festering hold thy father lies,
> of his bones New England pews are made,
> those are altar lights that were his eyes. (1997)

Hayden's lines represent what Caribbean writer Edouard Glissant calls the "point of entanglement" (1999, 15). For Glissant the point of entanglement is a multilayered space of conjuncture, a collective unconscious where structures of memory and feeling collage. In "Middle Passage," discourses and temporalities are polyvalent. Ocean depths, like the unconscious they haunt, are plumbed. Expressive cultures cross. The lines echo, yet revise, *The Tempest*'s "Full fathom five thy father lies." We are, thus, confronted by the phantasmagoria, the memory and desire, of the transatlantic slave trade. Hayden's poem carries us not only to the "festering hold" of the trade, but also to its fountainhead: "New England pews." The pews are synecdoche for *Christian capitalism,* an oxymoronic capitalism, a "holy avariciousness" that was a prime mover and sanction for political, mercantile, manufacturing, and exchange relationships that devastated Africa and compromised, beyond apology or revision, the ethics of the Enlightenment. The transatlantic trade violently displaced millions of Africans from complex, stable societies and transported them into New World plantation slavery. In its barbarous operations, the trade gave birth to race. In *The Slave Ship: A Human History,* scholar Marcus Rediker writes:

> Sailors . . . "produced" slaves within the ship as factory, doubling their economic value as they moved them from a market on the eastern Atlantic to one on the West and helping to create the labor power that animated a growing world economy. . . . In producing workers for the plantation the ship-factory also produced "race." At the beginning of the Middle Passage, captains hired a motley crew of sailors, who would, on the coast of Africa, become "whitemen." At the beginning of the Middle Passage, captains loaded on board the vessel a multiethnic collection of Africans who would, in the American port, become "black people" or a "negro race." (2007, 10, 40)

Fictions of *race* were, and remain, by-products of greed disguised as Christian mission. Novelist Chinua Achebe's *Things Fall Apart* narrates the process perfectly. First come the missionaries. They anoint the path. There follow magistrates, merchants, and marauders of enslavement and colonization. A venerable adage reads: "When the missionaries came, we had the land; they had the Bible. When they departed, we had the Bible; they had the land."

The University of Alabama symposium titled "Race and Displacement" (Tuscaloosa, October 1–3, 2009) was dedicated to scholarly investigation of global, historical, and present-day manifestations of violent dispossessions and constructions of race like the transatlantic slave trade.[1] The following pages present outcomes of that symposium. Where *race* and *displacement* are concerned, the latitude of the symposium's presentations was potentially infinite. Therefore, it may seem a narrow course for a foreword to confine itself to the transatlantic trade and, as a corollary, to invoke diaspora studies as a privileged form of intellectual address. Let it be clear from the outset, however, that the "Race and Displacement" symposium and its investigations were in no way narrow in compass or limited in scope. It seems a given that to confine scholarly inquiry devoted to race and displacement exclusively to the familiar dichotomy "the West and the rest of us" is to beg critical questions and miss the global operations of race and displacement that are beyond such a dichotomy. Race and displacement have had devastating consequences in Darfur, Palestine, Turkey, India, the Balkans, Rwanda, and other venues.

However, narrowing the focus of a foreword to the transatlantic trade and its diaspora provides a window on New World plantation economies. It also facilitates attention to expressive cultural resonances that record, respond to, and resist the exploitation and confinement of such plantation economies. One of the most accomplished exemplars of such responsive expressivity is Richard Wright. Race and displacement are hallmarks of Wright's corpus. He conscientiously traces their effects in his autobiographical *Black Boy* as well as his folk history *12 Million Black Voices*. No one has better represented the displacement and brutal "push factors" that drove southern blacks from rack-rent plantation abjection into claustrophobic northern urban systems of white ownership and control. Wright brilliantly fathomed the connections between Enlightenment fictions and racial abjection. He knew racial brutality and impoverishment were global and *enduring*. They constitute their own *longue durée*. Born on a plantation near Natchez, Mississippi, in 1908, Richard Wright chronicled the New World consequences of the transatlantic trade.

Wright's childhood was a series of interruptions. The abject poverty of black southern life made sharecropping exploitation and white violence the enforceable "ethics of living Jim Crow." Driven by poverty to seek a better life for his family, Nathan Wright insisted on migrating from plantation economics to southern urban existence in Memphis, Tennessee. But the lures of Memphis captivated Nathan, and the result was family dissolution. An orphaned existence followed for Richard and his younger brother when their mother Ella could no longer support the household.

Eventually fleeing the South altogether, Wright dreamed of breathing space and clarity in a black settlement in the North. His expectations were pure *desire* born of dread and stolen literacy. Wright's reading, and the new habits of mind it created, produced an outlaw ache and rebellious determination. He would, by any means necessary, *displace himself* from the ethics of Jim Crow and seek a liberating human community elsewhere, a fellowship bonded by intellectual purpose and common cause. He dreamed that such a space might be a northern *black community*.

What Wright discovered on arrival in Chicago, however, was the urban equivalent of the slave ship's "festering hold." Blacks lived badly. In the Windy City, the black majority was housed in the "zone," which the urban sociologist Robert Park et al. describe as a site of smokestacks, ashes, deteriorating housing, dehumanizing population density, crime, vermin, violence, and disease (Park, Burgess, and McKenzie 1926).[2] Psychologically, there was no black or human clarity to tap into. From Wright's stunned, displaced, racial, and radical perspective, Chicago's northern urban black populace seemed "locked down," financially blasted, and psychologically bereft of any sense of common purpose. Black intellectual and resistive impulses of racial advancement seemed erased by alienating white, urban economies. There was, to be sure, a cadre of black professionals and businessmen, some of them tracing a genealogy of family accomplishment and acquisition of more than a century. But the fiscal resources of the group as a whole were pitifully disproportionate to the wealth and power of even the lowest echelon of what today is the Forbes 400. Their cultural and economic capital was a pittance and scarcely philanthropic in its dedication. In his scathing critique *The Mis-Education of the Negro,* Carter G. Woodson (1933) fully analyzes the inefficacy of what W. E. B. DuBois calls the "Talented Tenth."[3] The community and purpose Wright sought seemed bitterly denied by the city and its "Bosses of the Buildings." It was Wright's comprehension of the dynamics and causes of the virtually imprisoned and comatose state of mid-twentieth-century urban blackness that erupted into his novel *Native Son.*

Published in 1940, *Native Son* was an instant global success. It has maintained canonical status to the present. Briefly, one might suggest that *Native Son* is an ethical, expressive, resistive *explication* of the transatlantic slave trade written as a novel of black urban existence. It is situated, that is to say, at the point of diasporic displacement and strategic entanglement. Dominant in Wright's novel are cross-temporal spirits of the unconscious. They find focus in matters of ownership and estate. *Native Son* brings scintillatingly to twentieth-century attention the consequences attendant upon ship captains and missionaries bearing Christianity as prelude to the appropriation of land and bodies. *Real estate* (in *longue durée*) is the beating, thematic heart of Wright's urban masterpiece.

Dalton Real Estate, the company that holds controlling interest in the South Side Real Estate Company (the Thomases' landlord), is the transatlantic trade's "charter company" *recidivus,* an urban variation of plantation exploitation and mastery. Boris A. Max is the defense attorney for Bigger Thomas, Wright's protagonist, who has been indicted for the murder of Mary Dalton. Max demands of Mr. Dalton: "Now Mr. Dalton, it has been said that you donate millions of dollars to educate Negroes. Why is it that you exact an exorbitant rent of eight dollars per week from the Thomas family for one unventilated, rat-infested room in which four people eat and sleep?" (Wright 1940, 326).[4] Later, Max demands: "Mr. Dalton, do you think that the terrible conditions under which the Thomas family lived in one of your houses may in some way be related to the death of your daughter?" (328). Bigger has smothered Mary Dalton in her bedroom, to which he has carried her because she is too inebriated to walk. He places a pillow over her head to silence her, fearing Mrs. Dalton will discover his presence as "criminal" in the girl's bedroom.

Mr. Dalton is stunned beyond comprehension by Max's questions. They seem to shake him, no matter how briefly, from his conviction that he is a man of "ethics," that he follows an "acceptable" economic law of "supply and demand." He considers the ghettoization of blacks as natural as his own occupancy of a mansion on Drexel Boulevard. "Well," he says, "I think Negroes are happier when they're together" (Wright 1940, 327). Devoted singly to capital profits, Mr. Dalton might, through ghostly ventriloquisms of the transatlantic, have said: "I think the festering hold is where they belong. Certainly that is where my supply of them brings the greatest demand." His *real* estate is racial terror and violent incarceration of a "raced" people. Tragically, but predictably, Mr. Dalton's faux Christian philanthropy of sending Ping-Pong tables to the ghetto and responding to Negro appeals for educational funding cannot forestall the exacting retribution of *chattel violence.* Murder is the return from the *real* world.

No one, of course, could have predicted from Richard Wright the remarkably executed and psychologically resonant representation of race and displacement that is *Native Son.* He was the son of an illiterate sharecropper expected by "men of wealth and property," as attorney Max phrases the matter (Wright 1940, 390), to spend his life stoop shouldered, slack mouthed, and dumber than a mule. But like many thousands gone before, Richard Wright tapped into the unconscious created by the transatlantic, that point of opaque entanglement producing orders of understanding that will provide work for diaspora studies for countless years to come. Race and displacement produce striking analytical and expressive returns. Brokers of global real estate should always wear more than one steel helmet.[5]

If we pause Wright's career at *Native Son* for the sake of concision, we can suggest that what he captures and forecasts about the displacement of "the wretched of the earth"—denied formal employment, decent housing, and a living wage—is bleakly manifest in the state of our planet in the twenty-first century. The Thomas family lives in a slum profitably and corporately under the executive aegis of *real estate* with its transatlantic echoes. In *Planet of Slums,* Mike Davis writes: "Altogether, the global informal working class (overlapping with but non-identical to the slum population) is about one billion strong, making it the fastest growing, and most unprecedented, social class on earth. . . . Among researchers, there is a base consensus that the 1980s crisis—during which informal-sector employment grew two to five times faster than formal-sector jobs—has inverted the relative structural positions, establishing informal survivalism as the new primary mode of livelihood in a majority of Third World cities" (2006, 178).

Agrarian subsistence enterprise (such as "sharecropping") is disrupted by highly mechanized corporate agribusiness. The impoverished seek refuge in cities. Erstwhile communally organized rural domains become depopulated targets of predatory armies (for example the Ku Klux Klan and Janjaweed Militia). The armies are in service to the state, or merely nonuniformed civilian thugs, purveyors always of what scholar Achille Mbembe, in his compelling study *On the Postcolony* (2001), calls "necropower."[6]

Displacement to urban domains yields the intense marginality of smokestacks, ashes, and the vicious unpredictability of the informal economy, meaning: illegal vending, sweatshops, unregulated day labor, unlicensed transport, sex trade, and narco-trafficking. Displaced millions migrate daily in search of minimal recompense and a square of earth to sleep on. Davis writes: "Instead of cities of light soaring toward heaven, much of the twenty-first-century urban world squats in squalor, surrounded by pollution, excrement, and decay . . . [by] 2015 Black Africa will have 332 million slum dwellers, a number that will continue to double every fifteen years" (2006, 19).

"Bigger," the name Wright chose for his protagonist in *Native Son,* was not accidental allegory. Race and displacement are monumental and omnipresent. Slums and their inhabitants are *bigger* and far more disastrous in our century than Wright could have imagined. Idealism, desire, and expressive brilliance were his stock in trade, seasoned with a Marxist grain or two. He believed if he wrote passionately and analytically enough, people would listen, and change. However, he knew indisputably that transatlantic *real estate* had produced a "Negro" and a "Negro Condition" that are metaphors for global race and displacement. War, incarceration, and chaos were standard processes of the transatlantic. They continue in the slum economies of our millennium.

In the absence of economic reparations, urban reform, and global, governmental, and juridical reconciliation, what end can our century anticipate? *Planet of Slums* concludes with a meditation on military and think-tank scenarios of the future. Mike Davis provides a vision of apocalyptic urban conflict. To the end of time, slum "insurgents" battle military counterinsurgents of the formal economy. *Native Son* concludes in less sensational fashion. Sentenced to death by the court, Bigger sits on a cot in Chicago's Cook County Jail. His idealistic defense lawyer has departed: "[Bigger] held on to the bars. Then he smiled a faint, wry, bitter smile. He heard the ring of steel as a far door clanged shut" (1940, 430). This is Wright's prophetic ending.

In our millennium, the scenario of African American ghetto insurgents in combat with global military forces is a pathologically irresponsible fantasy. There are no black liberation armies of the night in U.S. zones of ashes and excrement. There are surely narco-traffickers and their allied "gangs," but not a single Black Panther brigade in sight. Even "suspected" ghetto insurgents are now in lockdown by the American prison-industrial complex. There are more men, women, and children incarcerated in the United States than in any other country on the planet: a staggering 2.2 million souls. The prison-industrial complex is on the stock market's "big board" and deeply imbricated in the global economy. Its managers and brokers are *real estate* entrepreneurs who warehouse human *commodities* for profit. This land is their land, and they competently extend services globally.

In his essay "How Bigger Was Born," Wright avers: "The Southern scheme of oppression was but an appendage of a far vaster and in many respects more ruthless and impersonal commodity-profit machine" (2005, 441). Wright had studied the "factories" of displacement and race production known as slave ships. He had also taken the measure of the alienating and enduring trauma those transatlantic ships produced for people of color. The slave trade's legacy upon such people was, in Wright's view, a "burden of impressions and feelings" that he "recast . . . into the image of Bigger" (449).

In giving birth to *Native Son,* Wright plumbed ocean depths and the opaque collage of the black diaspora unconscious. He wrote not only a dread forecast of our millennial planet of slums, but also eloquently represented the symbolic and psychosocial conditions of modernity's dynamics of race and displacement. He dwelled at the point of entanglement. His spirit and intellect, even if implicitly, informed the University of Alabama's "Race and Displacement" symposium. Other authors, topics, and histories were present as well. The following pages are rich in their wisdom.

Notes

1. I am grateful to Professors Phil Beidler, Merinda Simmons, and Maha Marouan for their gracious invitation to deliver the keynote lecture for the "Race and Displacement" symposium. Their hospitality was nonpareil.

2. Park and his coauthors elaborated an account of the "human ecology" of the city, suggesting that "zones" of the urban evolve differentially through "evolution." The quality of resources, occupations, and character of a zone's inhabitants determined the zone's evolution. Implicit in Park et al.'s account is an aura of Darwinian "survival of the fittest." The Darwinian echoes have drawn fire for their anthropocentricism and too deterministic transfer from "the human" to "the urban." Of interest to my present reflections is *The City*'s observation that "*The city cannot fix land values, and we leave to private enterprise, for the most part, the task of determining the city's limits and the location of its residential and industrial districts*" (1926, 5; emphasis mine). Richard Wright was an informal student and partisan of the Chicago School of Urban Sociology led by Park. In Wright's *12 Million Black Voices,* the narrator depicts Park's industrial "zone" in terms of smokestacks, ashes, and black overcrowding.

3. W. E. B. DuBois labels the black elite the "Talented Tenth" in his 1903 classic *The Souls of Black Folk.*

4. I have chosen to use the edition handsomely edited by Professor Arnold Rampersad. Professor Rampersad's thoroughness of annotation and biographical notes are wonderful scholarly tools. Further, Professor Rampersad's inclusion of "How Bigger Was Born" in the edition makes it an extremely valuable addition to the critical canon.

5. I am borrowing here from Ralph Ellison's narrator in *Invisible Man,* who cautions that whenever an interlocutor begins to speak of intentions and greater "designs" of history, it is time for acolytes and listeners to put on steel helmets because things are surely about to *boomerang.* In the vernacular: "What goes around comes around." In scripture: Sow the wind; reap the whirlwind.

6. "Necropower" is the power to produce death. Mbembe writes: "What distinguishes our age from previous ages, the breach over which there is apparently no going back . . . [is] existence that is contingent, dispersed, and powerless but reveals itself in the guise of arbitrariness and the absolute power to give death any time, anywhere, by any means, and for any reason" (2001, 13).

References

Davis, Mike. 2006. *Planet of Slums.* New York: Verso.

Glissant, Edouard. 1999. *Caribbean Discourse: Selected Essays,* edited and translated by J. Michael Dash. Charlottesville: University Press of Virginia.

Hayden, Robert. 1997. "Middle Passage." In *The Norton Anthology of African American Literature,* edited by Henry Louis Gates Jr. and Nellie McKay, 1501. New York: Norton.

Mbembe, Achille. 2001. *On the Postcolony.* Berkeley: University of California Press.

Park, Robert E., Ernest W. Burgess, and Roderick D. McKenzie. 1926. *The City: Suggestions for Investigation of Human Nature in the Urban Environment.* Chicago: University of Chicago Press.

Rediker, Marcus. 2007. *The Slave Ship: A Human History.* New York: Penguin.

Woodson, Carter G. 1933. *The Mis-Education of the Negro.* San Diego: Book Tree, 2006.

Wright, Richard. 1940. *Native Son.* Edited by Arnold Rampersad. New York: Harper Perennial, 2005.

———. 2005. "How Bigger Was Born." In *Native Son,* edited by Arnold Rampersad, 431–62. New York: Harper Perennial.

Acknowledgments

This volume is the result of the "Race and Displacement" symposium that took place October 1–3, 2009, at the University of Alabama. We owe a great debt of gratitude to all those who made that conversation among scholars a success.

We extend our very deepest thanks to Robert Olin, dean of the College of Arts and Sciences, and Jimmy Williams, associate dean of Multicultural Affairs, for the financial and institutional backing for the symposium. Thanks, too, to the Bryant Conference Center, which served as the ideal venue for the weekend's conversations.

The symposium would obviously not have been the resounding success that it was without the involvement of those who were part of the program itself. Our very sincere and humble thanks go to Houston A. Baker Jr. for his inspiring keynote address that kicked off the conference weekend; Queen Quet for her creative performance, an undeniable highlight of the events; and Trudier Harris, whose participation fostered a productive and rousing roundtable, a finale to the symposium that encouraged a continuation of the dialogue between new and established scholars in the fields of transnational and diaspora studies. Our heartfelt thanks go to the exceptional moderators who participated in the panels and made true conversations out of the various paper presentations: Nikhil Bilwakesh, Brittney Cooper, Yolanda Manora, and Stacy Morgan.

The symposium was the thirty-third installment of the University of Alabama's Symposium on English and American Literature series, housed within the Department of English. We thank the English department, under the leadership of Chair Catherine Davies, for its invaluable support. Nancy Calvert was a key resource and point person where financial logistics were concerned. Norman Golar, a PhD candidate in English at the time (now English department chair at Stillman College), was a wonderful help in assisting with the transportation of several of the symposium participants to and from the Birmingham airport.

The Department of Religious Studies, a cosponsor of the event, was a source of invaluable support. We would like to thank specifically Russell McCutcheon, who served as department chair while we worked to organize the symposium. We also had the benefit of stellar student workers—Keke Pounds and Jaci Gresham—without whose help in organizing conference materials the planning would have been a far more difficult task. Within the Department of Religious Studies, special thanks go to administrative assistant Betty Dickey, who oversaw the student workers and helped us with so many logistical details throughout the planning process. Additional thanks are extended to Markus Harris, student in religious studies and African American studies, who worked the video equipment during the symposium and preserved all of the wonderful presentations on film.

We would most especially like to thank our fellow organizers on the coordinating committee. Phil Beidler (professor of English) drafted the initial call for papers, helped in the communications and arrangements with participants, and oversaw with wonderful efficiency various elements in the construction of this volume. Jessica Lacher-Feldman (curator of rare books and special collections at the W. S. Hoole Special Collections Library at the University of Alabama) was absolutely indispensable. She created and managed the blog and Facebook page for the symposium and managed the multifaceted advertising of the event. Additionally, we must recognize the artistic genius of Jessica Peterson, a graduate of the University of Alabama's MFA program in Book Arts and the visionary behind our logo and graphic design. Thanks, finally, to Dan Waterman, editor at the University of Alabama Press, who has overseen the production of this volume with remarkable efficiency.

The symposium and the volume are the results of the energies and boundless generosity of everyone listed above. We have been so pleased to work with all of you.

Introduction

Philip D. Beidler

Originally conceived of and entitled the Alabama Symposium on English and American Literature, the University of Alabama symposium series sponsored by the English department and the College of Arts and Sciences, begun in fall 1974, may now be said manifestly in its own substantial scholarly record of nearly four decades to trace out the radical evolution of the discipline and of critical inquiry over the period. Most visible in both relations has been the growth of cultural studies, highlighted by the new intersections, professional and theoretical, of scholarship and discourse in the traditional fields of language and literature with those of philosophy, linguistics, psychology, sociology, anthropology, religion, politics, and economics; nor is this to neglect exciting evolutions in the idea of disciplinary work itself in such fields as race, gender, postcolonial, and material culture studies.

Accordingly, the early years of the symposium series itself included a sequence of inquiries on current critical issues in the works of major individual figures: William Shakespeare, Geoffrey Chaucer, Samuel Johnson, Mark Twain, William Faulkner, Ezra Pound, and others. Within the first decade, however, in keeping with what may now be properly called the theory revolution, the purview quickly extended into contemporary problems and topics: rhetoric and literacy, theoretical feminism, postmodern poetry and poetics, critical theory futures. Representative titles included "After Strange Texts: The Role of Theory in the Study of Literature," "The Differences Within: Feminism and Critical Theory," "Our Academic Contract: The Conflict of the Faculties in America," and "Myth, Memory, and Migration: The Black South in the Cultural Imagination." A more recent, thematically connected set of programs and resultant publication series was entitled Signs of Race, with titles ranging from "Writing Race across the Atlantic World" to "English and Ethnicity" and "Eruptions of Funk." The latest event, in 2011, brought together an array of international researchers and writers on the corpus linguistics.

A central feature of the symposium project throughout was the attempt to combine the authority of established scholarship with the innovative work of younger figures. In the first case, the programs over the years came to include such eminent invitees (to name just a representative sampling), as Northrop Frye, D. W. Robertson, Cleanth Brooks, Alfred Kazin, M. H. Abrams, Hugh Kenner, Kenneth Burke, Geoffrey Hartman, Jane Marcus, J. Hillis Miller, Helen Vendler, Fredric Jameson, and Jacques Derrida. In the second initiative, selected participants in earlier stages of their careers included Stephen Greenblatt, Barbara Johnson, Jonathan Culler, Gayatri Spivak, Annette Kolodny, Peggy Kamuf, and Farrah Jasmine Griffin. For selected programs, major literary figures joined the invitees. These included Denise Levertov, Louis Simpson, William Gass, Alice Walker, and August Wilson.

In light of the above history, the intended—or, perhaps better, the aspirational—reach of the 2009 symposium was to continue and enlarge the process of evolution so described in a number of respects. Its wide-ranging call for papers, with the intention of attracting submissions from a potentially novel assortment of fields and research communities, announced a focus "on the concept of racial diaspora—removals, migrations, colonial and postcolonial geographies, and transnational identities, both individual and collective. What is the relationship between race and place in the various senses of those terms? What does race have to do historically with place? What is the place of a given race, 'its' place geographically, historically, in terms of social, educational, economic, and political traditions, hierarchies, power relations, and so on? What is the 'place' of a person in relation to race as well as in regard to other forms of difference—gender, sexuality, ethnicity; class, labor, ideology?"

A second, related innovation, also described in the announcement, was the proposed focus of conference presentation and participation on the core work of beginning scholars. To this end, the call for papers was addressed and promulgated exclusively to graduate students in all relevant fields, with program and prospective volume selections to be chosen by competitive submission. To establish further a project of conversation between scholarly and professional cohorts, participation was invited from two preeminent senior figures in the field, Houston A. Baker Jr., Distinguished University Professor at Vanderbilt University, and Trudier Harris, J. Carlyle Sitterson Professor of English Emerita at the University of North Carolina at Chapel Hill. Organizers included a senior professor from the sponsoring Department of English, with research interests in the Atlantic world of the contact era, and two faculty members, one from the Department of Gender and Race Studies, specializing in literature and religions of the African diaspora, and the other from the Department of Religious Studies, specializing in women's narratives of racial diaspora. The latter two, Professors Maha Marouan and Merinda Simmons refereed the competitive paper submissions and now serve as organizers and coeditors of this volume.

The success of matching aspiration with achievement is to be measured by the essays included here, a record of the proceedings, revised and thematically arranged into four groupings: "Race and Bodies," "Race and Place," "Race and Nation," and "Race and Imagination." These are presented within the conceptual framing of work by the conference's major invitees. The foreword by Professor Baker discusses Richard Wright as a modernist point of access to navigating economic, physical, and imaginative displacements in the transatlantic slave trade and the ideologies of subjugation faced on plantations in the New World. In the process, he further opens up a larger conversation about how these conflicts play into present-day notions and configurations of race and displacement. In such structural and thematic alignments, he engages "race" and "displacement" as mutually constructing and complicating forces, paying particular attention to the transatlantic world and the way the economics of the Middle Passage shaped (and still continue to shape) notions of racial identity. Next, in brief introductory reflections arising from her participation in the conference as both performance artist and independent scholar, Queen Quet Marquetta L. Goodwine of the Gullah/Geechee Nation addresses specific issues of displacement and the racial imagination—linguistic, cultural, and historical—in relation to the Sea Islands off the coast of the southeastern United States. Her presentation thereby touches on a diasporic South and its connection to Africa, Europe, and the Caribbean. Then, at the volume's conclusion, Trudier Harris's afterword addresses the work of the symposium itself as a basis for new and continuing conversations dealing with "race" and "place." At once a reprise of the opening sections by Baker and Queen Quet and a set of synthesizing critical reflections on themes and issues presented in the cycle of core essays, she leaves us with a moving meditation that delves into "the complexities of home" and the way place and migration shape understandings of personal and political identities.

In the body of the text, with the work of new scholars working in myriad cultural studies' fields, we find texts covering an extraordinary range of scholarship and original inquiry. In the form of fourfold statement—"Race and Bodies," "Race and Place," "Race and Nation," and "Race and Imagination"—the organization presented, as with the conference itself, is intended to reimage the discussion as a complex conversation, a provisional ordering of discourses still allowing for the fullest play of creative juxtaposition and supplementation. Tracing the roles of "race" from the corporeal and material to the imaginative, the essays thus provisionally chart the new ways whereby concepts of origin, region, migration, displacement, and diasporic memory create understandings of race in literature, social performance, and national policy, to name just a few. According to the editors, the volume thus, in its multilayered analyses and approaches, begins a new conversation about race and place in the way it reconceptualizes the relationship between racial formations and territorial notions of identity, thereby placing the concept of the diasporic subject at the heart of questions concerning postmodern individual and political identity.

Accordingly, in "Race and Bodies," Regina N. Bradley, Ashon T. Crawley, Deborah Katz, and Matthew Dischinger locate their work of analysis in what might be called the immediate political domain of the racialized body by using literary and oral narratives to consider and complicate relationships between race and corporeality. Specifically, these authors couch discussions of African American communities and narratives in relation to a broader diasporic context. In so doing, they further explore transnational histories of migration and performance in relation to religious traditions and embodied subjectivities. In "Lady Eve's Garden Sings the Blues: Spirituality and Identity in Gloria Naylor's Bailey's Café," Regina N. Bradley makes a compelling case for incorporating historical African diaspora practices into critical readings of Naylor's work. In a related but politically transhistorical fashion, Matt Dischinger's "Returning from 'Beyond the Bridge': Postcolonial Hybridity in Gloria Naylor's *Mama Day*" looks more broadly at Naylor as a "postcolonial" author, arguing for a contextualization of *Mama Day* as a major postcolonial statement. Meanwhile, Deborah Katz in "The Practice of Embodiment: Transatlantic Crossings and Black Female Sexuality in Nella Larsen's *Quicksand*" explores literary and cultural expatriation through constructions of black female bodies in the transatlantic world, and Ashon T. Crawley in " *Blackqueer Aesthesis: Sexuality and the Rumor and Gossip of Black Gospel*," with a focus on black male gospel singing, discusses constructions of black male sexuality in black churches through gossip and rumor.

In the essays in the section "Race and Place," Lauren Vedal, Melanie Fritsch, and Walter Bosse explore the way racial and cultural identities are challenged and transformed by larger spatial relationships. Their work challenges the nature of identity and community constructions and the way they complicate essentialist understandings of race. Walter Bosse's "Upon the Public Highways: Travel and Race in Charles W. Chesnutt's *The Marrow of Tradition*" explores the cultural and racial relevance of spatial mobility in the twentieth century, looking at the relationship between "roots and routes" and exposing the constraints of racial categories in America, while Lauren Vedal's "Immigrant Desire: Contesting Canadian Safety and Whiteness in Dionne Brand's *In Another Place, Not Here*" takes us to Canada, examining the notion of that country as a "safe haven" and the foundation of this belief, which has relied on white standards and epistemologies. Vedal's essay poses an important question: Does entering Canada's physical boundaries offer safety? Melanie Fritsch's " Beyond Race and Nation: The African American Barbary Captivity Narrative of Robert Adams," in which she considers early nineteenth-century African American texts in their broader historical contexts as they relate to Enlightenment thought and appropriate it to challenge the contradiction between the emancipatory promises of the Enlightenment and the existence of slavery and racism.

In the third section, "Race and Nation," the authors interpret race and its configurations in the historical and political dimension of national policy, as racial labeling and categorizations become necessary for the creation and implementation of federal regulation and immigration laws that control spatial and social boundaries. Delia Hagen's "Nations, Migration, and Métis Subsistence, 1860–1940" looks at the way federal laws and market capitalism reworked the physical landscape, decimated the agricultural system of the indigenous population, and transformed the possibility of them accessing their ancestral homeland, while Abigail G. H. Manzella's "Disorientation in Julie Otsuka's *When the Emperor Was Divine: The Imprisoned Spaces of Japanese Americans during World War II*" addresses the displacement of Japanese Americans by the U.S. government during World War II, a time when racist policies that constructed Japanese Americans as racially foreign were fashioned. Cassander L. Smith takes us to the transatlantic world of sixteenth-century Panama where the Spanish, the English, and the Cimarrons interact in complicated ways. In "Washing the Ethiop Red: Sir Francis Drake and the Cimarrons of Panama," Smith discusses the ways in which the Cimarrons challenged Drake's construction of social space and racial identity as he struggled to establish his own English, Protestant identity.

The final section, "Race and Imagination," invites dialogue about the role that new imaginative projections may play in shaping understandings of race and place. In "Moreau avec Cuvier, Kant avec Sade: Saint Domingue, Sara Baartman, and the Technologies of Imperial Desire," Jonathan Glover discusses the relationship between, as he calls it, "sexual desire and scientific duty" in French colonial contexts that emphasized exoticism and imperial power. Yumi Pak extends this obsession with "exotic" bodies into a discussion of the convergence of migration, tropes of lynching, and modernist sensibilities in "An Oracular Swan Song? American Literary Modernism, Modernity, and the Trope of Lynching in Jean Toomer's *Cane.*" Lastly, Kathrin Kottemann offers a discussion of how postcolonial identities are constructed and de-centered in "Cultural Schizophrenia and Postcolonial Identity in Derek Walcott's *Dream on Monkey Mountain* and Bernadine Evaristo's *Lara.*"

Such is the work of a volume, it is hoped, comprising at once a set of challenging individual reflections and a thematic collection eventuating in a whole that is greater than any sum of its parts. These essays not only raise questions about race and displacement as signifying tropes and lived experiences, they also offer constructive avenues for conversations about race, displacement, and migration both inside and outside the academy. Taken together, they become a kind of case study in dialogues across disciplines, providing insight from scholars with various interests in diaspora studies, postcolonial studies, literary theory, race theory, gender studies, and migration studies. Such multivocality allows for a nuanced discussion, one that was certainly evident in the "Race and Displacement" symposium. As a written record of that symposium, revised, restructured, and cooperatively edited, this volume becomes an invitation to the reader to join this important exchange of discourses. More properly—or, in this case, improperly, to choose the words of Houston Baker—it comprises the best kind of unruly conversation—among disciplines, cohorts, discourses—that has now become the true work of scholarship.

Reflections on *Race and Displacement*

Queen Quet Marquetta L. Goodwine

Transnational identity is not always dynamic within the discussion of race in the United States. However, the "Race and Displacement" symposium held at the University of Alabama, Tuscaloosa, in October 2009 incorporated this crucial aspect in the discussions. The symposium focused on the concept of racial diasporas—removals, migrations, colonial and postcolonial geographies, and transnational identities, both individual and collective. In order to begin with the premise of displacement, we must first recognize that there is an initial place where people belonged in order for them to be displaced and placed in yet another location. So, as an entry point into the discourse on displacement I examine the following definitions of place: (1) "any portion of space regarded as measured off or distinct from all other space or appropriated to some definite object of use; position, ground, site, spot"; and (2) a "rarely unbounded space" (*Merriam Webster English Dictionary* 2004). I take particular interest in the second definition given that I come from the Gullah/Geechee Nation where we still live in what is considered "unbound space" or "open space." The term is used to refer to planning and development as well as environmental protection for areas lacking buildings and gates. Rural communities are largely spaces that are unbound and where there are minimal fences and boundaries from one area to the next.

Gullah/Geechees have managed to preserve and perpetuate the African traditions of our ancestors by continuing to live in open and unbounded spaces that allow us the freedom to spiritually connect to and be bound with the land and the waterways over which we consider ourselves stewards. Interestingly enough, the Gullah/Geechee culture grew from the soil of the Sea Islands (located in the Atlantic Ocean off the coast of the United States from Jacksonville, North Carolina, to Jacksonville, Florida) as a result of the displacement of numerous African ethnic groups from that continent to North America. Africans from the Senegambia region down to Angola, from Madagascar, and from inland parts of the continent were captured and kidnapped and then enslaved on the Sea Islands, or what became the largest Carolina Gold rice, Sea Island cotton, and indigo plantations of North America. Given the environment of the Sea Islands and the extreme similarities of the marshlands to Africa, enslaved Africans brought to this region were largely able to continue many of the agricultural practices they had already known as well as sea work practices and architectural techniques. The fact that the Africans rapidly became the "black majority" in the region, outnumbering the Anglo people who were enslaving them, allowed them to preserve and maintain numerous Africanisms instead of being assimilated into the mores of the European enslavers.

In analyzing the history of the displacement of African peoples in the Sea Islands, I examine the word *displace,* which is defined as "to take over the place, position, or role of (someone or something); force (someone) to leave their home, typically because of war, persecution, or natural disaster; remove from a job or position of authority against their will" (*Oxford English Dictionary* 2006). The roles Africans had played in their homeland as leaders, heads of households, scientists, healers, and the like were changed to a uniform position of chattel by virtue of the transatlantic slave trade. The jobs and positions of authority that Africans held on their own continent were not to be a part of their existence after they were transported across the Atlantic Ocean and sold on auction blocks in Charleston, South Carolina, which became the number one "slave auction block" in the British colonies of North America. In fact, the roles that Africans played and the knowledge they brought with them were never acknowledged as they went from being African people to being "slaves." This new marker was an attempt to force them to become merely farm tools, chattel, and breeders, and not to be considered as whole human beings. Those who continued to preserve their collective consciousness were able to reconstruct their villages on the Sea Islands, or what is called now "family compounds." These are the "places" and "spaces" in which the Gullah/Geechee culture, language, polyrhythms, and heritage have evolved and flourished. Even natural disasters such as hurricanes and floods have not dissolved these communities—many people merely migrated temporarily, returning to rebuild their compounds on the islands, which remain there to this day.

As is the case with many disenfranchised minorities around the world, maintaining family compounds is replete with complexities: How do you obtain land and provide shelter and food for your family? If you have land, how do you keep ownership of it and ensure that you are not displaced to yet another place? Part of the process of owning and maintaining that land is also related to the way in which people identify with the land and with those who live in proximity to them. These questions are all too familiar to people who have been identified as the "Negro" or "black race" in the United States. Richard A. Couto in *Ain't Gonna Let Nobody Turn Me Round: The Pursuit of Racial Justice in the Rural South* writes:

> Because landownership was central to other changes, it was withheld. Twice the federal government distributed land to African Americans in the South, in the 1860s [via William Tecumseh Sherman's Special Field Order Number 15] and the 1930s. . . . The largest number of African Americans in the South, however, were landless farmers . . . they rebelled frequently from the repression and subordination that marked their landless condition. Their efforts exposed the violence beneath their economic condition. The various land-reform efforts were successful in various ways even though they served a very small portion of people who needed them. (1991, 162)

These efforts to bring change involved sustained economic empowerment, which is always a major aspect of freedom, civil rights–era mobilization, and the current human rights efforts that are being led to protect land rights and "food security" while also protecting African Americans' human rights as ethnic, linguistic, and national minorities. The Gullah/Geechee leadership in this case is an example.

This symposium "Race and Displacement" allowed us to examine and reexamine the dynamics of these issues around land and identity, economics, and decisions that were made regarding races of people and their choice or lack of choice in relation to their own displacement. I am talking not only about physical and geographic displacements but what I call "the displacement of the soul." Each time "black folks" within the United States began to settle in place, there seemed to be a mechanism that came forth to bring their souls to a point of unrest once again and they were then faced with another dilemma of displacement. When they were removed and moved to the new place, they had to once again figure out how to identify with a new place and in relation to it. Among the most examined periods of migration for people of African descent in America are the U.S. Civil War and the Reconstruction Era. As wars came to the Sea Island region prior to and during the Civil War, the people were often displaced. During the American Revolution and the War of 1812, Gullah/Geechees migrated with the British to the northeast and to Nova Scotia, Canada. Some settled in Liberia and even Freetown, Sierra

Leone, as parts of repatriation acts. Others migrated westward or into southern parts of Florida, while some went to other islands of the Caribbean. There were those who stayed near family members who were still on the plantations; they banded together with indigenous Americans and formed maroon colonies, raiding the plantation islands. Eventually these Gullah/Geechees became part of the Seminole Nation. The word *Seminole* means "wild" or "exiled," in reference to their constant displacement from one part of the Southeast to another. While some remained in Florida, others went to Mississippi, Alabama, Texas, Oklahoma, and Mexico. John McIntosh, the leader of the "Patriot forces," wrote a letter to the U.S. secretary of state, James Monroe, in regard to this alliance between Africans who had escaped enslavement and indigenous Americans. He stated that something must be done about this alliance and its power before word reached the plantation communities and brought about "a revolt of the black population of the United States." Understandably, the government was concerned about uprisings against a system that used race to keep blacks "in their place"(Guinn 2002, 34).

One of the questions raised in the closing roundtable of the symposium was that of agency and representation, as much of the anthropological work conducted regarding the Gullah/Geechee Nation remains problematic, bearing a stereotypical outsider's perspective that constructs this culture solely through the lens of the transatlantic slave trade, ignoring the transnational dimension of the Gullah/Geechee experience. Even contemporary works have been shaped and colored by literature composed by those standing on the outside of this unique cultural community, looking in with or without permission to do so. If outsiders are not truly permitted to enter the space of another group, many of the things that are important to that group may not be discussed or documented. A prime example of this is the lack of examination of the transnational identities of the Gullah/Geechees who live in Mexico: they are not fully considered Mexican citizens and have been basically forgotten by the United States, although the people themselves believe that they have rights to land across the border in the United States. These Gullah/Geechees also feel entitled to dual citizenship, since their ancestors fought for the United States and many of them were also hired to fight for Mexico at different points in time. The Muscogo, as they are called, consider themselves part of the African descendants of the United States. However, their displacement from their family within the Gullah/Geechee Nation has caused them to lose contact with the actual places from which they were displaced in the Carolinas and later in Florida. Neither of the countries that they belong to agrees to offer benefits to those who are considered black, Latin American, or Indian people because no one "knows their place."

The symposium "Race and Displacement" placed us in an unbound space that brought about examination not simply of race and displacement but also of the possibility of restoration and reconnection. Interestingly enough, the University of Alabama at Tuscaloosa is located in the Deep South—a place that many identify with racial violence, segregation, and a great deal of blood spilled for civil rights. The very name of the city means "Black Warrior," and it was here that the diverging issues associated with race converged in a unique examination of how the construct of race has become such a crucial mechanism used to displace and disenfranchise people in numerous ways over centuries. The knowledge shared that weekend allowed us to transcend what had become standard boundaries of race, space, and institutionalized discourse, resulting in our "replacing" our thought patterns and behaviors in relationships to race, place, and displacement.

References

Couto, Richard A. 1991. *Ain't Gonna Let Nobody Turn Me Round: The Pursuit of Racial Justice in the Rural South.* Philadelphia: Temple University Press

Guinn, Jeff. 2002. *Our Land Before We Die: The Proud Story of the Seminole Negro.* New York: Tarcher.

Merriam Webster English Dictionary. 2004. Springfield, MA: Merriam Webster.

Oxford English Dictionary. 2006. Oxford: Oxford University Press.

I
RACE *and* BODIES

Lady Eve's Garden Sings the Blues

Spirituality and Identity in Gloria Naylor's *Bailey's Café*

Regina N. Bradley

A prevalent theme that connects the various experiences of women in the African diaspora is the sense of displacement, a peculiarity that saturates the stories constructed about their lives. The single-dimensioned representation of being either hypersexual or asexual left little room for expressing the multidimensionality of black women. The memory and search for an identity untainted by the expectations of the Africana female body fill volumes of works by women writers of color. Women's narratives like Harriet Jacobs's and later works of fiction like *Dessa Rose* and *Beloved* offer self-constructed stories of torture and suffering from their unique viewpoint of lived experience as women slaves. What women of color are attempting to achieve is what Patricia Hill Collins refers to as the definition of self, or a space where "by being accountable to others, African American women develop more fully human, less objectified selves" (2002, 113). What Collins suggests here is that while black women are often restricted and constrained to a space of expected performance, there is a sense of empowerment when women of color are given the opportunity to establish their own networks and connections with others. This sense of independence is embedded within the notion that black women are nurturers and look out for the well-being of their loved ones. Black men, facing their own peculiar experiences with blackness, often do the opposite—they search for outlets of independence that allow room for uncensored mobility and expression. By challenging the stereotypical expectations of black manhood, men of color establish a space of visibility within American society. The desire to remove the physical body from social oppression is especially prevalent in the migratory narratives of black men written during the early twentieth century. Collins argues that while men of color focus on establishing identity based upon rebellion and opposition, black women thrive on the interconnectedness of individuals.

A large part of the foundation of the interconnection that Collins observes is embedded in a narrative of suffering—those traumatic experiences that dictate and often overpower the lives of black women. Perhaps the largest chunk of this narrative remains embedded in slavery discourse. One approach to this observation is the acknowledgment of a marginalized voice of women of color to relay their experiences from a firsthand account. As previously stated, we have Harriet Jacobs as a primary source for a look into women and slavery, but most of the written accounts are by men. Frederick Douglass, for example, speaks of the horrific treatment of an aunt because she snuck off the plantation to meet with a lover: "[N]o words, no tears, no prayers, from his gory victim, seemed to move his iron heart . . . the louder she screamed, the harder he whipped" (2003, 20). Douglass's aunt's desire to connect with another body on a human level beyond romantic attraction overshadowed her acknowledgment of being considered property. The horrendous whipping she received because of her attempts at human contact was the retribution of a master who feared rebellion and loss of control over her body and mind.

Gloria Naylor's literary canon bridges the suffering and trauma of slave narratives with contemporary Africana women's experiences. She investigates and acknowledges the connection between slave women and their current-day descendants. Further, Naylor not only carves out a space for teasing out the anxieties and issues facing those slave women, she also bridges the gap between generations of women who may face similar anxieties. Naylor searches for ways to reconnect women of color through a space of understanding that does not shun the painful afflictions that make the black woman her own entity. To pay attention to such afflictions and other unique experiences, Naylor creates an imaginary space in order to make the invisible black female body visible. The strongest trope that weaves through Naylor's works is the presence of a supernatural female figure. She uses this almost omniscient woman-God to blend the stories of the other women's lives that surround her; she is like the Rosetta Stone for deciphering their experiences. A reoccurring trope in the construction of the supernatural woman is her linkage to slavery. Because of the mystery, intrigue, and confusion surrounding slave discourse, Naylor crafts her superwoman character to blur the boundaries of reality and the supernatural. Sapphira Wade from *Mama Day* (1988) is Naylor's portrayal of the empowered black slave woman. She keeps watch over a secluded island community: "Willow Springs. Everybody knows but nobody talks about the legend of Sapphira Wade." Because her identity and African heritage remain intact, Sapphira is a threat. Sapphira "18 & 23'd" her way into legend and history and could not be oppressed or contained by her white owner Bascombe Wade.[1] Her description as a "true conjure woman: satin black, biscuit cream, red as Georgia clay" symbolizes her embodiment of all women of color as well as the ability to change her appearance and motif according to her beholder (3). She has a self-constructed identity and maintains control over her own body, which projects power.

Naylor slightly shifts direction for the construction of Eve in *Bailey's Café* (1992). She gives a traditionally white patriarchal space—the Bible—an Afrocentric reading to speak specifically to the susceptibilities and peculiarities faced by women of color. A complementary approach to navigating Naylor's reinterpretation of the biblical Eve is Theresa Washington's analysis of Àjé in her study *Our Mothers, Our Powers, Our Texts: Manifestations of Àjé in Africana Literature* (2005). Washington pulls from Yoruban spiritual beliefs and entities to help understand black diasporic texts. A descendant of Èsù, a trickster and creation spirit, Àjé is "the furtive force the Great Mother used to create life and ensure evolution. She shared her force with deities and select humans so that they might ensure that the world maintains its structure and balance" (4). Washington's fascinating concept of selection by a female deity to carry on the work of evolution and balance connects to the importance of African ancestry in the understanding or "knowing" of the woman of color's past. While it is unclear if Naylor purposefully pulls from Yoruban religious practice, pairing Washington's study with an Afrocentric and black feminist reading of Naylor's redressing of the Eve archetype is useful as a critical framework because of Washington's focus on the relationship between Africana women, spirituality, and independence.

Naylor's remake of commonly recognized archetypes—the Jezebel, Madonna, and Eve—demonstrates the problematic readings and applications of the Bible and suggests the peculiarities of using the Eurocentric (traditional) approach to the Bible to discuss the experiences of women of color.[2] Trudier Harris suggests that the re-creation of black female characters by black writers responds to the degradation that slave women faced in the past. Harris notes the challenge black writers face "in representing these women who have never had the luxury of being put on a pedestal or incorporated into anyone's concept of what true womanhood meant" and in "present[ing] these characters as perhaps freer to redefine themselves or to 'invent' themselves" (2001, 10). The idea of inventing an identity distinctly representative of their own experiences resounded strongly in black women's writing, including Naylor's.

Eve's character inverts and dismisses the understandings of the biblical Eve. Naylor's Eve is bold, cunning, sassy, and straightforward in her treatment of both men and women. She reaches a point of self-actualization in the city of

New Orleans. And while she can be viewed as a surrogate mother to those who live in her brownstone, what is most fascinating about Eve is her omniscient understanding of the plight her tenants experience. Eve's brownstone garden is an Edenic space that dually serves as a site of rehabilitation. Each flower is grown wild and represents a tenant; she refuses to grow domesticated species. Eve's garden symbolizes the critical need for women of color to reinvent themselves by their own standards and not those of outside (white) influence. Black women need to resist accepting an inferior and subservient position within the constraints of patriarchal society. This notion is symbolized triumphantly in the center of Eve's garden by the circle of lilies that consumes a barren tree stump: "[W]here that large tree stump sits, spring, summer, or fall you're gonna find circles and circles of lilies. Day Lilies. Tiger Lilies. Madonna lilies. Canna lilies. Lilies of the Valley. They grow in low clusters and on stalks; they vine up the stump of her only tree. Brown. Striped. Lilies-of-the-Nile. Stars of Bethlehem. . . . And none of them have a price. But all of her other flowers are for sale" (92). It is no coincidence that Eve's flowery representation is the lily, a symbol of resurrection from the dead. The colors and references to resurrection and rehabilitation also point toward the rejuvenation of the black woman in *all* forms. These flowers represent Eve's journey and her ability to redeem herself and others. Naylor teases out other, more exotic (wild) forms of the flower that reflect her own characteristics. Unlike the biblical Eve, Naylor's rendition suggests Eve as uncensored and able to present herself freely and in different forms.

The focal point of the lilies is the tree stump they encompass. The stump symbolizes the aftermath of Eve's purging of the rigidity of structured religion. Eve's stump represents the powerlessness of patriarchal and Christian knowledge over her identity. It is the idea that, once removed from the traditional white Christian construct, women of color are able to proudly display their self-resurrection and independent identity. She has cut down the tree of knowledge that condemned the biblical Eve. Her pilgrimage to New Orleans as a result of exile/displacement from Godfather's Pilottown helped Eve transcend religion and its impact on secular constructs of gender representation. Her experiences are priceless lilies. These flowers represent the resurrected, the transcended, and the redeemed. Because Eve's tenants are on the journey she has already completed, other flowers—still beautiful and meticulously crafted by Eve—must suffice.

Naylor charts Eve's transition, however, through the biblical lens of the original Eve. She is forced to accept and obey the wishes and commands of a man she solely refers to as "Godfather," a stern man with a frightening and malicious laugh. In similar fashion to Naylor's interpretation of the Bible,

Washington also suggests that the all-powerful God is not male, white, or patriarchal. Instead, the creation spirit is gender neutral and cares only about the balance of earthly men and women. Àjé is complex and cannot be constrained to a suggested space or position. Even more important, Àjé is a reflection of the Great Mother, who challenges the notion of an all-powerful male God. In African American women's literature, Àjé can be used to represent the connection to an ancestral past, purposely erased by slavery, and its continued relevance in establishing black female identity. Àjé threatens the static role of black femininity in patriarchal white society—it does not fit into traditional Christian beliefs and seeks out a balance between men and women of color.

Like Sapphira Wade, Eve is one of the Great Mother's chosen few who carry on the work of progression and balance. In order for her to ascend to this role, Eve must remove herself from the restraints of gender roles and the perceived performance of black women's identities. Washington argues that Àjé is "a biologically derived force that men and women can inherit. . . . in the grip of *alien, patriarchal, imperialist indoctrination,* it apparently became important to differentiate spiritually empowered females from their male counterparts" (2005, 6; emphasis added). Àjé does not fall into static representations of male or female. Disconnect between male and female Àjé, between men and women of color, resulted from the slave trade. This act removed the balance in identity and authority that was previously shared.[3] Whites (both European and American) pressed their views and ideologies onto people of color, leaving no room for ancestral influence or independent views of themselves. In "Eve's Song," we trace Eve's journey of self-discovery through her painful purging of masculine and Christian expectation and her eventual realization of a purpose that is uniquely her own.

Eve's relationship with her guardian, "Godfather," frames the trajectory of her narrative. Her description of Godfather alludes to the creation story found in the book of Genesis: "Godfather always told me that since I never had a real mother or father and wouldn't be alive if it weren't for him, *he* would decide when I was born . . . the very day he said he found me in a patch of ragweed, so new I was still tied to the birth sac and he had to bite off the umbilical cord with his teeth and spit it out to save me from being poisoned" (83). Godfather embodies the God of Christianity. His authority—lodged within hidden knowledge of her origins and identity—reflects Eve's total dependence on him.[4] Eve never reveals Godfather's name, suggesting either her ignorance of his identity or Godfather's fierce protection of such a powerful secret.[5] Godfather lacks affection, gruffly speaks to and supports Eve during her childhood and adolescent years, and is an authoritative figure in Eve's hometown of Pilottown, Louisiana: "The town had only three buildings that qualified as such: the school, the cotton exchange, and the church. He was the preacher in one, the scale foreman, and bookkeeper in another, and no one attended that drafty school past the ninth grade" (85). Godfather serves in every capacity—teacher, preacher, and provider.

Eve's burgeoning sexuality—a natural occurrence—finally challenges Godfather's hegemonic authority. Because he cannot control Eve's development into womanhood, Godfather removes her from his home: "He said I was going to leave him the same way he'd found me, naked and hungry. . . . He purged me with jars of warm water and Epsom salts, to remove, he said, every ounce of food his hard work had put into my stomach" (88). A direct result of Godfather's banishment is Eve's abrupt dismissal from Pilottown because people are afraid to take her in and face Godfather's wrath. There are two critical points in this scene—Eve's exile alludes to the biblical Eve's banishment from Eden and Naylor's Eve's loss of humanity because of her removal from a Christian social construct. "To be thrown out of his [Godfather's] church was to be thrown out of the world," Eve recalled (85). Eve loses the sense of identity constructed *for her* by Godfather. Without it, she is forced to search for self-actualization.

As she wanders toward New Orleans, Eve makes a conscientious effort to lock away her memories of Godfather and the security she was forced to abandon. Eve also recognizes that "she had no choice but to walk into New Orleans neither male nor female—mud. But I could right then and there choose what I was going to be when I walked back out" (91). Eve's description of her sexuality as a "body of mud" triggers the reading of this passage as Eve's realization that gender is performance based. She no longer acknowledges traditional gender roles that restrained her to a specific category.[6] She reaches a balance of understanding the male and female characteristics within her being. Instead of accepting Godfather's declaration of her life as his creation, Eve affirms, "I was born of the delta" (90). Eve's metamorphosis in New Orleans is no accident. One of the oldest cities in the United States, New Orleans is known as a city of death, hoodoo, and supernatural occurrences. Eve resurrects herself in the city that was taboo because of its distance from a traditional Christian-based community. The power of hoodoo, or conjuring, and life in the city of death awaken Eve's supernatural entity. She becomes Àjé and once her self-discovery is complete, wanders in search of a new challenge—"New Orleans was child's play. But it was my first real city and there I learned about any city in the world. I wanted out because I was bored. If I could get through all I'd gotten through, then I was overqualified to be the mayor of New Orleans. And much too overqualified to be the governor of Louisiana"

(91). Eve's migration from New Orleans and her remembrance of "delta dust" follow her to her new residence next to Bailey's Café. Her new challenge is helping other women of color achieve her level of power.

In the beginning of Eve's narrative she talks about delta dust and its relationship to her thousand-year journey: "[I]t's not a part of me—it is me. I became it, on that long walk from Pilottown to Arabi. The walk that took a thousand years. When people ask me how old I am and I say, About a thousand years, they think I'm being coy. But it's the gospel truth" (82).[7]

Eve questions a potential tenant's knowledge of delta dust to help her decide if the woman can stay. Like the phenomenon "18 & 23," Naylor does not pinpoint a concrete definition of delta dust. I would like to propose that delta dust is a composition of traditional characteristics of (black) womanhood that hinder women from transcending to an unrestricted state of being. Eve describes her own accruing of delta dust during her migration: "[T]he delta dusts exists to grow things, anything. . . . The dust sought out what wetness it could and clung to the tiny drops of perspiration in my pores . . . Up my thighs and deep into my vagina, so much mud that it finally stilled my menstrual blood" (90). The delta dust stills Eve menstrual cycle, the major identifying biological and social trait of women, which signifies the end of her restriction to womanhood. It is also important to note here the end of Eve's ability to bear children. Naylor cuts Eve's connection to her biblical predecessor and her attached stigmas. She also breaks away from the stereotypical role of black women as breeders. Although Eve is physically incapable of producing her own children, it does not suggest that her maternal instincts will go unused.

This is evident in her interactions with the tenants and prospective boarders. A battered woman seeking refuge from a man's hand, her own addiction, or some other vice doesn't interest Eve: "[T]hat kind of woman hated men. And there was no more room available for that kind in my boardinghouse. . . . Besides, with all that this woman had been through and would still keep going through—they always manage to keep going through—she didn't know, just didn't know, about delta dust" (82). As Àjé, Eve searches for those women who wish to transcend and rebalance their current lives. That journey includes interaction—physical, mental, and emotional—with men.[8] Delta dust helped Eve evolve out of Godfather's creation into her own entity. Eve's observations of the "few grains at the bottom of the tub" also signify her *continued* growth as Àjé and her continually shifting surroundings (82). In choosing women to accept as tenants, Eve does not look simply at the severity of their need. She searches for traces of the delta she trudged so many years earlier in search of herself and inner peace.

One of the characteristics Àjé possesses, useful in understanding Naylor's trajectory of Eve's character, is multidimensionality. Àjé possesses "a plethora of harmonizing tools and skills and . . . if necessary, they will use debilitation and painful didactics to institute gender balance and social harmony" (Washington 2005, 165). The darker representation of Eve as Àjé appears in the narrative of Jesse Bell, a play on the biblical Jezebel.[9] Jesse Bell's open sexuality, addiction to heroin, and obliviousness to the world around her embody the stereotype of the hypersexed black female body. Outside of "Sweet" Esther, the shadowy and illusive tenant of Eve's basement, Jesse Bell serves as Eve's biggest challenge. Eve recognizes that her approach to helping Jesse Bell will have to be strict, sinister, and avant-garde.

Eve's initial encounter with Jesse Bell occurs in a women's prison. Through Bailey, Naylor describes the sub par condition of the isolation cells where Jesse is imprisoned: "The stench is something awful. Alcoholics. Junkies. Hysterics. The problem population. The women crouch in wire-mesh cages among the watery stools from overflowing toilets. If they're not too sick to care, they push their floor mattresses away from the corners where they have to vomit. Because if they're not too sick to care, they've tried to keep the one sink clean enough to allow them to drink from the faucet" (133).

Eve's descent into the bowels of the prison places her as a figure of light in the darkness. As she walks through the isolation cells, Eve represents opportunity and guidance through the darkness of the women's own despair. One approach to analyzing the relationship between Eve and the isolation inmates is to view their surroundings as parallel to the slave ships and Middle Passage. The crowdedness, stench, and presence of death—in all forms, spiritual, physical, and emotional—align with the historical Middle Passage and the oppression slave women faced en route to the plantations of the Caribbean and United States. Referred to as "the problem population," female inmates are removed from *respectable* (Eurocentric) society in the same manner as black women upon their arrival at the plantations. Both the inmates and slave women are dehumanized and cast away from the world, condemned to wallow in their own hopelessness. These women, though dirty, often do not have the delta dust Eve claims is necessary for admittance into her brownstone: "[M]any times she'll walk back up that hall without having spoken to one of them or handed out a single card. . . . And there's no need to waste directions on someone who's just going to spend her life staying lost" (133). In retrospect, Eve is the liaison between the living and the dead, the ancestry and hope, there to revive the women's spirits and sense of worth.[10] She brings her cards only for women she feels are ready to benefit from her assistance and embark on their own redemptive journey.

A somewhat sober Jesse searches for Eve at Bailey's Café. After hearing Jesse's run-of-the-mill story, an irritated Eve warns her of what lies ahead:

"I never waste my time. Never. And if you don't come off the dope, then I've wasted over an hour listening to you claim that you will. . . . [Y]ou've put me into the position of ensuring that I have not wasted this hour" (137). Jesse's detoxification process, a vividly described and horrific encounter, speaks to Eve's powers as a supernatural being. She presents Jesse Bell with a dark void and demands that she see something, anything. Jesse, unbelieving and in need of a fix, has a vision that takes her back to childhood, incorporating both memory and fantasy. The opulence and grandeur of Jesse Bell's childhood fantasy bathroom initially appears to be a pleasant memory. It is the conversation between Eve and Jesse, however, that suggests Eve's ulterior motives:

> —I dreamed of a bathroom like this when I was a little girl.—I did too, Eve said.
> —None of this can be real. Where am I?
> —Hell. (138)

Eve's use of fear to intimidate an otherwise strong black female character suggests her sensitivity to approaching her tenants from a perspective of familiarity. In Jesse Bell's case, Eve utilizes Godfather's mannerisms—she is gruff, cold, and distant—to force Jesse to recognize and fight her drug addiction.

Eve's persona in this section of the novel resembles Jesse's own—she is a tough woman from the docks who does not submit to anyone's standards of civility. Her hardness is reflected strongly in Eve's first response to Jesse while she is incarcerated: "[F]or some reason she stopped at Jesse's cell. And no, she wasn't moved by her story. But when she was tired of wallowing in her own shit, come and find her" (133). Each time Jesse kicks her addiction, Eve is waiting, watching to see if she is truly ready for a new beginning. And each time Jesse falls again to her demons. Eve supplies Jesse with heroin, each gift more potent and richly presented than previously. At the end of Jesse's second high using a silver kit, Eve reminds Jesse of the temptations around her:

> —The needle is gold this time, isn't it?
> —It's gold, said Eve.
> —And if I made it through, I suppose I'd get platinum. Would that be the end of the line?
> —Remember where we are; that's only the beginning of what's available here. (142)

The surface response to Eve's reply "Remember where we are" suggests a tough-love reproach to Jesse's previous pleas of being clean and desiring to quit for good. Deeper analysis suggests duality in Eve's words. While she implies that

Jesse's stay in hell is far from over, Eve also inadvertently suggests that her boardinghouse as a site for redemption and revival of Jesse's spirit—if that is what Jesse desires. Both temptations—a readdiction to heroin and salvation—are available in the space. This is representative of the duality of Àjé, a balance between peace and violence when deemed necessary. Eve's command over time and place reemphasizes her supernatural power as well as her ability to choose to help or not to help those who need assistance.

Eve in *Bailey's Café* manifests the critical need for black women to remove themselves from the restrictive constructs of gender within patriarchal society. Eve, like Àjé, desires to harmonize and restore the sacredness of black women's worth and spirits. The manifestations of Àjé dictate the representation of a blended spirit of God and mother, a being that transcends race and gender. Naylor's text challenges the reader to reconsider the powerful presence of spirituality in the construction of the black woman's narrative. Black women's spirituality and identity do not exist solely within the stagnant narratives of the Bible. There must be a continual reaffirmation of a spiritual connection not only with a higher being but with other women of color. The imaginary spaces suggested in Naylor's texts demonstrate the separation of black women and our fragmented stories. In order for our lives to retain their validation, we need to reconnect so that a fragmented body becomes whole.

Notes

1. Naylor leaves the definition of "18 & 23" to the discretion of the reader. In the opening paragraph of the novel, 1823 appears to be a year of acts that Sapphira performs to control and dominate Bascombe Wade: "1823: she smothered Bascombe Wade in his very bed and lived to tell the story for a thousand days. 1823: married Bascombe Wade, bore him seven sons, in just a thousand days to put a dagger through his kidney and escape the hangman's noose, laughing in a burst of flames" (*Mama Day* 1988, 3). In Willow Springs, "18 & 23" serves not only as an acknowledgment of Sapphira's power but also as a warning to those who are acting indecently.

2. Mae G. Henderson's analysis of Toni Morrison's use of the Bible in *Beloved* is especially useful in understanding how to approach reclamation of biblical scripture in black women's literature. Henderson suggests that Morrison uses the Old and New Testaments to "problematize the nature of the relationship between the past and the present, but also thematizes the importance of historical reclamation and repossession. Morrison seeks to repossess the African and slave ancestors after their historic violation" (1991, 64).

3. In her study of black women in slave communities, Angela Davis argues that treatment of black women built up resistance and anger toward whites, but they (slave

women) ultimately wanted to uplift and remain equal with black men: "[I]t was not her comrade brother against whom her incredible strength was directed. She fought alongside her man. . . . She was in no sense an authoritarian. . . . On the contrary, she herself had just been forced to leave behind the realm of female passivity in order to resume her place beside the insurgent male" (1971, 4).

4. This passage can also be analyzed in terms of the social hierarchy established in slave society—Godfather symbolizes the white male slave owner who creates an identity for black slave women. She is renamed and manipulated into believing her existence begins as his property. The slave owner deifies himself in the slave woman's eyes, forcing Christian beliefs and erasure of previous influences outside of his patriarchal society. Because of displacement—physical and emotional—the slave woman assimilates herself for survival.

5. The interaction between Eve and Godfather regarding her mysterious past is intriguing for two reasons—Godfather presents himself as Eve's creator and he remains powerful because of the knowledge he possesses about Eve, which makes him appear all-knowing. The trope of naming is also significant in this passage. Eve knowing Godfather's name would balance their relationship and make them equal. Because Eve does not know about her past, it is quite probable that Godfather named Eve, which alludes to Genesis 2:20: "Adam names his wife Eve, because she would become the mother of all the living." Man names woman first, coincidentally giving him authority over her. It should also be noted here how Godfather's anonymity parallels God's—his name is never mentioned.

6. Because she considers herself mud, Eve also considers herself equal to any man since she was from the Earth (dust). Naylor inverts the allusion to man's creation to signify both man *and* woman's creation.

7. This passage shares a lot of similar characteristics in the embodiment of wisdom with August Wilson's Aunt Esther. She is a prominent character in Wilson's play *Gem of the Ocean* (2003), set in 1903 in Pittsburgh, Pennsylvania. Aunt Esther tells people she is over three hundred years old. Both Eve and Esther serve as liaisons between the past (ancestry) and the present.

8. Bailey and Eve's relationship stands as a prime example of the balance and harmony of gender that Eve works to instill in her tenants. Bailey is responsible for leading all of Eve's tenants to her home. In Eve's narrative, he describes his role as that of a guide in the women's road to Eve's boardinghouse. Hidden in Bailey's directions to Eve's house is a disclaimer: "[W]hen you see the garden—*if* you see the garden," an indication of Bailey's understanding of Eve's selection process (81; emphasis added). Eve's garden, symbolic of her self-constructed paradise, represents Naylor's answer to the biblical Eve's expulsion from Eden by God.

9. For the biblical story of Jezebel, see 1 and 2 Kings. Trudier Harris argues that the Jezebel figure "locked black women into the uncontained lustiness of sexuality and

animalism in which they were stereotypically considered to lead upstanding, Christian white men astray during and after slavery" (2001, 2). In Jesse Bell's narrative, however, the "upstanding white man" is her husband, a member of the higher-class King family. Jesse discusses the use of her sexuality to keep her husband interested. Because of Jesse's blatant sexuality and lower-class standing, her marriage into the King family infuriates Uncle Eli, the feared patriarch of the family. I believe Eli is Naylor's exaggerated rehashing of W. E. B. DuBois and his theories on class and racial essentialism. Eli's control over his family and the direction of their lives reintroduces the ideologies of whiteness, power, and authority in the black community. Instead of wealthy white men, it is educated, upper-class black men who dictate the boundaries of respectability and the acknowledgment of one's humanity. The major indicator of the latter is the socioeconomic standing of the one in question. Because Jesse fails to meet both of these standards, Eli isolates her from her family and, in broader terms, society. She blames Uncle Eli for her misery, citing him as the cause for her displacement from her family and ultimate drug addiction.

10. Karla Holloway's definition of ancestry remains a valuable resource for investigating its role in black women's literature (1992).

References

Collins, Patricia Hill. 2002. *Black Feminist Thought.* New York: Routledge.

Davis, Angela Y. 1971. "Reflections on the Black Woman's Role in the Community of Slaves." *Black Scholar* 3 (4): 2–15.

Douglass, Frederick. 2003. *Narrative of the Life of Frederick Douglass, an American Slave.* New York: Barnes and Nobles.

Harris, Trudier. 2001. *Saints, Sinners, Saviors: Strong Black Women in African American Literature.* New York: Palgrave.

Henderson, Mae G. 1991. "Toni Morrison's *Beloved*: Remembering the Body as a Historical Text." In *Comparative American Identities: Race, Sex, and Nationality in the Modern Text,* edited by Hortense J. Spillers, 62–83. New York: Routledge.

Holloway, Karla F. 1992. *Moorings and Metaphors: Figures of Culture and Gender in Black Women's Literature.* New Brunswick: Rutgers University Press.

Naylor, Gloria. 1988. *Mama Day.* New York: Vintage.

———. 1992. *Bailey's Café.* New York: Vintage.

Washington, Teresa N. 2005. *Our Mothers, Our Powers, Our Texts: Manifestations of Àjé in Africana Literature.* Bloomington: Indiana University Press.

Wilson, August. 2003. *Gem of the Ocean.* New York: Penguin.

Blackqueer Aesthesis

Sexuality and the Rumor and Gossip of Black Gospel

Ashon T. Crawley

In this essay I consider the sound of religious music in relation to a sociosexual understanding of queerness as nonnormative, resistant, and utopist. Influenced by aesthetic and sound studies, this essay investigates the relation of aurality to subject formation and personhood that both anticipates and escapes subjection (Moten 2003, 1). In the notational devices of Western music, harmony is graphed through the treble and the bass clefs. Clefs indicate register and pitch for notes. But more than that, on a written score, the clefs reference space—intervality, proximity, closeness, nearness—*between* notes. Thus, it seems that the clef announces, by way of representational arrest on the page, the capacity of sound to hold space and time, intervality and temporality, or what we might simply call spatiotemporality. It is in the spatiotemporality that, I will argue, rhetorics circulate, curiously revising the past in the present.

This is true for the well-circulated, un(der)documented secret: the idea that most black men who perform gospel music are gay. This idea has found much currency: in fictional accounts by writers like James Baldwin, in movies like *First Sunday,* and in churches by pastors and preachers who openly *call* out—with the desired *response* of laughter—"dykes," "bull-daggers," and "sissies" in the choir and in the missionary departments.[1] When gossip and rumor are shared, what cultural histories are performed, contested, and calibrated by demarcating who is and who is not acceptable by way of this sound? Gossip and rumor circulate regarding the spectacular sexualities, the abject lives of the "church queens," creating a narrative form through which certain figures crystallize. The narrative, like the musical score, is arresting, attempting to represent the always-abundant excessiveness of performance. The narrative seeks seizure of queer aesthetics, though this queering narrative exists previous to action.[2] This narrative is both foundational for the bodying forth of a certain type of abject, queer subject and functional for a certain mode of resistance. The black queer subject is thrown into a narrative as irreducible incoherence while he concurrently grounds a narrative of black, Christian normativity. Rumor and gossip—as narrative—are a technology of queering potentiality. I use the term *queering* intentionally to speak to the nonnormativity and indexing of difference that "queer" announces. Queering is a verb and, by way of narrativizing, anyone can be queered if they occupy a certain socio-sonic space. Other works think about queerness with relation to blackness and religiosity, such as Marlon Moore's (2008) argument foregrounding the performance of various masculinities between preacher and musician in black churches.

Though I am writing about male-identified persons, I am interested in the various constructions and narratives around *voice* that is related but not reducible to body. Bodies matter, we might say, but differently based on the enunciative voice. Charles Nero (2005) attempts to "queer" W. E. B. DuBois's *The Souls of Black Folk,* which begins with a hum in the short story "The Coming of John"; that hum allows Nero to think about the turn of twentieth-century discourses about gender inversion and film. He relates the sound of a hum to a possible splitting of a subject that yields a duality and inversion—a queering. While I am similarly interested in the production of sound, I am hoping to linger in the materiality of sound that literally emanates—and is not split off from—individuals.

It appears that in black churches,[3] peculiar sexualities suture to aurality and then converge on particular bodies. But more than converging *on* bodies through the circumscribing, voyeuristic imaginings of others, aurality and sexuality are compressed, as it were, *in* the bodies and literally sound *out* of them. The antitheses of gossip and rumor are not truth and honesty, in my view, but rather a noise, a particular type of overt announcement that everyone can hear, that is not hushed. That is to say, gossip and rumor are not always merely lies; at times the sound of the voice functions as the narrative confirmation. Sissies singing in sanctuaries on Sundays and sinning in secret societies on Saturdays serve an important purpose in congregations. The sound created by these imagined queer subjects create the sonic background, the soundtrack, upon which the holy can be realized during a church service. The circulation of rumor and gossip and concurrent repudiation of those abject persons who create those ever-important sounds does important excavatory work. What factors contribute to making voice/tone sound queer but also alluring? What occurs when sound queers bodies; what are the contexts of such work? How does sound matter for and materialize in the aural, ecstatic, and aesthetic religio-cultural life? Extending Judith Butler's important work (1993), I want to explore "aurality that matters," aurality that has historically marked identity and difference through categorizing enunciative sound.

Rumor and gossip create, and are curiously created by, a common narrative of deviant sexualities out of, upon, and through which—at the moment of performance—aural utterances matter and materialize. The voice announces the uniqueness of the self, *plus more.* The surplus entails the proclivities declared sinful, lascivious, and salacious. But the voice likewise announces what is purportedly not in the subject, what is a deficiency: of control, rationality, holiness. What are the implications for a resilience wherein one constructs personhood through this narrative that is both contained within and exceeds that narrativity?

I am not making an argument essentializing certain tones and notes as queer (for example, "When a black man sings the note A in a black church, he is gay," because that is terribly reductive and wrong); I rather seek to understand uttered sound in sonic context. Here, then, sound, subject, and scene are mutually constitutive. If antiphony—feedback, passionate response to impassioned call, call and response—is important to the formation and understanding of black music generally, it seems appropriate to analyze gossip and rumor as a particular sort of background noise that serves as the foundation for certain persons to matter and materialize.

Most analyses of black gospel music (BGM) give particular attention to lyrics and oral utterance as somehow separated. That is, some analyses scrutinize the lyrics but not the aesthetics attached to them; others analyze the aesthetics without regard for the referential quality of the lyrics (Boyer and Yearwood 1995). I seek to broaden the discussion by thinking about the sonic quality of voice as a matter and material of concern. I also attempt to consider the consequences arising from the narratives told *about* those subjects during their moments of performance. *The Gospel Sound* by Anthony Heilbut (1971) seems to be the only history of gospel published that addresses—head-on and without apology—the issue of sexuality and its relation to the creation of BGM, while he gives equal attention to aurality. In the book, queer people as the animating force of BGM, particularly of the Holiness/Pentecostal churches, were mentioned but not by name. Though Heilbut's work was first published in 1971 and documents the history of the BGM, it seems that scholars have offered scant attention to the issue of sexuality after Heilbut, though choir directors, singers, and gayness are often the topics of conversation in barbershops, salons, and on the Internet. It is this theoretical gap that this chapter attempts to fill.

BGM is considered moving, particularly for its listeners: churchgoers and religious persons. Listeners in the church often describe it as heartfelt, convicting, convincing, and healing. Movement is bound up with this particular mode of black aesthetics: you've gotta pat your foot, clap your hands, bob your head, sing along, stand up, move your body, dance as God's spirit compels you. But a fundamental question lingers: if the music can move, can it also queer? That is, can the tones emanating from seemingly unholy persons invade the body of others; can that sound force others to move in "unholy" ways as well? Is gossip, as circumscribing rhetoric, really about the worry of contamination? It appears that a theological construction of personhood—where the Spirit of God can come into and animate the body, where Satan can oppress and possess—possibly grounds the ideology of aesthetics as a force that can invade. As such, sound—as one deployment of aesthetics—can be dangerous because it forces its way into bodies that want to shore up against porosity; the sound is penetrative. This contradicts the dominant cultural logic and understanding of gay men as always penetrated and, as such, given to effeminate, womanly pleasures. This is not to devalue penetration but to explicate how those things that seem to "pertain to a woman," within this religio-cultural domain, are seen as subordinate to a masculine, manly, patriarchal, misogynist mindset. If the sound of unholy men penetrates the religio-cultural space, and this penetrability is foundational to theological problems, it appears that undergirding such ideology is a disdain for women, the feminine (as category and performance), and maternity. Is this why there is such a brash disdain for the "effeminate" male character?

Pastor and author Michael Stevens has much to say on this topic that elucidates some of the concerns with femininity, porosity, and the black gospel sound (BGS). In an interview conducted by GospelCity.com, he answered the question, "In gospel music, do you think we have a big problem with homosexuality?" as follows:

> Absolutely. As a matter of fact, it's a little more flamboyant in the gospel music industry than it would be in the, let's say, traditional pulpit. . . . But there seems to be a little more of a flamboyancy, a little bit more of a pride and . . . there's not as much need to be on the downlow in the gospel music industry as much as it would be, maybe, in the pulpit . . . and because there's more of an acceptance in the gospel music industry, yeah, you do see the flamboyancy, you do see the arrogance almost, when it comes to being feminine and when it comes to being homosexual. . . .
>
> There is still a very feminine gospel within the black culture church. Everywhere from our music to our preaching style to our lavender colors in our pulpits to the flowers. We still have a very feminine environment in the church. . . . And preaching, we're more emotional, more sensa-

> tional. Of course, women are a little bit more inclined to that . . . and oh, they're hollering, "oh this is God, thank God," they're screaming and crying . . . whereas in our church if we kind of be a little bit more masculine in our approach, logical, analytical, challenging, even, if need be, I think it would attract more men and dissolve the feminine spirit in the church. (2007)

There are many different people I could quote who espouse similar sentiments, from pastor and gospel artist Rev. Clay Evans to a missionary evangelist in the Church of God in Christ (COGIC) Evangelist, Frances Kelly; from Bishop Alfred Owens of the Greater Mount Calvary Holy Church calling on all the "real men" who aren't "sissies" or "faggots" to parade around the church to Rev. Willie Wilson stating that "lesbianism is about to take over the [black] community" to Bishop Iona Locke questioning "why I got to look at you and wonder if you male or female?" (Locke 2007; Kelly 1998; Evans 1994; Wilson 2005; Owens 2006). Then there is Jamal Harrison Bryant, pastor of Empowerment Temple African Methodist Episcopal (AME) Church in Baltimore, who has stated that gay men in the black church "took on that posture or their spirit because they never saw a man in church worship God. They only saw women praise God. So, they began to clap like their mamas, shout like their grandmothers and took on an effeminate spirit"(quoted in Williams 2003).

Stevens's ideologies are not shocking or spectacular to those familiar with black church parlance—they are quotidian, mundane, very much ordinary in thought and expression, though no less accusatory, unfounded, and problematic. It appears that Stevens is worried by a particular mode of sociality that ruptures not just religion but culture generally. What would it mean to not marginalize the feminine, not to look for its dissolution but, rather, to privilege it? The disruption he envisions occurs by way of a feminine/feminizing spirit that announces and disburses through *aesthesis* and has all sorts of potential that Stevens can only register as ontic and social death. Aesthesis/aesthesia as I am deploying it deserves a bit of clarification. Aesthesis and aesthesia are the antitheses of anesthetic and anesthesia. Understood as the blocking of or temporary alleviation from sensation, anesthetic devices are used in medicine to reduce distress and pain felt during a medical procedure such as surgery. In this essay, aesthesia refers to one's capacity to have or perceive sensation; the aesthetic will be those sensations, and aesthesia the openness to feeling, sensing, or perceiving the aesthetic.

What intrigues me about Stevens's interview is how the artistic, social, sensual, affective, spiritual norms of the black church register as aesthetic aggression. These norms are detected by clothing, color choices, emotionalism, screams and hollers that are read as feminine—and thus deadly. That femininity—embodied in and disbursed by homosexuals—is a spiritual problem that must be overcome bespeaks a desire to shore up against porosity or penetrability. This is, of course, confusing, particularly when stated by a person like Stevens who is part of the Pentecostal Church of God in Christ, a denomination that privileges the "movement of the Spirit" and the theology of the "baptism of the Holy Ghost," which is most evidentiary through speaking in tongues.

No names were mentioned in the airing of this broadcast, but that, of course, both propels rumor and gossip and diminishes the particularity of the material bodies affected by such circulatory rhetorics. For Stevens and others of his ilk, the feminine registers in a whole range of aesthetic practices, music being no exception. In fact, music is wholly implicated in this process and could be thought of as the prominent example of these issues: for it is when the singer—in the interview, most definitely male—performs that one witnesses the clothing, one hears the sound, one sees the body movements, one listens to the screaming and hollering, one witnesses the effect. If the black church is conceived as one that privileges movement, but movement—of the body, of the voice, of the aesthetics to the ecstatics—is bound up with the feminine, and thus the nonanalytic and nonrational, the black church itself approaches its own declination. This movement, of course, is quite fine for women but certainly not for men. The movement of men—of their body, of their voice—is entirely a feminine, gay, transgressive, transgendered, unholy, ungodly thing that must be forestalled. Is there a contradictory impulse at play here? There is the desire both toward and away from the feminine on the part of the institutional black church; there is the necessity of the marginal character to give meaning to the central figure. That is, the marginal character(istics) are both centripetal and centrifugal coterminously. The circulation of rumor and gossip creates a narrative about abject sexualities in ways that highlight the complicated and contradictory ideologies at work in the black church, as there is both a valuation of the body and a devaluation of (some of its) movements.

Eric Lott's thought-provoking writing regarding blackface minstrelsy assists in articulating some contradictory and complicated sexualized impulses at work through his excavation of the various ways in which people thought about blackface minstrelsy throughout its life in the United States. For example, he states, "Minstrelsy brought to public form racialized elements of thought and feeling, tone and impulse, residing at the very edge of semantic availability, which Americans only dimly realized they felt, let alone understood" (1993, 6). I believe the circulation of rumor and gossip participates in a similar process of highlighting and elucidating—via public rhetoric and discourse, regardless of how hushed or rushed and quiet that discourse is—the testing of sexualized boundaries for what it means (or could possibly mean) to be black and Christian.

Fred Moten offers this: "What is it to be an irreducibly disordering, deformational force while at the same time being absolutely indispensable to normative order, normative form?" (2008, 180). It appears that these queer subjects are disordering, deformational, *and* dysfunctional but no less necessary for the religio-cultural coherence. Black queer men are one sort of testing ground for pushing boundaries, for exploration—via imagination and fantasy—of a utopian movement away from boundedness. And the force of such testing congeals, at least partially, around the enunciative voice, how it leaps and descends, trembles and quivers. What is apparent in Stevens's interview is "the honesty and clarity with which [he] expressed what [seems] to be a rather profound alienation from his own corporality, his so-called [blackness], alienation that is focused and transmitted precisely through [homophobic] discourse." This discourse illustrates "an anxiety engendered by his will to recapture normality in the face of the intense sense of vertigo that [is] shared" (Reid-Pharr 2001, 90). Just under the surface of this rumor and gossip is a more fundamental concern: how do the queered subjects establish personhood in the face (and hushed narratives) of impossibility; how can the religio-cultural world castigate the queer subject only to mine it as a resource?

Rumor and gossip—such as that voiced by Stevens—marginalize persons by creating a discourse that enframes them and relegates them to the domain of the sinful. More, these very queer subjects do not operate simply in a black and queer aesthesis (two oppositional forces, queerness always already read as a "white" thing), but in a "blackqueer aesthesis" that is wholly part of, wholly bound up with and easily definable in the black radical aesthetic tradition. Blackqueer aesthesis operates by way of an aesthetic escape, by way of the capacity to give. Though Stevens conceives of femininity as weakness, when men perform it, it is downright criminal. The desire for its removal at any cost bespeaks its irreducible strength, the strength of the radical openness, radical feminine we find in blackqueer aesthesis. The black male's voice—within its context of the black church space, as bare materiality that precedes song—recovers the feminine that Stevens seeks to dissolve.

Adriana Cavarero elucidates this concern by discussing maternity and voice: "Before making itself speech, the voice is an invocation that is addressed to the other and that entrusts itself to an ear that receives it" (2005, 169). Cavarero speaks about the voice in terms of its uniqueness to each individual. She utilizes an infant/mother relationship to explicate how there is relationality of the voice. For Cavarero, "There is . . . a cadence of demand and response—or, better, a reciprocal invocation in which the voices [of the mother and the infant] convoke one another in turn. This cadence has its temporal rhythms, its communicative soundtrack, its la-la melody—it has a certain measure, if not yet a law" (170). Steven Feld's writing about acoustemology is similarly helpful: "Hearing and voice are connected by auditory feedback and by physical resonance, the immediate experience of one's presence through the echo-chamber of the chest and head, the reverberant sensation of sound, principally one's own voice" (Feld and Basso 1996, 97). And is not call and response—what Cavarero terms a reciprocal invocation, what Feld discusses as auditory feedback and physical resonance—integral to the BGS? Cavarero establishes for us a mode of social life that, depending as it does on sonic convocation and invocation, obscures the normative binary of male/female, masculine/feminine. The mode of social life Cavarero finds for us depends upon cry and anticipation. The child cries out with sound (call) with expectation that someone will hear (response). This anticipatory mode of social life that desires relationality with others without depending on that preestablished relationality for action is about the capacity for such enactment. This reciprocal invocation of voices convokes and, I will add, constitutes the other because "in the uniqueness that makes itself heard as voice, there is an embodied existent, or rather, a 'being there' [*esserci*] in its radical finitude, here and now" (Cavarero 2005, 173). You gotta be there to hear it, to sing it, to clap to it, to experience it, gotta be there to have *being* there. But, in return, if these black men have *being* by way of their performance of and through blackqueer aesthesis, the voice critiques the theology of their valuelessness, of their beinglessness.

The voices of black men who sing BGM—as part of the blackqueer aesthetic ensemble—convoke and constitute the other, the congregation that listens. Of course, for Stevens, the convoking and constituting by invoking the Spirit through a blackqueer aesthetic sets off all sorts of problems. Aurally, this blackqueer aesthetic is the fugitivity of voice, the uncontainable interiority of the subject sounding out once emitted, a seeming lawlessness found in aesthetics, a sound that is itself ecstatic and calls for the ecstasy in others, a movement of Spirit that allows the vocalist to operate as a preface and perforce to *ekstasis* in the vocalist *and* congregant. This fugitivity, this lawlessness, bodies forth through a *form*, through music as an organizing principle. This form is regulative and restrictive. By way of blackqueer aesthesis, the voice resists regulation and restriction at the moment of performance. The strictures of religio-culture create the queer subject at the scene of musical performance by making enjoyment and amusement impossible, by making the condition terminal, by making sensuous sound by particularly biologically determined bodies abject. This fashioning of the blackqueer male subject in the context of the black church expresses through sound the pain caused by these hateful and hate-filled rhetorics. Our personhood, though, exceeds this process: we withhold our consent to these conditions while outpouring the burden in sound; the pain is joy, the ashes are beautiful, the mourning becomes song. So even in the space of impossible enjoyment, we smile and dance and laugh and sing. It is not false consciousness or merely cathartic. It is a working of something new in the conditions that oppose you. The blackqueer aesthesis Stevens critiques is "given in the register of the merely sensual"—evidenced by Stevens's focus on attire, color, and affect—but this mere sensuality is a rhetorical blush, it hides his just-below-the-surface melancholic desire to understand and, quite possibly, identify with (Moten 2007, 221). And it is this seeming "mere sensuality" of excess that sets off the readings, desires to know, to regulate and force conforming upon blackqueer ecstatics, rumor and gossip functioning as a means toward all these concurrently operational aspirations.

Queer men in the cultural imagination are thought to have nothing to *give*. We are thought to obscure manhood and masculinity by becoming physical, bodily receptors who *choose* this state of being rather than have it befall us at the time of conception (that is, biologic determinism). From being conceived as sex inverts to embodied perverts, homosexual men are all thought to be bottoms (though there's nothing wrong with being a bottom). However, I argue that the voice of the blackqueer men—within the context of the black church—*gives* in a way that ruptures a normative conceptual framework of what it means to be, and to be queer. This giving results in the spirited, spiritual ability to move others outside oneself through ecstasy. We are masc and fem, top and bottom, giver and receiver, flamboyant and undetectable, seen and unseen, dangerous and holy, hated and loved, undervalued and appreciated, feedfront and feedback. This is a different mode of sociality, to be sure, and it contradicts everything thought (im)possible. It is friendship as a way of life.[4] Thus, blackqueer aesthesis, voiced by the voice, displays the viability and tenacity of a life force that is thought to be nothing other than the drive toward death.

Of course, the status, the condition of/as "the homosexual" is seeming lawlessness and unregulated pleasure that occurs, as it were, previous to behavior, it is "a sexuality whose criminality lies in and before the fact that it is" abominable (Moten 2007, 234). The status and condition of/as "the homosexual" (and all of its pejorative synonyms) require the faculty of imagination to create and sustain such circumscribing, voyeuristic rhetorics. Thus, at the moment of performance, the voice of one imagined as "the homosexual," the voice of the queered subject, is a relay and oscillation between the vulgarity and the virtuosity in the same breath. The ways in which queerness is imaginatively linked to the sounds particular persons make instantiate the infinite range of possibilities—of sexuality of melisma, falsetto, moans, groans, inversions; the multitudinous configuration of relationships found in the imagination; the limitlessness of the fantastic—found in and as any voice. The sound is the enunciation of the uniqueness and singularity of one's personhood, by way of a criminality that is anti- and ante-, which is to say against and before, the law. This before and against the law brings into operation the rumor and gossip that would so desire to function as regulatory.

The circulation of rumor and gossip regarding black men who sing BGM performs the same sort of stripping of identity—by way of the sonic materiality.[5] Placed into a collective identity that is marginalized, the particularity of identity is dismissed because each person who belongs to this collective needs to change his sinful behavior, lest he continue to live in sin. The radical nature of singing anyhow—of choosing to sing when the world tells you that you should not or that you could not—is diminished because all black men who sing are relegated, are framed, in this particular mode of being. That is, everyone is a pervert, a psychopath, a pedophile. But singing anyhow allows for an escape from the enframement, it allows for a radical disruption of the circulatory rhetorics. The blackqueer aesthetic's potential energy is transformed into kinesthesia through the voice, the voice announces the uniqueness of the individual, the uniqueness of the individual refuses others' refusals to hear.

And stripping is an important framing for the famed fairy tale "The Emperor's New Clothes," which finds much circulation in children's lives, even today. Two swindlers come to town to dupe the emperor; they fashion clothes out of nothing and proclaim that only the intelligent and worthy will be able to see and feel them. The emperor agrees to their wishes because he wants the finest robes made from the most extravagant fabrics, though doubtful of their claims. When he sends members of his court to view the progression of the fabrication, they literally see the untruths of the new "clothes." However, no one wants to be thought of as stupid or an unfit courtier and each forthrightly proclaims that he can see what isn't visible, that he can feel what isn't tangible. Eventually, the swindlers have the emperor try on his new threads, and his court acclaims the raiment: "They didn't dare let on that they couldn't see a thing" (Andersen and Nunnally 2005, 94). The emperor walks through his court, people professing the wondrous works of the swindlers, the beauty of those new clothes. But everyone knows this simple fact: the emperor is naked.

I always have been fascinated by this story because the emperor walks through the streets, celebrating his *au naturel*-ness it seems, head held high rather than appearing inane, inept, or disturbed by the townspeople's astonished stares and smiles as they regard him. It is not simply the nakedness that intrigues me but the circuitous narratives that buttress the fairy tale. The townspeople were all talking about the exquisiteness of the emperor's new clothes before they saw them, based on the rumors they heard, and it takes the announcement of a child—"But he doesn't have anything on!"—to set in motion another cycle of storytelling: "And one person whispered to the next what the child had said" until the entire crowd was decrying the Emperor's lack of clothing" (Andersen and Nunnally 2005, 94, 95). What immediately strikes is the power of the word to create truth, the ability of rhetorics to create narratives that the entire community accepts. It seems that knowing and telling serve two different functions, the oral utterance working in concert with and against the emperor's performance of conviction and pride.

The lack of cloth, of materiality, occasions the circulation of rumor and gossip in the fairy tale. The clothing—that layer which hides the "private parts" from the world, the layer that culturally encodes bodies with meaning—is removed, the emperor risking the inquiry into his intelligence and character through the materiality of cloth. Everyone knows of the emperor's nakedness but he chooses to stride through town, seemingly impervious to the jeers. But the nakedness of the emperor does not affect just the visual domain, but the sonic as well. When he walks down the street, people whisper to one another and a child exclaims. The visual is augmented by the sonic, and the sonic—by way of whispers and exclamations—occasions the circulation of the narrative.

Hans Christian Andersen was well acquainted with the removal of clothing to appease an audience's insatiable desire to *know* rather than simply *tell*. When he was young, this soon-to-be writer of tales was a singer with a melodious, moving soprano voice and he used this voice to entertain workers to support the income of his working-class mother. This working-class background created the condition for the necessity of his work but also led to a peculiar assault on Andersen's personhood. "So beautiful was his high-pitched voice that [the workmen he entertained through song] soon decided that he must be a girl, and forcibly undressed him to find out" (Andersen and Nunnally 2005, xix). He fled the scene and his mother promised that he need never return. The emperor's narrative demands reconsideration with Andersen's history in mind, a revaluation of the nakedness, the pride and the aloofness with which the emperor moves. Is it possible that Andersen wished to revise his own story wherein nakedness would not mean shame? Where song would not lead to shaming?

Andersen's life and the emperor's narrative both give critical attention to the circulation of rumor and gossip; they both inquire into the difference between knowing and telling. But more, the emperor's narrative of being naked and unashamed revises Andersen's shaming through forced nakedness. It seems that Andersen's stripping as a result of his voice as well as his revision of the meaning of nakedness, rumor, and gossip give a way to analyze the circulatory praxis of queering sound in BGM. Like the emperor's lack of clothing posited as something "new," so too is the rhetoric that claims that the many gay, lesbian, bisexual, and transgender people visible in black churches are "new," but that is not the case.

Disco singer Sylvester knew all too well the damaging, stripping effects of rumor and gossip on personhood but chose to sing anyway. Born September 6, 1947, Sylvester (James) was reared in the Palm Lane Church of God in Christ. By the age of three, he would go to the choir stand to sing with others, though he was far too young. If removed from the choir, Sylvester would simply run back until the fatigued congregants allowed him to sing. His was a voice that must be heard, and he knew this from an early age; it was a voice that refused others' refusals of it.

> Like a lot of church kids, Dooni [Sylvester] was banging on the piano and singing by the time he was three. It turned out he could sing quite well, pretty and soprano-high, and he seemed to have made a decision very early on that he would be heard. "If you said no," his mother said, "he was determined to let it be yes. That was just his own personality." You had to be eleven to join the choir, but Dooni, years too young, would wait until the choir came marching in and jump into line from the pew. Someone in the choir would put him out, but usually he would come right back in the side door. They'd put him out again, and he might still slip himself back in. "He would just *make* them listen to him, 'cause he was so determined to sing," his mother said. (Gamson 2005, 20)

Sylvester used the materiality of his voice—high soprano, falsetto—to force others to contend with his material body. His body mattered, and the enunciation of the voice was used to compel others to deal with his personhood: and others listened. Is it possible that the congregants tried to shield Dooni from living a narrative about queerness that already circulated in black religious circles? It is, I think, at least probable. Maybe they looked at his aesthetic choices—from composure to comportment when he sang, when he walked, when he talked, when he played—and decided that if he utilized his voice, his queerness would be solidified. But Dooni was unrelenting, and what is more probable is that he recognized within himself a difference that he did not want to withdraw from but to rehearse and revise publicly through song.

Not only did folks listen to Dooni but they were moved by him in and out of church: "Everywhere he went he made a name for himself singing 'Never Grow Old.' When he got through, everybody would be shouting," his mother said. "He would just *dismiss* church, then he would run off and play in the parking lot" (21). His ability to dismiss the church through song did not protect him from the church's dismissal of him when he outgrew being a "pretty little thing" during puberty, when his mannerisms were more than an indication of a youthful zeal.

> It turned out that Dooni had discovered not just God but sex at Palm Lane. By the age of eight, Sylvester later told . . . [that] he had been introduced to "the life"—homosexual life—by a choir leader. Sylvester never named the man publicly, and he didn't tell his family about it until many years later. . . . But at Palm Lane, people began to talk about Dooni. . . . His effeminacy was now hard to write off as child's play, and Dooni wasn't working very hard to be like the other boys. His voice was changing, but he still preferred to sing in the high range. Rumors circulated, too, that he was doing unmentionable things upstairs with a man from the church. (23)

Sylvester enacted a refusal of others' refusals to hear him, using the striving toward the falsetto range, a soprano voice even when, physically, he had "outgrown" it. For Sylvester, the striving toward the falsetto would continually be used throughout his lifetime as a singer and would distinguish him from other singers. In both cases, there was a blackqueer aesthetic choice to exceed the limits of the predefined, prescripted, prescribed aurality placed on men. Is this nothing other than the desire to create something new out of the voice's materiality? Falsetto and new worlds? This is Nathaniel Mackey's realm: "[T]he deliberately forced, deliberately 'false' voice we get from someone like Al Green creatively hallucinates a 'new world,' indicts the more insidious falseness of the world as we know it. . . . Like the moan or the shout, I'm suggesting, the falsetto explores a redemptive, unworded realm—a meta-word, if you will—where the implied critique or the momentary eclipse of the word curiously rescues, restores and renews it: new word, new world" (1986, 51–52). In a world that marginalizes queer possibilities, Sylvester turned to and utilized the voice to give place and meaning to his personhood; he utilized voice to critique the world in which he lived and imagine a new world that was fully inhabitable. This ability to critique and live was smuggled in by aesthetic choice.

Like the emperor, materiality is important to queering the BGS. Whereas the absence of the material of cloth sets off the dominoes of rumor and gossip in Andersen's tale, the absence of a seeming normative gendered/sexual materiality (masculinity, bravado, straightness, heterosexuality) of voice sets off the dominoes of rumor and gossip in the BGS, Sylvester's example as illustrative. The materiality of his voice secreted the presence of blackqueer aesthesis. The materiality of the voice is what is implicated as queer itself and sets into motion all sorts of tattling, from the inappropriateness of his voice to the inappropriateness of his upper-room sex. Cultural meaning is ascribed to the voice when performed under certain restraints.

But he chose to sing anyhow. It is tantamount to our revaluation of the value of nakedness, writing a children's story wherein the emperor proudly walks around the town naked, aware of his nakedness. Singing anyhow, knowing that a narrative exists before you ever pick up a microphone, is a powerful and potent revaluation of the value of rhetoric that seeks to circumscribe behavior. Rumor and gossip, behaving as a stripping of sorts, make possible the detection and disbursement of what is thought of as the *merely sensual* of blackqueer aesthesia that we can hear. So heard, blackqueer aesthesia announces the personhood *anyhow,* declares the value of those who have being that homophobic theologies cannot refuse to hear.

To sing anyhow is to refuse the role of an object that has no interiority and to refuse the role of collaborator in one's own marginalization.[6] Rather, as artists who create art and are art—art by way of blackqueer aesthesia—singers who sing anyhow achieve "a near perfect balance of behavior and self-consciousness" that arises from the "degree to which [one can] both *express* [one's] state of mind and also self-consciously acknowledge it" (Piper 1996, 92). In singing anyhow—utilizing the voice under rhetorical and often violent constraint—aurality, through blackqueer aesthesia potential, is transformed to kinesthesia, moving congregations. A theological conviction and sonic proclamation of one's worth despite what others perceive are declared. Those who invoke and convoke others are worrisome: they worry the line musically to worry the religio-socio-cultural boundaries. They recover the feminine/maternal that some seek to dissolve by way of creating a prophylactic covering against the feminine. Blackqueer aesthesis refuses to be refused.

Notes

1. See Baldwin 1979; Talbert 2008.

2. "Previous to" is from Nathaniel Mackey's work (1986).

3. I use the term *black church* to refer to Christian assemblies in the United States with ministries that serve predominantly black congregations. This is not to say that

all black churches share the same theology or aesthetic practices, but to index the historical conditions of constraint under which many were created.

4. Michel Foucault's interview "Friendship as a Way of Life" has been very influential to my thinking through modes of sociality with regard to queer sex and friendship. See Foucault and Lotringer 1996.

5. For useful studies on the relation of queerness to musicality, see Hubbs 2004; Gill 1995; Brett et al. 2006; and Whiteley and Rycenga 2006.

6. See Adrian Piper's "Untitled Performance in Max's Kansas City" in Piper 1996.

References

Andersen, H. C., and T. Nunnally. 2005. *Fairy Tales.* New York: Viking.

Baldwin, J. 1979. *Just above My Head.* New York: Dial.

Boyer, H. C., and L. Yearwood. 1995. *The Golden Age of Gospel.* Washington, D.C.: Elliott & Clark.

Brett, P. et al. 2006. *Queering the Pitch: The New Gay and Lesbian Musicology.* New York: Routledge.

Butler, J. P. 1993. *Bodies That Matter: On the Discursive Limits of "Sex".* New York: Routledge.

Cavarero, A. 2005. *For More Than One Voice: Toward a Philosophy of Vocal Expression.* Stanford: Stanford University Press.

Evans, C. 1994. *Immorality in the Church—Homosexuality.* Chicago: J.-P. Records.

Feld, S., and K. H. Basso. 1996. *Senses of Place.* Santa Fe, NM: School of American Research Press.

Foucault, M. 1996. "Friendship As a Way of Life." In *Foucault Live: Collected Interviews, 1961–1984,* edited by S. Lotringer, translated by J. Jonston, 308–12. Semiotext(e) Double Agents Series. New York: Semiotext(e).

Gamson, J. 2005. *The Fabulous Sylvester: The Legend, the Music, the Seventies in San Francisco.* New York: H. Holt.

Gill, J. 1995. *Queer Noises: Male and Female Homosexuality in Twentieth Century Music.* Minneapolis: University of Minnesota Press.

Heilbut, A. 1971. *The Gospel Sound: Good News and Bad Times.* New York: Simon & Schuster.

Hubbs, N. 2004. *The Queer Composition of America's Sound: Gay Modernists, American Music, and National Identity.* Berkeley: University of California Press.

Kelly, F. 1998. "Women's Day Sermon, 82nd COGIC International Convocation." Memphis.

Locke, I. 2007. "Abyssinia Christ Centered Ministries—Iona Locke Ministries." http://www.ionalocke.net (accessed November 18, 2007).

Lott, E. 1993. *Love and Theft: Blackface Minstrelsy and the American Working Class.* New York: Oxford University Press.

Mackey, N. 1986. *Bedouin Hornbook.* Charlottesville: University Press of Virginia.

Moore, M. 2008. "Black Church, Black Patriarchy, and the 'Brilliant Queer': Competing Masculinities in Langston Hughes's 'Blessed Assurance.'" *African American Review* 42(3–4): 493–502.

Moten, F. 2003. *In the Break: The Aesthetics of the Black Radical Tradition.* Minneapolis: University of Minnesota Press.

———. 2007. "Taste Dissonance Flavor Escape: Preface for a Solo by Miles Davis." *Women and Performance: A Journal of Feminist Theory* 17(2): 217–46.

———. 2008. "The Case of Blackness." *Criticism* 50(2): 177–218.

Nero, C. 2005. "Queering *The Souls of Black Folk.*" *Public Culture* 17(2): 255–76.

Owens, A. 2006. *Fan or Follower.* Washington, D.C.: Greater Mount Calvary Holy Church.

Piper, A. 1996. *Out of Order, out of Sight.* Cambridge, MA: MIT Press.

Reid-Pharr, R. 2001. *Black Gay Man: Essays.* New York: New York University Press.

Stevens, Michael. 2007. "Special Feature—Interview with Michael Stevens." Gospelcity.com.

Talbert, D. 2008. *First Sunday.* Sony Pictures Home Entertainment.

Whiteley, S., and J. Rycenga. 2006. *Queering the Popular Pitch.* New York: Routledge.

Williams, Leslie. 2003. "Panel Explores Sex, Power, Spirituality." *The Times-Picayune,* July 4.

Wilson, W. 2005. *You've Got a Right to be Free.* Washington, D.C.; Union Temple Baptist Church.

The Practice of Embodiment

Transatlantic Crossings and Black Female Sexuality in Nella Larsen's *Quicksand*

Deborah Katz

The Diasporic Mulatta Body

In *The Practice of Diaspora: Literature, Translation, and the Rise of Black Internationalism,* Brent Edwards argues that the central question of Harlem Renaissance writings should be how "black expression between the world wars . . . was molded through attempts to appropriate and transform the discourses of internationalism" (2003, 3). Figuring Alain Locke's "New Negro" as a "new" black internationalism, he writes, goes against mainstream scholarship on black culture in the 1920s, "which has tended to emphasize U.S. bound themes of cultural nationalism . . . and uplift" (2–3) rather than considering the ways in which cultural nationalist movements were always shaped by global race politics. In a challenge to nationally bound histories of black art and politics in this period, Edwards's paradigm of diaspora privileges "outernational" cosmopolitan geographical spaces, like "the European metropole," which offered "a special sort of vibrant, cosmopolitan space for interactions" (4) between black expatriates.

Edwards's premise is indebted to Paul Gilroy's *The Black Atlantic: Modernity and Double Consciousness,* which provides an oceanic framework for black modernity. Gilroy's focus, "the history of the black Atlantic . . . continuously crisscrossed by the movements of black people—not only as commodities but engaged in various struggles towards emancipation, autonomy and citizenship" (1993, 16), foregrounds the political bent implicit in both his and Edwards's modes of reading. For Gilroy, people of African descent who undergo transatlantic crossings become agents who enact their liberation even as they remain captured commodities. Consequently, when Edwards writes that "black radicalism *is* an internationalization" (2003, 243), he also suggests that the opposite is true: black "internationalization," or geographic "boundary crossing," is by definition "radicalism." In both Gilroy's and Edwards's formulation of the black Atlantic and black diaspora, respectively, Atlantic crossings were a historic and historical apotheosis of black political interaction and resistance.

Because of this focus on black transatlantic movement, Edwards and Gilroy would appear to offer a possible vocabulary with which to map the transnational shuttlings in Nella Larsen's novel *Quicksand.* Published in 1928, *Quicksand* tells the story of Helga Crane, a young woman born of a black American father and a white Danish mother who, feeling ever dissatisfied with and entrapped by her various local communities, leaves her teaching position at Naxos, a black school in the rural American South, for her hometown of Chicago, then moves to Harlem, across the ocean to her dead mother's native Copenhagen, and back to the United States. But while both Gilroy and Edwards mention Larsen in passing, neither of their formulations account for two crucial aspects of *Quicksand*'s transatlantic crossings: the corporeality of Helga's biracial subjectivity and objectification, and her physical discomfort with black community. As I will discuss later in this chapter, both of these experiences are largely shaped and exacerbated by Helga's struggles with white definitions of blackness as visual, embodied performance.[1] When Gilroy asks, "What of Nella Larsen's relationship to Denmark?" (1993, 18), he poses the question in the context of Copenhagen's underground political radicalism,[2] suggesting that Denmark warrants more critical attention as a site of "counterculture." However, figuring the relationship of Nella Larsen—or that of *Quicksand*'s protagonist—to Denmark as one of political insurgency against modernity fails to account for the apolitical, anticommunal diasporic position narrated through the complicated representations of Helga's body.

Moreover, while Edwards usefully concedes that Larsen's fiction critiques "the ways the black modernist modes of imagining expatriation and migration are always gendered" (2003, 141), his greater attention to "institutional formations of black internationalism" (11) necessarily privileges the political motives for furthering black community abroad over the psychic and physical experience of a body in transit. As a result, his brief mention of *Quicksand* cannot sustain a consideration of the crucial ways in which gender shapes Helga's vexed relationship to black bodies in various geographic locations. In this essay, I argue that *Quicksand*'s diaspora, routed through Helga's initial aversions to embodiment, her later embrace of it in Copenhagen, and her eventual suffocation from it in an unnamed rural town in the American South, in fact reveals the novel's ambivalence toward such ideological conceptions of diaspora. In other words, Helga Crane's physical movement between the United States and Demark, paralleled by her discomfort with black *bodies,* elucidates not Edwards's practice of "diaspora" but a practice of *escaping* diaspora, an attempt to flee black community.

While critical response to Helga's uncomfortable body has been rich and substantive, missing in this generative analysis is a consideration of the ways in which that body adapts to and is shaped by transnational movement and location. In order to recenter the crucial component of embodiment in these black transatlantic crossings, I turn to Lauren Berlant's brief reading in *The Female Complaint: The Unfinished Business of Sentimentality in American Culture* of Larsen's novel *Passing,* published one year after *Quicksand.* Berlant argues that "the way the citizen conventionally acquires a new body by participation in the political public sphere" is an impossible task for anyone who cannot claim the "implicit whiteness and maleness of the original American citizen" (2008, 110). Therefore, the black woman, and "the mulatta" in particular, is the "most abstract and artificial of *embodied* citizens . . . the paradigm problem citizen" (111). Irene Redfield, the middle-class mulatta protagonist of *Passing,* refuses to move with her husband and sons to Brazil, insisting, "She was American. She grew from this soil, and would not be uprooted" (235). In response, Berlant writes that Irene's "will . . . to flee her body by embracing the Liberty Tree suggests . . . her desire to shed" her racially marked, gendered body through "identification with the state" (111). While both Helga and Irene are biracial African American women with vexed attitudes toward their "racially marked" and sexually legible bodies, the national loyalty that interests Berlant in *Passing* cannot be said to inform Helga's imagination of the United States as "home." Despite migrating to and settling in a southern town as a preacher's wife by the end of the novel, Helga remains skeptical about the land of America itself: she still thinks of America as "this vicious, this hypocritical land" (Larsen 1986, 130), a poor place to raise her black children. Therefore, Berlant's reading of Irene's nationalism in *Passing* usefully highlights the contrast between the protagonists of these two works, suggesting the centrality not only of American soil but of international travel in *Quicksand*'s narrative of mulatta embodiment.

This essay stages its intervention at the discursive crossroads of these two modes of reading, Edwards's and Gilroy's geographic and transatlantic on the one hand and Berlant's emphasis on the body and disembodiment of the "mulatta" subject on the other, to ask what such an intersection might reveal about the troubled specters of "diaspora" and black female sexuality in *Quicksand.* I will begin this analysis with a consideration of why Helga's transatlantic attempts to evade "diaspora"—meaning a global network of black community—

occur concurrently with her feelings of repulsion to black bodies, and her desire to flee them, both others' and her own. To do so, I will briefly examine instances of her disavowal of bodies that motivate her departures from Harlem, and then explore the allure of consumer subjectivity that leads her initially to accept embodiment as a black, aestheticized object in Copenhagen. I will conclude with a discussion of the ways in which transatlantic travel affords her an agency that is lost upon her reimmersion into a rural black community in the American South. I will argue that her permanent settling there, where she becomes reduced to nothing but her body, signals the impossibility of disembodiment providing an escape from the confines of diasporic identification.

From Escape to Embodiment

Feminist critics of *Quicksand* have read Helga Crane's discomfort with black bodies and her own sexuality as Larsen's response to popular representations of African American women as sexually debased. In her introduction to the American Women Writers Series' edition of *Quicksand,* Deborah McDowell argues that Larsen belongs to a coterie of "black women novelists" who have responded to "the pattern of social and literary myths perpetuated throughout history about black women's libidinousness . . . by insisting ferociously on [the black woman's] chastity" (1986, xii–xiii). In *Bodies That Matter,* Judith Butler agrees that Helga's distaste for physical intimacy is a correlative of her reined-in sexuality, adding that this portrayal has autobiographical motivations: "Larsen herself appears to be caught in that very dilemma, withholding a presentation of black women's sexuality precisely in order to avert the consequences of its becoming exoticized" (1993, 174).

While the correspondence between Helga's flight from the body and her flight from "diaspora" is suggested by the proximity of these events in the plot of *Quicksand,* the variance in her reaction to black bodies, particularly in Harlem, sheds further light on the motivation for her departure. After she leaves Naxos and then Chicago, the potential nearness of black bodies when she first arrives in Harlem actually exhilarates her: "She stood in the doorway, drawn by an uncontrollable desire to mingle with the crowd. . . . As she stepped out into the moving multi-colored crowd . . . she felt . . . that she had come home" (Larsen 1986, 30). *This* mass of "dark molds of flesh" appeals to and even grounds Helga with a sense of place and "home" in part because she can displace her embodiment onto others via a physical proximity that is safe because it is *contained.* These pedestrians are not only anonymous, their bodies are fully covered, a far cry from the hypersexualized music and dancers in the Harlem dance club or the flailing black bodies she will later witness in Copenhagen. In contrast, the disgust that causes Helga to escape black community is always in response to overtly sexual or otherwise *excessive* bodies in which she fears seeing something of herself. When "more and more she made lonely excursions to places outside of Harlem" (47), it is because "as the days became hotter and the streets more sweltering, a kind of revulsion came upon her. She recoiled in aversion" (48) from "the dozen or more brown faces, all cast from the same indefinite mold, and so like her own . . . pressing forward against her. . . . It was as if she were shut up, boxed up with hundreds of her race" (54). It is this intimate enclosure with hundreds of naked faces identical to "her own" that incites Helga's horror over the imagined constriction on her bodily mobility.

In a Harlem nightclub, the tantalizing closeness to the throbbing, overt sexuality of black bodies temporarily incites an excitement in Helga that quickly turns to the same aversion. As Helga listens to the club's music, "The essence of life seemed bodily motion. And when suddenly the music died, she dragged herself back to the present with conscious effort; a shameful certainty that not only had she been in the jungle, but that she had enjoyed it. . . . She hardened her determination to get away." This passage is notable for its portrayal of "bodily motion" as the conduit of her psychic movement into the sensual "jungle" and as the motivation for her departure from the club (and soon thereafter from the United States). When the "swirling mass" of dancing black bodies closes in on her, Helga feels physically "strangled by the savage strains of music" (Larsen 1986, 59). "After surrendering to the music, [Helga] longs all the more to flee to Europe" (Gray 1994, 262); in response to both her "shameful certainty" of her connection to the black music and her fear of asphyxiation by the overtly sensuous black bodies, she becomes "purposely aloof and a little contemptuous" (Larsen 1986, 60), emotionally preparing for her escape to Copenhagen.

Given that the first sections of the novel chart Helga's flight from black bodies, we might expect the Copenhagen chapters to narrate a continuation of this drive for disembodiment. However, as Helga's is the only black body in her aunt and uncle's middle-class circles, her social value depends on her embrace of that body as an exoticized, commodified spectacle. The Naxos chapters of *Quicksand*, which suggest that Helga's body has always been cast as aesthetic object, explicate the ease with which she undertakes the transition in Copenhagen. The novel opens with Helga in her room at the school, "well fitted to the framing of light and shade" (Larsen 1986, 2), like a painting. With the abundance of her exoticized possessions, "the blue Chinese carpet . . . the oriental silk" (1), "the text slips between her own aesthetic appreciation of beauty, and her exhibition by others" (Snaith 2007, 216) as it foreshadows Helga's exhibition as commodity in Copenhagen.[3] At Naxos, Helga strikes the others as "odd" because her belief that "bright colors *were* fitting . . . dusky skins" (Larsen 1986, 18) implies that black bodies are particularly suited for display as art.

Therefore, upon her arrival in Copenhagen, when her late mother's sister, Katrina Dahl, tells her, "You must have bright things to set off the color of your lovely skin. Striking things, exotic things," she is only echoing Helga's own beliefs about the appropriateness of black exhibitionism and the role of "exotic things" in demonstrating cosmopolitan consumer status. She also designates Helga as *the* exotic thing that will "play in advancing the social fortunes of the Dahls." Notably, the first article of clothing Helga dons after her fitting with her aunt is a Chinese red dressing gown, which "suits" her, according to her aunt (Larsen 1986, 68). Those silks that indicated her cosmopolitan status in America turn her into an exotic commodity in Copenhagen (Snaith 2007, 216): in her "shining black taffeta with its bizarre trimmings of purple and cerise . . . Helga felt like a veritable savage . . . nothing so much as some new and strange species of pet dog being proudly exhibited" (Larsen 1986, 69–70). While Helga feels torn, she "had to admit that Fru Dahl was right about the dressing gown. . . . and her feet *were* nice" (69); at this point, the opportunity to be admired seems worth the dehumanizing humiliation of being put on display.

The crucial difference from her exhibitionism at Naxos is that here, its purpose is to "make an impression" on the white Danes rather than to make her fellow working-class blacks "uncomfortable" (Larsen 1986, 18). Due to Copenhagen's European colonial legacy, foreign uniqueness and class privilege, as opposed to loner status, facilitate the commercial success of Helga's exoticism. As Jeffrey Gray argues, Helga's "embodiment as black American" takes place in Copenhagen (1994, 265) rather than in America because she "is carrying on a tradition . . . of exhibiting 'exotic' African females at European social gatherings" (262). Helga's idealization of a raceless Copenhagen where "there were no Negroes, no problems, no prejudice" (Larsen 1986, 55)—no uncomfortable physical intimacy with other black bodies—demonstrates her ignorance of that colonial, class-striated history that propels her to local celebrity. On the boat to Copenhagen, free from the stifling presence of black bodies in America, she "enjoys that blessed sense of belonging to herself and not to a race" (64). And in contrast to Harlem's "glimmering" avenues "swarming with people, merging into little eddies" (30), Copenhagen streets, Helga initially observes, are "toy-like," filled not with bodies but with "bicycles" (66), and distinguished by "amazing orderliness" (79).

In "Helga Crane's Copenhagen," Arne Lunde and Anna Westerstahl Stenport contend, "Helga's phantasmagoria of an all-white ethnically homogeneous stability far from a conflicted heterogeneous America contradicts not only Denmark's history as a colonial power and involvement in the trans-Atlantic slave trade, but also the documented presence of Afro-Caribbeans in early twentieth-century Copenhagen" (2008, 231). The Colonial Exhibition of 1905 in Copenhagen, they point out, "presumably led to a fairly substantial presence, clearly coded in terms of class, of Danes of color to the city" (232).[4] However, these working-class black bodies are nowhere to be found in the novel; instead, Helga's light skin contributes to her exoticization within the Dahls' middle-class social set as surely as it distinguishes her from the invisible black working class. In one telling encounter, a friend of the Dahls', Fru Fischer, complains that the Hotel Vivili where Helga meets her for coffee "was getting so common, always so many Bolsheviks and Japs and things. And she didn't—'begging your pardon, Helga'—like that hideous American music they were forever playing" (Larsen 1986, 80). But while it is clear that jazz and other aspects of international culture *are* infiltrating the Copenhagen that Helga blithely envisions as racially homogeneous, Helga's view of Denmark's residents remains, quite literally, whitewashed: "Here the doorsteps were always white from constant scrubbing. . . . Here were no tatters and rags, no beggars" (75). Helga can maintain her lucrative status as exotic foreigner as long as she does not acknowledge a reality beyond the middle- and upper-class circles that grant her social currency.

As she becomes a commodity for Copenhagen's white middle class, Helga realizes that her cash value is hers to spend: "Always she wanted, not money, but the things which money could give, leisure, attention, beautiful surroundings. Things. Things. Things" (Larsen 1986, 67). Denmark allows Helga the paradoxical position of both consumer subject and objectified body. Although she has fled the United States because "Negroes were not people" (82), here, seduced by the promise of material wealth, she gamely accepts her embodiment as a "Negro" art object: "Helga was incited to make an impression, a voluptuous impression. She was dressed for it, subtly schooled for it. And after a while she gave herself up wholly to the fascinating business of being seen, gaped at, desired" (74). Helga understands not only the importance of performing her exoticism visually, but also the necessity of wearing her sexuality on her "voluptuous" body. Rejecting the version of sexual embodiment that would lead to motherhood, she becomes a participant in the "business" of her childless exoticization: "How stupid she had been ever to have thought that she could marry and perhaps have children in a land where every dark child was handicapped at the start by the shroud of color! . . . She now believed sincerely that there was a law of compensation, and that sometimes it worked" (75). Although Gray writes that Helga "accepts the body as given and fails to see its constructedness" (1994, 260), her belief in a "law of compensation" indicates not only that she is highly aware of her body's construction in Copenhagen but also that she feels entitled to benefit from it. Helga understands that this embodiment-as-commodity and her subsequent material gain are contingent on her presence in Copenhagen. "Yes," she tells herself, "if I hadn't come away, I'd be stuck in Harlem. Working every day of my life" (Larsen 1986, 81). In Copenhagen, by embracing her role as commodity, she escapes the drudgery of the African American working class.

Her disillusionment about the viability of her commodified body as a source of material gain—and, consequently, about Copenhagen as a city where she can escape the burden of her blackness—begins to take shape during the marriage proposal from Axel Olsen, the Danish artist who has asked to paint her portrait. It becomes clear to her that the consumer subjectivity she has gained through her exoticized embodiment will always be subservient to her objectification. Gilroy's statement that the "shape of the Atlantic [is] a system of cultural exchanges" (1993, 14) suggests an egalitarianism between two nations that is lacking in Helga's degrading exchanges with Axel. From the start, their relationship is based on his admiration for her as an art object: "He looked at her for what seemed to her an incredibly rude length of time. . . . 'Yes, you're right. She's amazing. Marvelous,' he muttered" (Larsen 1986, 71). Positioning himself as her marketplace superior, Axel tells her in his proposal, "You have the warm impulsive nature of the women of Africa, but, my lovely, you have, I fear, the soul of a prostitute. You sell yourself to the highest bidder." With her response, "But you see, Herr Olsen, I'm not for sale. Not to you. Not to any white man. I don't at all care to be owned. Even by you" (87), Helga declares that the "extravagant things" paid for by her embodied commodification in Copenhagen come at too great a cost (74). As the sexual and racial exploitation of Helga's body in the service of white Danish financial gain becomes explicit, Denmark's history of involvement in the slave trade, generally hidden below the cosmopolitan surface of the novel's middle-class Copenhagen, comes to light. As Lunde and Stenport claim, "Between the lines of his proposal, Olsen reveals his sublimated fantasy—playing the role of slave-owning colonizer—and Helga rebels against her assumed role in this sexualized colonial economic exchange" (2008, 237).

While critics have read Helga's refusal as a mysterious gesture of "loyalty" to her race or an assertion of "a new transnational identity" (Lunde and Stenport 2008, 237), I contend that Helga is not so much affirming a racial or national identity as she is rejecting her commodification. But as she cannot articulate this motivation to white Danish society or even to herself, she translates it into a rejection of superficiality. The explanation that she gives both Axel, "It's deeper, broader than that. It's racial" (Larsen 1986, 88), and her aunt and uncle, "It's just something—something deep down inside of me" (91), cites a motivation *below* the seen façade of her body. Axel's painting of her "wasn't . . . herself at all, but some disgusting sensual creature with her features" (89), demonstrating the force with which Axel and Danish society can understand her only as visualized embodiment, an art object without interiority. Precisely because she recognizes that her embodiment can be comprehended only as surface appearance, she realizes she will never be satisfied in Copenhagen. Significantly, "her definite decision to go" takes form at a concert of Dvořák's "New World Symphony," where the "wailing undertones" of "Swing Low, Sweet Chariot" "struck into her longing heart" (92). Not just the music but the *undertones* of the black spiritual speak to Helga's desire for depth and her realization that, in Copenhagen, it cannot be had.

Conclusion: The Quicksand of Diaspora

Even the most careful and sensitive of critical responses to *Quicksand* are at a loss to account for Helga's shocking transformation from the cosmopolitan traveler who longs for "something deeper" in Copenhagen to the rural black preacher's wife who is "used . . . up" (Larsen 1986, 123) by the endless production of children. Although the close of the novel, in which Helga "began to have her fifth child" after barely surviving the birth of her fourth (135), comes as a surprise to the reader, I would like to suggest that Larsen represents Helga's switch as a transition, albeit a rapid one. When Helga returns to Harlem from Copenhagen, she first refuses the possibility of ever becoming a mothering body: "Why *do* Negroes have children? Surely it must be sinful. Think of the awfulness of being responsible for the giving of life to creatures doomed to endure such wounds to the flesh" (103). But while Helga resolutely rejects the idea of reproduction, her focus on the *sin* of exposing a child to physical injury foregrounds the language of religion and the physical pressure that will convert her to black, Christian motherhood in a Harlem church.

Helga's visit to the church is driven by her failed attempts to escape her body upon her return to Harlem. After her illicit kiss with former Naxos principal Robert Anderson, her body is tormented by its newly awakened sensuality: "For days, for weeks, voluptuous visions had haunted her. Desire had burned in her flesh with uncontrollable violence" (Larsen 1986, 109). On a rainy evening, "[d]istracted, agitated, incapable of containing herself," Helga flees her room and heads in "no definite direction" to "escape" her internal torment, externalized as a brutal storm (110). She finds sanctuary in a storefront church, where her first physical reaction to the "endless, moaning verses" is cathartic release from the hostile weather: "Her nerves were so torn, so aching, her body so wet, so cold! It was a relief to cry unrestrainedly." Soon, however, she becomes swept up in the physical frenzy of the church service: "Men and women were swaying and clapping their hands, shouting and stamping their feet. . . . Without warning the woman at her side . . . leaped to her feet, waved her long arms . . . and then, in wild, ecstatic fury jumped up and down before Helga clutching at the girl's soaked coat" (112).

Here, I would like to return briefly to a scene in Copenhagen, where Helga encounters black performers at a vaudeville show. The "two black men, American Negroes undoubtedly . . . danced and cavorted . . . pounding their thighs, slapping their hands together, waving their abnormally long arms, throwing their bodies about with loose ease" (Larsen 1986, 82–83). The similarity of the descriptions of the "long arms" and physical agility of the vaudeville performers and the churchgoers is striking, as is Helga's contrasting reaction. There, "Helga was not amused. . . . She felt shamed, betrayed" (83), distanced from the black bodies' performance for a white audience, a spectacle in which she recognizes something of herself. Here, in an all-black setting, initially "Helga was amused"—that is, until she becomes caught up in the physical frenzy: "As Helga watched and listened, gradually a curious influence penetrated her; she felt an echo of the weird orgy resound in her own heart; she felt herself possessed by the same madness. . . . She fell forward. . . . The yelling figures about her pressed forward, closing in on her on all sides" (113). Helga's religious conversion by means of "penetration" in a spiritual "orgy" and her entrapment in a mass of black bodies officially render her previous strategy of disembodiment impossible; whereas before she refused to be "owned" by Axel Olsen, here her "salvation" is figured as the sexualized "possession" of her body by the spirit. Laura Doyle calls this scene "a swoon moment, invoking a bodily 'undoing' or 'ruin' that is often sexual and coded as feminine." The fainting dramatizes the transformation of the subject from her "old social identity" (1996, 544).[5] By falling forward and joining in the frenzy of sound and movement, Helga's previously secular female body is undone so that it can be "born again" in its new role as black mother.

In one influential reading of *Quicksand,* Helga's sexual repression ensues directly from "her entrapment between two equally disabling models of selfhood: the construction of the black woman as hypersexualized primitive and middle-class ideals of chaste 'ladyhood'" (Ngai 2005, 178–79). The critical attention to this opposition—hypersexualized primitive versus chaste lady—notwithstanding, I am suggesting that the binary that *Quicksand* itself most harshly critiques is the stifling imagination of black female sexuality as either whore or mother.[6] Helga's transition as sexually intelligible object, from a whorish commodity in Denmark and a "pore los' Jezebel" in the Harlem church (Larsen 1986, 112) to a rural Christian mother removed from the capitalist market of commodity exchange, begins when she acts on her sexual compulsions for the first time, after the Harlem church service. Acting every bit the whore, Helga easily seduces the Reverend Mr. Pleasant Green with a "faint provocative smile" and a press of her "fingers deep into his arms." This new embodiment as a sexually forward woman, however, first spells Helga's removal from the logics of capitalism that rendered intelligible her sexuality in Copenhagen, and consequently the loss of her consumer subjecthood. The next morning, "she thought, all I've ever had in life has been things—except just this one time. At that she closed her eyes, for even remembrance caused her to shiver a little" (116). Her physical response of disgust to the commodities that once incited her desire and excitement paves the way to her reembodiment as the Reverend Mr. Pleasant Green's wife in his impoverished diasporic community. In contrast to Copenhagen, where she simply did not recognize the existence of the working classes, here she responds to the overwhelming destitution by romanticizing the bodies: "The smallest, dirtiest, brown child, barefooted in the fields or muddy roads, was to her an emblem of the wonder of life, and of God's goodness" (121).

When she first moves to the rural South with her new husband, Helga is able to enjoy her newfound embodiment in the figure of the insatiable "whore." Although her husband's "finger-nails were always rimmed with black . . . he failed to wash his fat body, or to shift his clothing. . . . Helga somehow overcame her first disgust" (Larsen 1986, 121) because that dirtiness occasions her sexual passion: "Emotional, palpitating, amorous, all that was living in her sprang like rank weeds" (122). But when her embodiment as "whore" transforms to embodiment as "mother," converting her voracious sexual activity into an equally voracious production of children—three children "all in the short space of twenty months" (123)—her troubled relationship with bodies returns. The third child renders her ill and bedridden, giving her a feeling of "suffocation" and "of asphyxiation," and her husband triggers her "deep and contemptuous hatred" (134). Despite this sensation of bodily repulsion, Helga's captivity by her body is permanent: "And hardly had she left her bed and become able to walk again without pain, hardly had the children returned from the homes of the neighbors, when she began to have her fifth child" (135). Whereas previously, her transatlantic movement allows her to escape the bodies of black communities, now her body reinforces the permanence of her imprisonment in this black rural town.

Ultimately, Helga's transatlantic crossings do not save her from a devastating fate. As Doyle writes, Helga's "story signals the flaw in any assumption that transnational travel will in itself offer liberation from anything, including race" (1996, 551). Such readings complicate the assumption that the practice of diaspora, as Edwards and Gilroy would contend, is best understood as a global, emancipatory mode of antiracist resistance. In its opposition to a narrative of black diaspora that centralizes the formation of transnational political subjecthood, "race" in *Quicksand* becomes embodied (and gendered) precisely through the capitalist market logic that renders Helga either a black commodity for sale or a physically overburdened black mother.

Helga's acquiescence in her damning embodiment at the end of the novel emphasizes Larsen's indictment that no matter the diasporic community, black female sexuality cannot be made legible outside of the global, patriarchal binary of prostitute versus mother. Thus, Helga can never "embody a body" free of the signification that precedes and informs her, nor escape the pervasive mode of racist sexism through which her sexuality is always read. The mode exercises a frightening universality, informing, through slightly different valences, wealthy white Copenhagen and a poor southern American town alike. The expansive reach of this disempowering binary suggests another, far more disturbing "diasporic" ideology, one that condemns the expression of black women's sexuality, particularly for mixed-raced women like Helga Crane, to the twofold nightmare of physical asphyxiation and geographic immobility.

Notes

1. In Denmark in particular, her objectification as an art object by her white relatives and friends and the black vaudeville performance she attends among an entirely white audience emphasize the racist logic that undergirds her uncomfortable, claustrophobic relationship to black bodies, including her own.

2. Gilroy briefly describes Norway in terms of its radical political activity, the place "where George Padmore was held in jail in the early 1930s and which was also the home base of his banned paper the *Negro Worker*, circulated across the world by its supporters in the Colonial Seamen's Association" (1993, 18).

3. Helga's taste for exotic, Oriental commodities that represent membership in a cosmopolitan class continues in Harlem. There, she meets Anne Gray, the avid "race woman" who later marries Robert Anderson, Helga's principal at Naxos. Helga "approved of" Anne's "brass-bound Chinese tea-chests . . . lustrous Eastern rugs . . . Japanese prints" (Larsen 1986, 44). Despite having "irked her with great irksomeness" with all her "racial ardor" (49), she has to concede that Anne, with her "blue Chinese jars . . . *did* have such lovely things" (56).

4. Timothy Mitchell's reading of exhibited Egyptians in *Colonising Egypt* suggests the ways in which this history offers a fitting cultural background for Helga's experiences in Denmark. Adapting Heidegger, Mitchell describes nineteenth-century European world exhibitions of Egypt as the "spectacles" that "set up the world as picture. They ordered it up before an audience as an object on display, to be viewed, experienced and investigated" (1988, 6). In the same way, Helga's foreign, exotic body on display complements the white, middle-class Danish colonial vision of "the world" as something to be viewed.

5. Doyle situates the "swoon moment" as a correlation to the "trope of an Atlantic crossing": the character "swoons" because she is "overcome with an experience of violation." Thus the swoon "distills the 'undoing' effects of Atlantic violence arising from slavery, deracination, and the Atlantic's unanchoring, sink-or-swim . . . economy" (1996, 544). In Helga's case, the refashioning of her violated body allows her to survive the violent encounter.

6. As Butler puts it, "*Quicksand* exemplifies [the cost of uplift for black women] as a kind of death in marriage . . . [revolving] on the impossibility of sexual freedom for black women" (1993, 178).

References

Berlant, Lauren. 2008. *The Female Complaint: The Unfinished Business of Sentimentality in American Culture.* Durham: Duke University Press.

Butler, Judith. 1993. *Bodies That Matter: On the Discursive Limits of Sex.* New York: Routledge.

Doyle, Laura. 1996. "Transnational History at Our Backs: A Long View of Larsen, Woolf, and Queer Racial Subjectivity in Atlantic Modernism." *Modernism/Modernity* 13 (3): 531–59.

Edwards, Brent. 2003. *The Practice of Diaspora: Literature, Translation, and the Rise of Black Internationalism.* Cambridge: Harvard University Press.

Gilroy, Paul. 1993. *The Black Atlantic: Modernity and Double Consciousness.* Cambridge: Harvard University Press.

Gray, Jeffrey. 1994. "Essence and the Mulatto Traveler: Europe as Embodiment in Nella Larsen's *Quicksand.*" *Novel: A Forum on Fiction* 27 (3): 257–70.

Larsen, Nella. 1986. *Quicksand* and *Passing.* Edited by Deborah McDowell. New York: Rutgers University Press.

Lunde, Arne, and Anna Westerstahl Stenport. 2008. "Helga Crane's Copenhagen: Denmark, Colonialism, and Transnational Identity in Nella Larsen's *Quicksand.*" *Comparative Literature* 60 (3): 228–43.

McDowell, Deborah. 1986. Introduction to *Quicksand and Passing,* by Nella Larsen, xi–xxxvii. New York: Rutgers University Press.

Mitchell, Timothy. 1988. *Colonising Egypt.* New York: Cambridge University Press.
Ngai, Sianne. 2005. *Ugly Feelings.* Cambridge: Harvard University Press.
Snaith, Anna. 2007. "C. L. R. James, Claude McKay, Nella Larsen, Jean Toomer: The 'Black Atlantic' and the Modernist Novel." In *The Cambridge Companion to the Modernist Novel,* edited by Morag Shiach, 206–23. New York: Cambridge University Press.

Returning from "Beyond the Bridge"

Postcolonial Hybridity in Gloria Naylor's *Mama Day*

Matthew Dischinger

In *The Empire Writes Back,* Bill Ashcroft, Gareth Griffiths, and Helen Tiffin contend that the "'Black writing' model" should not find a home in postcolonial criticism because such a conflation would "overlook . . . the very great cultural differences between literatures which are produced by a Black minority in a rich and powerful white country and those produced by the Black majority population of an independent nation" (2002, 21). Since this text is frequently used as an introduction to postcolonial studies, Ashcroft et al.'s narrow definition of the field presents several problems. Where should we place a text like *Mama Day*—one that fits neither geopolitical model presented by Ashcroft et al.? I will argue that reading Naylor's text as postcolonial, despite its placement in the tradition of African American fiction, is not only helpful but also essential in understanding Naylor's investigation of hybrid identities. To do this, I will discuss George and Cocoa as characters interacting with two spaces—the so-called Western space of New York and the non-Western space of Willow Springs—and show how Cocoa is able to survive this navigation, both physically and ideologically.

Ashcroft et al. do well to point out that political context should be considered before one reads a text as postcolonial; if the term *postcolonial* is tossed about haphazardly without consideration for where it might land, there is danger of its becoming a non sequitur. However, one must question whether scholars should deny African American texts entry into the canon of postcolonial studies, if such a canon can even be said to exist. While a claim that the political climate of postcolonial Africa can be equated to that of the modern United States would be tenuous, one does not have to conflate the two settings to allow African American fiction to be examined through a postcolonial lens.

One must acknowledge that the ideological choice of cultural assimilation or Western exclusion faced by African Americans is akin to the choices faced by postcolonial subjects—above all: to either accept Western cultural and political ideas wholesale or face sociopolitical exclusion from the West.

Naylor uses the relationship between Cocoa and George to showcase two opposing worldviews available to African Americans in the twentieth century. Cocoa, who grew up in Willow Springs—the non-Western space where much of the novel is set—is able to bridge her childhood to her adult life in New York to form an identity that is shaped by both worlds. She recognizes the role that her communal family in Willow Springs must play in her life. In George, however, Naylor presents an orphan who values only Western notions of individualism. Naylor uses George's death to suggest that his rejection of his own ancestry is an act of ideological suicide. Instead, Naylor suggests that her characters—as well as real African Americans—should occupy a hybrid ideological space by allowing both modernity and an ancestral past to shape their lives in the West.

Before I begin my postcolonial investigation of *Mama Day*, we must pause to consider what makes a text postcolonial. While America was once a colony of England, it would be problematic to align America's postcolonial environment with that of Frantz Fanon's Martinique, for instance. While Ashcroft et al. contend that African American fiction should not be considered postcolonial, they do not hesitate to include T. S. Eliot, who, they claim, sought to deny his "origins in an attempt to become 'more English than the English'" (2002, 4). This argument seems to efface particulars of the high modernist movement to which Eliot was indebted; in doing so, it limits any author's goals to his or her subject position while failing to consider the mechanics of neocolonialism. In other words, American writers could be read as postcolonial only if their literature was seen as responding specifically to the British Empire. While the traditional American canon may well profit from these postcolonial readings, this essay will not attempt to read the body of American literature exhaustively. Rather, I will demonstrate how Naylor's novel may be made new by postcolonial readings.

If we are to define postcolonial writing only through the author's subject position while excluding an individual author's goals, then what business does J. M. Coetzee, a white South African, have in postcolonial studies? Ashcroft et al. address this concern through their discussion of postcolonial revisions, which the three authors suggest are central to postcolonial dialogues: "[T]he rereading and the rewriting of the European historical and fictional record is a vital and inescapable task at the heart of the post-colonial enterprise" (2002,

196). This definition would include Coetzee's *Foe,* for example, an indisputably postcolonial revision of Daniel Defoe's *Robinson Crusoe.*

Naylor's *Mama Day,* like Coetzee's *Foe,* can be read as a postcolonial revision. Missy Dehn Kubitschek persuasively argues for a reading of *Mama Day* as a revision of Shakespeare's *The Tempest* in her article "Toward a New Order: Shakespeare, Morrison, and Gloria Naylor's *Mama Day*" (1994). Kubitschek argues that Naylor uses the character Mama Day to critique Prospero's use of magic in *The Tempest,* noting that magic "remains a subset of natural powers, small and constituent of, not in control of, nature" (84). Kubitschek's broad claim is that Naylor is critiquing Western individualism; in this case, she uses Mama Day's relationship with nature to demonstrate her point. For her part, Adriane L. Ivey (2005) persuasively argues for a reading of *Mama Day* as a revision of the Passion of Christ in her article "Beyond Sacrifice: Gloria Naylor Rewrites the Passion." Ivey argues that Naylor presents an alternative to Western culture's idea of sacrifice, thereby subverting "the symbolism on which dominant [Western] ideology is based" and providing a socially "viable form of Christianity" (106). Another example of Naylor's use of revision is the island community's celebration of "Candle Walk" rather than Christmas and "standing forth" rather than funerals. Lene Brøndum discusses these two rituals as revisions of Christian rituals, claiming that Naylor uses Candle Walk, which celebrates the journey of the island's emancipator, Sapphira Wade, back across the Atlantic Ocean to Africa, to "replace Jesus Christ . . . with a fierce African slave woman" and change "the inflexible Christian ritual of celebration into a flexible, dynamic ritual" (1999, 158). The standing forth ceremony allows the people of Willow Springs to communicate with Little Caesar, a deceased Willow Springs child. As an outside observer, George admits that "[t]he church, the presence of the minister, were concessions, and obviously the only ones they were going to make to a Christian ritual that should have called for a sermon, music, tears—the belief in an earthly finality for the child's life" (Naylor 1988, 269). By creating these two ceremonies, Naylor revises strict Western rituals to fit Willow Springs. In doing so, Naylor seems to reinforce the importance of building a bridge between Willow Springs and the Western world to allow modern characters to function in both spaces.

Since I have established that *Mama Day* has been read—purposefully or not—using a postcolonial lens, I will begin my own investigation, which is expressly postcolonial. John Cullen Gruesser notes in *Confluences: Postcolonialism, African American Literary Studies, and the Black Atlantic* (2005) an area of postcolonial studies that seems to overlap overtly with relevant discussions of African American texts: hybridity. Gruesser explains hybridity as a counterbalance to "the negative connotations of displacement and its attendant identity crisis" present in colonization (6). Ashcroft et al. discuss the role hybridity has played in postcolonial dialogues: "Most post-colonial writing has concerned itself with the hybridized nature of post-colonial culture as a strength rather than a weakness. Such writing focuses on the fact that the transaction of the post-colonial world is not a one-way process in which oppression obliterates the oppressed or the colonizer silences the colonized in absolute terms. . . . It lays emphasis on the survival even under the most potent oppression of the distinctive aspects of the culture of the oppressed, and shows how these become an integral part of the new formations which arise from the clash of cultures characteristic of imperialism" (2006, 137). Ashcroft et al. suggest that a rigid expulsion of the colonized's former ideology problematizes that subject's survival in the newly created postcolonial space. *Mama Day* lends itself to a similar reading, since we are introduced to a generation of African Americans forced to choose whether they will accept a hybrid identity that embraces an ancestral past as a way of defining themselves within and outside the spatial boundaries of Willow Springs.

Naylor alerts the reader to the importance of using the past as a lens to understand the novel before the novel even begins. Naylor gives us a family tree dating back to Sapphira Wade, the "great, grand Mother" of the Day family and arguably the most important historical figure in Willow Springs (1988, 48). Naylor also gives us an apparent bill of sale from the transaction wherein Sapphira Wade was sold to Bascombe Wade, whom she is able to trick or convince into freeing his slaves. While Sapphira Wade is responsible for granting the Willow Springs slaves their freedom in 1823, none of the characters, not even Mama Day, know her name. Elizabeth T. Hayes points out that Sapphira Wade may not even be her original name: "'Sapphira' is merely the slave name assigned by her captors; 'Wade' is the surname of Bascombe Wade, the man who purchased her." Hayes's point is perhaps reinforced by the reminder that the bill of sale states only that she "is a woman 'answering to the name Sapphira'" (2004, 674). Sapphira Wade's adoption of the name "Day" seems to aid Hayes's argument; the choice allows Sapphira to "establish the cultural and racial nascence of Willow Springs" (Eckard 1995, 129). We must not overlook the importance of this material at the beginning of Naylor's novel, all of which demonstrates the importance of these events in shaping the rest of the novel—both as a form of narrative for a prospective reader and as a means of definition for the novel's characters.

The centrality of Sapphira Wade to the novel's plot becomes even more evident in the first page of Naylor's work. Naylor opens her novel with a discussion of "the legend of Sapphira Wade" (Naylor 1988, 1). She was a "true conjure woman" who "could walk through a lightning storm," "use the heat of lightning to start the kindling going under her medicine pot," and "turn the moon into salve" (3). The narrator's description of Sapphira is disparate; we are reading a community of descriptions rather than a unified perspective that a single narrator provides. The voice seems to be the communal voice of Willow Springs; incidentally, the name of the town is the first thing uttered by this communal narrator. If we can suppose that George's and Cocoa's sections each use a linear, Western style of narration, then the communal voice should be read as an alternative to that voice. The community's voice is meant to give us a complete vision of Willow Springs's past as a foundation for the novel.

The communal voice does not offer a consistent narrative for Sapphira Wade's emancipation of the slaves in Willow Springs, as we are told the emancipation occurs "somehow, some way" in 1823 (Naylor 1988, 3). The communal narrator offers three possible scenarios that could have resulted in Sapphira's freedom while stating that the story "ain't about right and wrong" because "Sapphira Wade don't live in a part of our memory we can use to form words" (3, 4). While the particulars of the story are located outside any verbal understanding, Sapphira Wade's indescribable ascension is relayed through concepts like "18 & 23." While the numbers obviously come from the year Sapphira Wade emancipated her fellow slaves, the meaning of "18 & 23" is fluid and adaptable. An attempt to map its location within a linear system of thought is unproductive and misguided. Naylor demonstrates this point through the communal narrator's discussion of "Reema's boy," a character who was raised in Willow Springs but has since departed in body and spirit and tries to classify the term within "'ethnography,' 'unique speech patterns,' 'cultural preservation,' and whatever else" to produce a formal definition of 18 & 23 (7). To classify 18 & 23 was to misunderstand its usage; it was used to say something that had meaning only in Willow Springs, so, in a way, it was indefinable beyond the bridge.

We can see an attempt to map Willow Springs more clearly through one of the novel's narrators: George Andrews. Naylor uses the contrast between George and Cocoa to demonstrate how African Americans might interact with their ancestry. George was raised in a shelter where he was told that "[o]nly the present has potential"(Naylor 1988, 23).This mantra for George's life is fitting, because he has been orphaned from his past. Mrs. Jackson, who runs George's shelter, gives George and his fellow orphans only a series of fragmented ideas within which the boys can understand their lives. George recites Mrs. Jackson's speech from memory: "I am not your mother. I am paid to run this place. You have no mothers or fathers. This is not your home. And it is not a prison—it is a state shelter for boys. And it is not a dumping ground for delinquents, rejects, or somebody's garbage—you are boys. Here you have a clean room, decent food, and clothing for each season because it is a shelter. There is a library in which you study for three hours after school—and you will go to school, because you are boys. When you are eighteen, the state says you are men. And when you are men you leave here to go where and do what you want. But you stay here until you are men" (26). George understands his life only through this series of facts. His mother was a prostitute. His mother is dead. He lived in a state shelter for boys. It was not his home. He later dissects his world as an adult using the same type of logic. George's analytical understanding of life as a series of unfolding events that quickly become obsolete explains his choice to become an engineer. When George first meets Cocoa in an interview for a job with his engineering firm, George asks how Cocoa, whose legal name is Ophelia, became "Cocoa." Cocoa explains that a pet name just "fits," so George quickly notices that Cocoa's "buttered cream" skin makes the pet name fit (29). George does not understand how a name could fit, just as he would not have been able to grasp the concept of 18 & 23. Both notions require a real belief in abstract concepts that cannot be fully articulated—not even by characters in Willow Springs.

While George grew up without a history, Cocoa was raised in a community built upon its history. Susan Meisenhelder describes Willow Springs as "a world outside white parameters, a place in no state, on no map, connected to the mainland by the flimsiest of bridges periodically destroyed by storms" (1993, 405). While George has been faced with the harshness of living in an urban environment without any historical concept of who he was, Cocoa is constantly reminded of the historical significance of Willow Springs, which has been physically estranged from the outside world. Even though Cocoa has left Willow Springs for New York, she does not put the community behind her. Cocoa is pulled in by Willow Springs annually during her life in New York, and she moves to Charleston after George's death. But just as Willow Springs seems to pull Cocoa, she is also pulled back "beyond the bridge"—a phrase the island's inhabitants create to describe the outside world, which is accessible only by crossing the bridge leading away from the island. After Cocoa and George are married and come to Willow Springs, Cocoa quickly shoots down George's half-baked plan to move to Willow Springs permanently (Naylor 1988, 222). Cocoa hears the voices of her ancestors tell her she'll break George's heart as she walks past the family plot. Instead of rejecting what the voices say, Cocoa wants only to "get out of there" by escaping back to New York (224). Cocoa seems to understand that she must allow her worlds to converge: she brings pet names and lavender perfume back to New York from

Willow Springs, and she brings George to Willow Springs from New York. She needs to build a metaphorical bridge between the two worlds to survive. Naylor's metaphor becomes more concrete, however, when Cocoa falls ill.

Before I investigate Cocoa's illness, however, I must examine Naylor's title character. We see the clearest glimpses of Mama Day herself, the daughter of the seventh son of the seventh son of Sapphira, in Naylor's sections featuring the communal narrator. Mama Day has a heightened awareness of nature, and therefore is the first to anticipate the hurricane that destroys the bridge to the mainland. The narrator's description of the impending hurricane suggests that the storm is a means of sectioning the African-rooted Willow Springs off from the Western world: "It starts on the shores of Africa, a simple breeze among the palms and cassavas, before it's carried off, tied up with thousands like it, on a strong wave heading due west. A world of water, heaving and rolling, weeks of water, and all them breezes die but one. . . . Restless and disturbed, no land in front of it, no land in back, it draws up the ocean vapor and rains fall like tears" (Naylor 1988, 249). The storm also seems to be a clear symbol of the slave trade, which "carried off" and "tied up thousands" of Africans to be sold in the West. Mama Day seems to recognize that Sapphira is communicating with her; in fact, Mama Day says she hears Sapphira's voice "in her soul" (250). The arrival of the hurricane coincides with Cocoa's declining health. After Cocoa falls ill, it is Mama Day who recognizes that it will "take a man to bring [Cocoa] peace" (263). Naylor seems to be emphasizing the strengths of ideological hybridity. Cocoa's life literally depends on an outsider's care, but in a way that only makes sense inside Willow Springs. To save Cocoa, Mama Day must rely on George's belief in his own supernatural power, and George must be willing to embrace an abstract healing method.

George is unwilling to fully participate in a non-Western method of healing Cocoa. He plans to escape in a rowboat to find help on the mainland, but Dr. Buzzard tells George his way across the sound "woulda been suicide" because of rough waters (Naylor 1988, 286). Dr. Buzzard's language is prophetic; George does not waver in his reluctance to accept any terms that are not his own. The suggestion that Naylor is making here, I argue, is that this choice to reject an ancestry he cannot understand ultimately leads to his death. When Mama Day presents George with her way to heal Cocoa—searching in the chicken coop for whatever is there before coming back to Mama Day—George rejects her collaborative method. George digs through the chicken coop but only ends up bloodied and confused: "There was nothing that old woman could do with a pair of empty hands" (301). Ivey argues that George's "inability to believe in [Mama Day's] solution" causes his "needless" death (2005, 104). George's final rejection of Mama Day's advice should be read as

Naylor not only emphasizing the importance of a community in healing, but also critiquing George's monolithic worldview.

One must then ask what these identifications regarding cultural hybridity mean for the text. Daphne Lamothe investigates this issue in her article "Gloria Naylor's *Mama Day:* Bridging Roots and Routes" (2005). One of the strengths of Lamothe's study is her discussion of Cocoa's "nostalgia for the island" as contrasted with her choice to live in urban environments in New York and Charleston (161–62). Lamothe explains Cocoa's place in defining a new, pragmatic definition of blackness: "This definition of blackness that acknowledges hybridity is nonetheless viewed through a historical lens . . . that refuses to erase the memories of violence and the misuses of power integral to African Americans' new world racial and cultural identity" (162). Cocoa's identity is as close as Naylor comes to presenting an ideological model that African Americans may rely upon safely—one that participates in modernity while remaining aware of the historical African experience in America. Cocoa carries her past with her in the present. In doing so, she occupies an ideological space that embraces and uses the difference of her historical position to inform her position in the modern world. Similarly, Naylor's text requires a reading that embraces a diverse application of theory—a reading that uses a postcolonial lens to inform the author's choices.

This reading of *Mama Day* would be nearly impossible if scholars lock African American texts outside the gate of postcolonial literary criticism. More important, one must question what such a gate is designed to do. If it is intended to keep postcolonial studies intact by keeping it in stasis, we must question whether this is a worthy cause. This type of move not only leaves us with problematic categories like Ashcroft et al.'s singular "'Black writing' model," it also keeps postcolonial studies from evolving within the wider field of literary criticism. For scholars interested in continuing to work with postcolonial theory, pigeonholing the field through essentialism limits its future application as literature and theory continue to trouble essentialism. Instead, we must look for new ways to appropriate the field while retaining its integrity. Rather than installing a bulwark that separates postcolonial studies from black diaspora studies and new southern studies, each of which would allow for texts like *Mama Day* to fit within its critical boundaries, critics should embrace the ways in which postcolonial studies are enriched by African American literature.

By way of conclusion, let us consider the ways this reading of *Mama Day* might enliven other critical fields as well. The novel makes crucial contributions to black diaspora studies when read through a postcolonial lens. What Houston A. Baker has referred to as an "unruly conversation" in African American literature—the conversation about how a single African American ideology is made—is of central importance to the way I have argued that *Mama Day* interacts with postcolonial hybridity. One reading of the text would suggest that it is, in fact, making some fairly rigid claims about black identity. If George's individualism is tied to a Western whiteness, then Cocoa's willingness to consider history alongside modernity is a new model. But rather than installing a new center, the novel might be read as destabilizing the notion of ideological centers by placing seemingly competing cultural centers together. Postcolonial hybridity buttresses this reading, thereby proving itself useful in understanding the ways in which black diaspora literature has and will reconfigure black identity. This is merely one possible opening. Using postcolonial theory will help us conceive of new readings within black diaspora studies, thereby deflecting questions of essential identity in favor of more nuanced readings.

References

Ashcroft, Bill, Gareth Griffiths, and Helen Tiffin. 2002. *The Empire Writes Back: Theory and Practice in Post-Colonial Literatures.* London: Routledge.

———. 2006. *The Post-Colonial Studies Reader.* 2nd ed. London: Routledge.

Brøndum, Lene. 1999. "The Persistence of Tradition: The Retelling of Sea Islands Culture in Works by Julie Dash, Gloria Naylor, and Paule Marshall." In *Black Imagination and the Middle Passage,* edited by Maria Diedrich, Henry Louis Gates Jr., and Carl Pedersen, 153–63. New York: Oxford University Press.

Eckard, Paula Gallant. 1995. "The Prismatic Past in Oral History and *Mama Day.*" *MELUS* 20 (3): 121–35.

Gruesser, John Cullen. 2005. *Confluences: Postcolonialism, African American Literary Studies, and the Black Atlantic.* Athens: University of Georgia Press.

Hayes, Elizabeth T. 2004. "The Named and the Nameless: Morrison's 124 and Naylor's 'The Other Place' as Semiotic *Chorae.*" *African American Review* 38 (4): 669–81.

Ivey, Adriane L. 2005. "Beyond Sacrifice: Gloria Naylor Rewrites the Passion." *MELUS* 30 (1): 85–108.

Kubitschek, Missy Dehn. 1994. "Toward a New Order: Shakespeare, Morrison, and Gloria Naylor's *Mama Day.*" *MELUS* 19 (3): 75–90.

Lamothe, Daphne. 2005. "Gloria Naylor's *Mama Day:* Bridging Roots and Routes." *African American Review* 39 (1–2): 155–69.

Meisenhelder, Susan. 1993. "'The Whole Picture' in Gloria Naylor's *Mama Day.*" *African American Review* 27 (3): 405–19.

Naylor, Gloria. 1988. *Mama Day.* New York: Vintage, 1993.

II
RACE *and* PLACE

Immigrant Desire

Contesting Canadian Safety and Whiteness in Dionne Brand's *In Another Place, Not Here*

Lauren Vedal

Canada is frequently imagined as a haven (for British Loyalists, runaway slaves, draft dodgers, and refugees, to name a few). Such an image presents a Canada that is by definition "safe"—or at least safer than the places that drive people there. Thus, safety and the nation become synonymous in Canada. However, despite its diverse population and institutional commitment to multiculturalism as policy, Canada remains a nation built on white identity: white Canadians comprise the mainstream that "tolerates" other populations. So as a haven, Canada functions as a "white nation" that accepts "others." What becomes clear in analysis is that the safety promised by the Canadian nation is contingent upon nonwhite immigrants' embrace of whiteness. More than a racial category, whiteness functions as a set of assumptions about what is normal and good. Thus, white racial dominance not only prizes the phenotypical characteristics of white people but also normalizes and glorifies the values of the dominant culture, while at the same time rendering that very process invisible. In her novel *In Another Place, Not Here* (1996), Dionne Brand writes immigrant subjectivities that do not embrace whiteness, exposing the coercive violence (both physical and psychological) at the heart of the notion of Canadian safety. Moreover, while she demonstrates how Canada fails to function as a haven, she interrogates the fundamental desirability of the kind of safety that this haven is supposed to provide in the first place. This troubles the conflation of whiteness and safety as being desirable states achieved within desirable nation-states.

Brand questions the *desirability* of this kind of safety by showing how desire for safety obscures oppression, violence, and trauma. Her novel suggests that coming to terms with trauma and loss is at odds with the "desirable safety" promoted by the Canadian idea of a haven, a suggestion with implications that go beyond critique of the Canadian national imaginary. Questioning the relationship between safety and whiteness, and what constitutes safety itself, reveals what is needed for healing on national, cultural, and individual levels. Healing, coalition, and conversation can be enabled only through desires that do not rely on a supposed safety.

Brand's novel opens in Grenada with the beginning of a lesbian relationship between Elizete and Verlia, both of whom are originally from the Caribbean (Elizete has lived there all her life, while Verlia immigrated to Canada at the age of seventeen). Verlia joins the Black Power movement in Canada, but comes to Grenada at age thirty to help with socialist organizing, and it is then that she becomes involved with Elizete. After Verlia dies in the U.S. invasion, Elizete immigrates to Canada (illegally) to make sense of Verlia and her death. Her arrival in Canada results in her homelessness, exploitation, and rape. At a shelter, Elizete finds Abena, Verlia's former lover, who is also from the Caribbean. Through conversation, Elizete and Abena come to a combined understanding of Verlia.

To make sense of the protagonists' choices, this essay focuses on the ways in which Verlia and Elizete's desires function as windows into their subjectivities. I base this analysis on Brand's own description of desire in her memoir, *A Map to the Door of No Return: Notes to Belonging* (2001). According to Brand, for people of the black diaspora, desire is complicated and contradictory, combining desire for revolution with faith and love. Desire for revolution and the love that accompanies it diverge from the idea of safety as defined by the Canadian nation. This alternative description of desire allows us to understand the actions of characters who do not desire the safety that is supposedly offered by immigration to Canada. Desire for something other than a normative lifestyle and the safety it bestows allows the two main characters to grow and heal, rather than simply survive. My goal here is to examine desire in terms of the central lesbian relationship depicted in the novel and in terms of immigration, the desire to leave as well as the desire to arrive. These desires demonstrate the interconnections between the personal and the political within each character's subjectivity, and how those subjectivities are at odds with dominant white epistemology. In doing so, I also examine the characters' relationships and encounters with whites, white epistemology, and safety.

The novel is structured around a central rupture, in which Verlia jumps off a cliff during the U.S. invasion of Grenada, a choice that is not so much a suicidal response to depression as it is an effort to escape overwhelming oppression. Elizete likens her loss of Verlia to the experience of a slave's trauma of arriving in the Americas, imbuing this moment with the historical legacy of slavery and colonialism. The jump echoes the Ibo Landing myth while also gesturing to the flawed epistemology of whiteness.[1] As myth, the Ibo Landing story proposes a collective alternative to the dominant white imaginings of slavery. White slave traders could not comprehend why African slaves would turn back to the sea upon arrival in the New World, rejecting the apparent safety of "civilization." Likewise, modern-day white epistemologies are blind to alternative subjectivities and desires, which are premised on a different idea of safety. Normative safety disregards the transgenerational effects of traumatic memory and the ongoing effects of oppression. Verlia's jump crystallizes the intersection of desire, safety, trauma, and race, and it suggests that there is a logic that cannot be understood from a normative white perspective.

Later, when Elizete immigrates to Canada, she conceives of her migration as a jump, like Verlia's, rather than as a move to somewhere safer. Multiple jumps link the two lovers, as both jump at different points, and for each, the jump represents a kind of joining with each other. At the heart of the rupture is a question: why jump? Their desires, coupled with their relationship to whiteness, will make legible the characters' various literal and figurative jumps. From a normative perspective, making the jump—departing—makes no sense. But once their desires for revolution and healing are taken into account, jumping becomes a logical and empowering solution. These initially illegible desires are revealed to be strategies for survival and growth for black women for whom the world (both the Caribbean and Canada) is a profoundly unsafe place. These desires challenge the relationship between nation and safety and also suggest that safety (as it is conceived of in terms of haven) is at odds with healing from trauma.

Whiteness and Migration

Elizete's experience of whiteness is directly connected to the history of slavery and colonialism. Her experience of whiteness makes a clear link between the history of slavery and the modern-day slavery of current immigration policies (McCallum and Olbey 1999). It is also explicitly connected to patriarchy and sexual violence. Her experiences map onto a clear schematic of domination. Assimilation is not an option for her. In fact, the intersection of capitalism, patriarchy, and racism constitutes a worldwide system, which is premised on her unassimilability. In Canada she is far removed from slavery (both temporally and from her job as a sugarcane worker), yet there is a persistence of economic exploitation, and it intersects with racism and sexual violence. Although Elizete resists, her resistance becomes increasingly futile in the face of overwhelming oppression. Her migration results in a descent into a world of violence, homelessness, and victimization. For Elizete, *here* is no different than *there*. She is equally disempowered in either place. Both places are physically unsafe for her, and in both places, she seems to exist only to be used, sexually and for her labor. Elizete equates the slaveholders cursed by her ancestors with the white people she encounters in Canada—both are irredeemable and cursed to unhappiness as a result of their own evil.

The first section of the book is entitled "Elizete, beckoned," and the title suggests that the main question concerning Elizete is "why come?" Why come to Canada? Her desire to immigrate is nonsensical in terms of the national narrative regarding immigration; it is an illegible jump. The second section of the novel is called "Verlia, flying," and it concerns a parallel question: why go? If Elizete's immigration is illegible, Verlia's constant departure, too, needs examination. In the course of the novel, she leaves the Caribbean, Sudbury, Toronto, two lovers and, ultimately, life. While for Elizete, whiteness is a fixed system of domination, and the myth of Canadian safety is simply a myth, Verlia has a more vexed relationship with both whiteness and Canada. Unlike Elizete, who is disempowered on virtually every front and multiply traumatized, Verlia is comparatively privileged. In the Caribbean, she has a family that takes care of her and she attends school. At the age of seventeen, she immigrates to Canada, where she is greeted and taken in by family; her way is paid and she immigrates legally. For Verlia, assimilation in Canada is at least partially possible, and many of the homogenized desires of national belonging (such as economic success) are attainable. However, Verlia faces her own struggles for safety, and this pushes her to go.

Verlia "can't remember ever sleeping soundly or without fear" (Brand 1996, 121). Verlia feels unsafe in her childhood home, where the legacy of colonialism and slavery has created a toxic environment of hopelessness (121–33). Like Elizete, her lack of safety is the result of a history of oppression, but unlike Elizete, this danger is represented as psychological. Elizete's physical peril teaches her that nowhere is safe, so she does not even try to find a safe place. Verlia, in contrast, begins a search for safety. She associates her childhood home and the Caribbean with despair, surrender, poverty, and fear. In response to this psychological unsafety, Verlia embraces binary oppositions, rejecting parts of herself in the process. She rejects her family. She rejects embodiment. Her first desire, it can be said, is to leave—to jump. For her, desire takes on an abstract, ideological form. Her desire becomes sublimated, and in its first iteration, her desire is white.

Verlia sees whiteness as something far away from her Caribbean home, and she embraces it. Both whiteness in general and Canada in particular represent a rejection of home. For Verlia, whiteness, at least initially, represents an attractive idea, one she desires. Upon arriving in Sudbury, Ontario, however, Verlia undergoes a radical shift in her understanding of whiteness. It becomes cold, sterile, and associated with fakeness, lack of love, and psychological death. Her aunt and uncle are intensely assimilationist. They moved to Sudbury from Toronto to distance themselves from black people and, in a sense, their own blackness. For her relatives, whiteness is equated with privilege and empowerment. Like Verlia, they "other" a part of themselves in the desire to escape. But their lives demonstrate that this sort of splitting is lethal.

In addition to literal death (her uncle's asthma and swollen heart, which Verlia attributes to their assimilation), there is also an emotional death. Verlia describes how their desire to create the perfect "white" family has distorted their ability to love. For her aunt and uncle, assimilation involves not only acquiring desired privilege (such as order, home, consumer goods, and opportunity) but also equating whiteness with normalcy (in this case, family). Her relatives have acquired the privilege, but not the whiteness, and they believe this is due to their childlessness: "[They] think that her addition will fill out some of the rest somehow, she senses, make them white in this white town" (Brand 1996, 141). Verlia lives with them for only three weeks. In this time, she comes to see assimilation as psychologically unsafe, and in fact as a kind of death. This leads to her next flight. She runs away to Toronto. This flight also coincides with another desire: blackness. So again, Verlia makes a choice between binary opposites. Her valuation of the binaries has reversed (now, black is good and white is bad), but her pattern is the same: to leave one place for another.

When she moves to Toronto to join the Black Power movement, Verlia maintains her binary worldview, and takes a black separatist position. At this stage, Verlia's understanding of whiteness is most similar to Elizete's, and she believes herself to be fundamentally different from whites (unassimilable), rejecting all whites and, she believes, all white epistemologies. However, Verlia's rigid binary thinking does not leave room for complications and conflicts. As these develop within the black community, Verlia again chooses to leave, rejecting the murkiness of political work in Toronto and going to Grenada to join a more concrete cause. Significantly, she sees staying in the black community in Toronto as seduction; in the community, she sees the same apathy that she saw in the Caribbean.

Verlia's binary view of the world originates in a rejection of part of herself (the poor, the black, the disempowered) and an embrace of whiteness. Even as her valuation of the binaries switches, the same structural thinking remains intact. Her worldview makes clear the way in which Verlia has internalized white epistemologies. In addition, her revolutionary thought is structured by Western and first world hierarchies. Despite her self-education in many different revolutionary traditions (Communist China, the African American civil rights movement, Ghandi, Che Guevara and other Latin American revolutionaries), Verlia believes it is her reading that makes her a revolutionary and fails to see how one can come by such knowledge in other ways. When she first met Elizete, "she thought that she was the one who knew everything, and how she was going to change this country woman into a revolutionary like her" (Brand 1996, 202). Verlia's initial misreading of Elizete indicates how her revolutionary thought is still grounded in imperialist (read: white supremacist) logic. Although Verlia is neither white nor originally from the first world, her worldview is very much structured by those logics.

In addition to internalizing the logics and sometimes the values of white supremacy, Verlia internalizes self-loathing. Like her acceptance of those epistemologies, it deeply structures her psychology and relationships. Ultimately, Verlia's binary, hierarchical worldview in which part of her is always degraded results in an emotional fragmentation that leads to her death—her final jump.

Desire and Healing: Women in Motion

Elizete and Verlia's experiences with immigration to Canada and with whites and white epistemology demonstrate not only that the idea of a Canadian haven is a myth but also show that even if this myth were true, it is not desirable. The safety offered by assimilation is available only in terms of normative desire, which does not enable healing. While Brand presents this problem, she also presents desire as offering a solution. In her memoir, *A Map to the Door of No Return: Notes to Belonging,* Brand lays out the role of desire in the black diaspora, and as such, provides a model of desire that is not based in white logic. In particular, in the section entitled "Arriving at Desire," Brand explains that desire is not simple, as it is often imagined, but is rather a combination of courage, resistance, embodiment, complication, and sense making (2001, 182–95). She conceptualizes desire in terms of two books that shaped who she is: *The Black Napoleon* (about the Haitian Revolution) and *Lady Chatterley's Lover.* Reading *The Black Napoleon,* she learns a history she had never been taught. She describes how two figures, Toussaint L'Ouverture and Jean-Jacques Dessalines, embodied two aspects of desire for her, faith and ferocity respectively. Reading *Lady Chatterley's Lover* had less to do with the content of the book (which she barely remembers) than with the context and experience of reading it. She describes a fluid sense of desire in which she identified with both male and female characters, additionally complicated by a third world double consciousness.

Desire involves both faith and ferocity, which I take to mean love and empowering vision, respectively. Moreover, it becomes a response to loss and trauma. Brand concludes, "Making sense may be what desire is. Or, putting the senses back together" (2001, 195). Desire makes sense of a world that does not make sense as it is (and we might think here of how white epistemologies lack sufficient explanatory power for the injustices we see around us). In addition, the idea of "putting the senses back together" seems to be an explicit reference to healing from trauma. If trauma is world destroying, putting the senses back together re-creates the self and the world after traumatic experiences. As a result, desire is tied to a history of oppression, but most important it is an embodied, complicated resistance to that oppression. Brand writes about a desire very unlike desires based in domination, ones that operate in the myths of Canadian immigration. She proposes desires that are not based on consumer desires (capitalism), desire to be recognized by the Other (that is, racism, master-slave dialectic), or sexual conquest (patriarchy). *In Another Place, Not Here* conceptualizes the potential for migration to be desire, in this contradictory, noncommodified sense, a part of healing rather than perpetuation of oppression.

For Elizete, desire grows out of the context of overwhelming disempowerment and trauma. The book opens with Elizete describing her desire for Verlia: "GRACE. IS GRACE, YES. And I take it, quiet, quiet, like thiefing sugar" (Brand 1996, 3). Elizete does not question desire, and this faith exemplifies one of the key characteristics Brand ascribes to desire in the black diaspora. Elizete jumps fully into love with Verlia because she knows what life has to offer her and she knows "grace" when she sees it. For Elizete, her love for Verlia is a leap of faith. For Brand, the figure of Toussaint L'Ouverture also represents faith: "Toussaint was a diplomat. When I was twenty-five or so, I would write in a poem, 'Toussaint, I loved you as soon as I saw you on that page.' I loved his faith, though it betrayed him" (Brand 2001, 187). In this way, faith is tied to both love and revolution. And it entails a jump.

The faith with which Elizete embraces her relationship with Verlia is not a faith in a simple kind of safety. While she observes that grace is "everything changing for good" (Brand 1996, 74), this change does not mean her life is physically any safer. In fact, she faces the very real threat of her husband murdering her as a result of her departure (5). It is clear, however, that material safety is not what Elizete desires. Moreover, Elizete's attraction to Verlia expresses her latent desire for revolution. Before they've even spoken, Elizete reflects: "Her look say 'I know you. I know you plan to sling off a man's neck and go to Maracaibo'" (13). Elizete feels recognized and known for her desire to kill her husband and change her life.

While Elizete is by no means uncritical of the injustices that have dictated her position in life, what Verlia gives Elizete is vision for change—the ability to envision what does not yet exist and to believe in that vision. This vision is not simply one of a "safer," more comfortable life; rather, it is a vision that refuses to take for granted the state of the world as it is: "Though she was not sure that she fully got Verlia's meaning, what was interesting about Verlia was what she suggested, abandoning the certainty of hardship, not because life had become better but because you recognized its compulsion, the beat beat of it which you did not control and one day you said, not enough, not enough at all" (Brand 1996, 102). Verlia brings Elizete vision by migrating from Canada to Grenada; however, this is not simply a matter of bringing first world knowledge to the third world. The creation of vision and a new way of making sense of the world is not a conclusion but a project, arrived at collectively.

Here, it is helpful to consider how the specifically lesbian relationship makes this collective project possible. In "Women and Honor: Some Notes on Lying," Adrienne Rich (1979) provides a way to understand the sense-making work of desire that Brand refers to. Rich writes: "There is nothing simple or easy about this idea [truth]. There is not 'the truth,' 'a truth'—truth is not one thing, or even a system. It is an increasing complexity" (187). Verlia brings a new complexity to Elizete's world. Rich adds: "Women have often felt insane when cleaving to the truth of our own experience. Our future depends on the sanity of each of us, and we have a profound stake, beyond the personal, in the project of describing our reality as candidly and fully as we can to each other" (190). Their love, then, is a project of better understanding the world they are in, which is evidenced in Elizete's desire to know Verlia, to complicate her world by understanding where she comes from and whether they are the "same": "Tell me what colour was the ground there, where you from, tell me what your mother's face look like. . . . And your hand, did you ever want to plunge it in the stones there. . . . I want to go against the ground, grind it in my teeth, but most I want to plunge my hands in stones." But this collective sense making is painful; Elizete recalls, "And she make things hard, she make me have to say everything, she make me have to tell everything. She want me to open up my head for hell to fly out" (Brand 1996, 76). Again Rich is useful; her description of honesty in a lesbian relationship is as pain: "When someone tells me a piece of truth which has been withheld from me, and which I needed in order to see my life more clearly, it may bring acute pain, but it can also flood me with a cold, sea-sharp wash of relief" (1979, 193). The work of love and making sense comes from the differences and distance between the women. It is not simply that Verlia gives Elizete a vision of something better, and the hope to reach for it. Rather, it is the contention between them that is so productive and that defines Elizete's love for Verlia.

The idea of love as struggle further complicates the idea that Canada's model of multiculturalism provides a haven for minorities. But rather than merely indicating the model's failure to reflect reality, the idea of love as struggle demonstrates a positive reality, one not visible in the model. In the Canadian model of multiculturalism, distinct yet internally homogeneous cultural groups coexist in harmony to create the "Canadian mosaic." This model assumes a uniformity and lack of internal conflict within cultural groups.[2] Likewise, there are widespread, generalized notions that lesbians somehow better understand each other than heterosexual couples (Jagose 1994). Both of these beliefs rely on the idea that sameness necessarily results in understanding (or even that certain categorical similarities result in sameness). The struggle of collective sense making shows that what makes these groups safe and meaningful is not the comfort of being with one's "own" (perhaps a traditional notion of safety), but rather it is the work and pain of trying to understand and make oneself understood despite difference. This does not mean that there is therefore no place for groups, rather that the meaning of those groups must be reconceptualized as places of contestation. Brand demonstrates that these intragroup contestations can result in healing, and that these struggles are painful. In other words, healing cannot be understood as simply attaining comfort.

If desire for Verlia allows Elizete to become empowered through the struggle of collective sense making, then Verlia's death is not only the loss of a lover but also the loss of Elizete's newly acquired vision and empowerment—her new sense of safety based not in security but in the belief that change is possible. When Elizete loses Verlia, she comes to Canada, but not to find safety, escape violence, or leave a traumatic past behind. Canada does not offer Elizete traditional safety; however, it allows her to remember Verlia and to engage in a healing process through sharing traumatic memories with Abena.

Elizete flies to Canada because life in Grenada after Verlia's death is untenable. The flight is linked with slavery through the Ibo Landing myth, in which, upon reaching the New World, the slaves turned around and either flew back to Africa or walked into the water, drowning themselves rather than live as chattel. Imagery of this choice abounds in the novel. Elizete sees coming to Canada as jumping off a cliff, like Verlia; coming to Canada is her way of jumping. The question is whether she died or flew. The novel in fact suggests both. On the airplane to Canada, Elizete hopes to die and "slipped into Verlia's skin until she could not tell who had died" (Brand 1996, 105–6). However, in some ways coming to Canada does represent flying back to Africa, albeit in a fallen way. If we believe that slaves did actually fly back to Africa, it was a return that also involved a loss. Even if they returned to Africa, nothing could make up for their loss and trauma. Likewise, nothing will return things to the way they were for Elizete. However, in Canada, she meets Abena and is able to find a way to come to terms with her loss. Canada itself is "no place," but her interaction with Abena makes it a place that enables recovery and a return to life, like the mythical Africa. So it is not Canada itself, imagined in the national narrative as the welfare state with "tolerant" white folks, that is a haven for her; rather it is Abena's presence, loss, and alienation from Canada that makes it a place of healing.

When Elizete finds Abena, who works in a shelter, however, this healing does not occur immediately. Abena misrecognizes her and her need: "[Elizete] had come here to give help or to get help and had got some kind of wisdom she didn't need and couldn't use. . . . She only needed a place to sort her head out" (Brand 1996, 232–33). Elizete's desire to "sort her head out" echoes Brand's assertion that desire may be "putting the senses back together." Elizete's desire to immigrate (born of a desire to die, on the one hand, and to maintain connection with the dead, on the other) turns out to be a desire for survival of trauma and loss through healing. It is only when Abena realizes that she needs Elizete in order to testify to her own trauma that recognition occurs and healing begins. Abena and Elizete are not lovers, and their testifying together does not make up for the losses that they have suffered; however, testimony functions as a kind of consolation, something that makes their lives survivable, allowing them to live and function with their memories. This recovery suggests the possibilities and need for community, but also its limits. Also, importantly, this healing has nothing to do with mainstream ideas about what makes Canada "safe."

Elizete's story proposes desire as a strategy for both survival and growth in the context of disempowerment and trauma. Verlia's desires present a more problematic case. Like Elizete, Verlia's desires are fundamentally bound up with safety, as the result of feeling unsafe in the world as it is. However, because Verlia's desires remain binary and fragmented, she is unable to use desire as a strategy for self-empowerment and healing as effectively as Elizete. Nevertheless, her failure is suggestive about what would need to change to allow true and meaningful healing for those who have one foot in and one foot out of the Canadian nation. As discussed before, Verlia is defined by binary oppositions, and she sublimates desire into the political. Verlia embraces the Black Power movement in the hopes that it will give her everything that assimilation has denied her. Her aunt and uncle's inability to love is contrasted with the "great feelings of love" she associates with revolution (Brand 1996,

165). It seems, then, that her political desires might do for Verlia what Elizete's romantic desires do for her. But this integration of love and revolution is, at best, temporary because she has rejected and devalued integral parts of herself.

Verlia rigidly divides love and revolution. The strict opposition serves to elevate the importance of revolution while devaluing the significance of love. Verlia's journal entries during her time in Grenada reveal that this binary is something that she struggles with, something she cannot resolve fully. She writes to herself: "If you're in the struggle you're in the struggle Verlia" (Brand 1996, 206) but can't find an answer to "What I want to know, Che, is if you ever wake up and it is all right" (214). Verlia's experience of desire does not map onto all she has read or onto her binary worldview. Her conception of romantic love excludes several of Brand's criteria for desire, including ferocity and sense making; but, most important, it lacks faith. It is this lack that dooms her relationships, and motivates her to keep leaving.

Verlia's lack of faith is directly proportional to her fear. Her fear comes about at the very beginning as the result of historical trauma and oppression and is continued by her internalization of whiteness. Despite thinking that Elizete is the woman she will be with forever, Verlia is fearful and withholds from her. Verlia's fear, along with her rigid binaries, causes her to reject the relationship between love and revolution. She relegates love and physical embodiment to a lesser experience, while elevating politics and revolution. In so doing, she refuses to let love inhabit the complicated space of desire articulated by Brand. Refusing to be Elizete's "grace," Verlia says: "I don't want to be. Look Elizete, don't try and seduce me. I don't believe in seduction. If you're coming you come with your head clear. Seduction is a thing between a man and a woman. There is no seduction between women. This is harder" (Brand 1996, 74). On the one hand, Verlia rejects seduction (one of her terms for assimilation and hopelessness) and gendered hierarchies. On the other hand, by demanding that Elizete "come with [her] head clear," she denies the possibility of faith and refuses to go beyond reason, a refusal that seems decidedly unrevolutionary.

On the day of her death, Verlia merges private and public, love and revolution, by allowing Elizete to take her hand when they go to join the other activists. If integrating these parts of her life seems possible in this moment, why does Verlia jump? As Elizete puts it, "She bet all she life on this revolution. She had no place else to go, no other countries, no other revolution" (Brand 1996, 114). However, more important, Verlia sees the U.S. invasion as an irreparable heartbreak, and in this moment of bringing love and revolution together, she sees both being taken away from her: "What did they think they were taking? Only her heart. . . . Well, let them take her heart too. If it was so important to some white man thousands of miles away, so important that all these planes were coming for it and all these bombs were going to kill it, let them have it" (117). The failure of the revolution, the overwhelming nature of the forces against it and her, confirm Verlia's sense that nowhere is safe. There is no place in this world where her desire, personal or political, can be realized or can exist without being violently suppressed.

In this moment Verlia tragically combines her political love with her romantic one. Verlia gets all the activists running toward the ocean, thinking: "[P]ushing and running and running and forgetting she felt someone behind her, 'Comrade, run! Comrade, sister, lover, run, not today, not today.' . . . Who was behind her. Who was she leaving. 'Run, comrade!'" (Brand 1996, 245). In her jump, she leaves Elizete but calls her to join. In this way, she blends revolution with love—Elizete is both comrade and lover—but only in escape and death, not in this world. As with Elizete, the jump's initial illegibility is resolved by a more complicated notion of desire, one that goes beyond the white normative desires that the national narrative assumes of immigrants. Verlia's jump is now legible in terms of a complex set of causes. Her fear is the result of a legacy of slavery and continued oppression. That fear results in her internalization of white epistemologies and values, which ultimately make it virtually impossible to integrate her life into a complete whole. While she is more privileged, assimilable, and "white" in relation to Elizete, Verlia has internalized racism and white epistemology, and Brand represents the psychological stakes of this. Her split desires represent a double bind where comfort equals psychological death and her unsafe revolutionary life results in literal death.

Immigration to Canada plays an important role in Verlia's trajectory. As I argued earlier, Canada functions as a place where Abena and Elizete are able to meet and heal from traumatic pasts (and in this way Canada does function as a sort of "Africa"). Being in Canada allows for something to happen within Verlia, too. In Canada, Verlia is able to reject whiteness as an ideal. Given the importance of desire in the novel, her rejection of her earlier desire for whiteness is both significant and liberatory, even if it is not entirely successful. In both of these instances, Canada is the site of significant transformation; however, it is not because it is a safe haven. Canada is not psychologically safe for Verlia, but it does change her and it facilitates her return to the Caribbean as a revolutionary.

If Elizete shows that the myth of Canadian haven is really only a myth, Verlia shows that this myth might be in fact true in a limited sense, but it is neither safe nor desirable. For Elizete, there really is no difference between Canada and Grenada; for Verlia, there is a difference, but that difference doesn't get to the "heart" of the problem. Moving to Canada does not allow her to heal from trauma or her inherited fear. In fact, it makes it worse by reinscribing the binary oppositions that caused her fragmentation and inability to heal and love.

While *In Another Place, Not Here* is a novel primarily about loss and is structured around the traumatic rupture of Verlia's jump, it also suggests that survival, healing, and love are possible. They are made possible by desire—not by homogenized, normative desires but by those that require struggle. The healing and growth that Elizete and, to a lesser extent, Verlia produce in their relationship come about through their contestation and struggle—their complicated and contradictory desires.

Notes

1. Particularities vary, but the myth contends that the newly arrived slaves turned around and walked across the water back to Africa. This connection has been discussed in Brand's work; see McCallum and Olbey 1999 and Smyth 1999.

2. This notion of Canadian multiculturalism has been amply critiqued. See Bannerji 2000 and Day 2000.

References

Bannerji, Himani. 2000. *The Dark Side of the Nation: Essays on Multiculturalism, Nationalism and Gender.* Toronto: Canadian Scholars' Press.

Brand, Dionne. 1996. *In Another Place, Not Here.* New York: Grove.

———. 2001. *A Map to the Door of No Return: Notes to Belonging.* Toronto: Vintage Canada.

Day, Richard J. F. 2000. *Multiculturalism and the History of Canadian Diversity.* Toronto: University of Toronto Press.

Jagose, Annamarie. 1994. *Lesbian Utopics.* New York: Routledge.

McCallum, Pamela, and Christian Olbey. 1999. "Written in the Scars: History, Genre, and Materiality in Dionne Brand's *In Another Place, Not Here.*" *Essays on Canadian Writing* 68 (Summer): 159–82.

Rich, Adrienne. 1979. "Women and Honor: Some Notes on Lying." In *On Lies, Secrets, and Silence: Selected Prose, 1966–1978*, 185–94. New York: Norton.

Smyth, Heather. 1999. "Sexual Citizenship and Caribbean-Canadian Fiction: Dionne Brand's *In Another Place, Not Here* and Shani Mootoo's *Cereus Blooms at Night.*" *Ariel: A Review of International English Literature* 30 (2): 141–60.

Beyond Race and Nation

The African American Barbary Captivity Narrative of Robert Adams

Melanie Fritsch

African American writings from the colonial and early national periods have traditionally been read through the lens of the antebellum fugitive slave narrative, and early black texts have often been reduced to mere precursors of the more popular autobiographical genre. The critical preoccupation with the autobiographical slave narrative has largely foreclosed a reading of those earlier texts within their broader historical contexts. Historian Philip Gould proposes an extension and revision of the African American canon, pointing to a group of life writings such as the narratives of John Marrant and Venture Smith, to which he refers summarily as "early black Atlantic autobiography."[1] The narrative that is at the center of this essay features Robert Adams, an African American sailor held captive in the Barbary States in the early 1800s, and belongs to the set of early black writings identified by Gould, whose discovery challenges the predominance of the antebellum slave narrative. *The Narrative of Robert Adams* (1816) prompts us to think of new approaches to early African American literature. Transcending critical categories developed from nineteenth-century slave narratives, Adams's account exemplifies the creativity and subversive character of such understudied texts whose complex strategies of life writing complicate their generic categorization and intervene in the continual process to outline the contours of an African American subjectivity. Significantly, it is the geographical mobility of the African American subject that renders possible the articulation of an alternative identity in the decades after the American Revolution.

This essay brings together two strands of recent criticism in African American literature: on the one hand, the critical impulse to think through the significance of geographical mobility within a transatlantic framework for African American literature; and, on the other hand, the attempt to establish a black literary tradition before the antebellum period as an independent field of study. In doing so, this essay builds on Gould's innovative work and on Gilroy's notion of the black Atlantic as a counterdiscourse to Western notions of modernity and the Enlightenment.[2] This does not mean, however, that this essay embraces Gilroy's idea that eighteenth-century African American literature should be juxtaposed with prevalent discourses of rationality within the European Enlightenment. Rather this essay proposes to extend the notion of the black Atlantic to consider the possibility that early African American writings include and appropriate Enlightenment discourses in order to challenge the contradiction between the emancipatory promises of the Enlightenment and the existence of slavery and racism.

Transcending Genre in Early African American Literature

The first publication of *The Narrative of Robert Adams* in Britain in 1816 sparked a heated transatlantic debate between British and American reviewers over the authenticity of Adams's alleged journey to Timbuktu, the mythical city that no traveler from the West had been able to reach before. After his arrival in Britain, Robert Adams, a free black from Hudson, New York, related his story of captivity in North Africa to a white amanuensis working for the African Company, a British association involved in the exploration of the African interior. He claimed that he was shipwrecked in 1810 near the African coast, taken captive by desert Moors, imprisoned by a band of dark-skinned Africans, and subsequently transferred to Timbuktu. Treated as a curiosity during his six-month stay in Timbuktu, Adams was able to move about the legendary city at his leisure. Ransomed again by a group of Moors, Adams was subsequently driven through the Sahara and forced to work for changing masters. He was finally redeemed by the British vice-consul Joseph Dupuis in Mogadore (Morocco) and made his way via Fez, Mequinez, Tangier, Cadiz, and Gibraltar to London, where his story was recorded. The third-person narrative that evolved was published in London with authenticating materials that occupied more than twice the space of the actual narrative.[3] British reviewers in the *Quarterly Review* and in the *Edinburgh Review* corroborated the authenticity of Adams's original narrative. In 1817, however, the *North American Review* printed a conflicting version of the narrative, which Adams had dictated to an American in Cadiz before he embarked for England. After an American reprint of the British version had become available in 1817 alongside the Cadiz narrative, the magazine published a trenchant attack on both versions, questioning the veracity of Adams's story. This condemnation, supposedly penned by the historian and educator Jared Sparks, revolved primarily around the exploratory aspects of Adams's report, especially his account of Timbuktu, which had aroused interest in Adams in the first place.[4] The narrative received attention not only for its sensational reports about the interior of Africa but also because it was the first (and would remain the only) account of Barbary captivity by a nonwhite American.

Recent scholars of Adams's account have been most intrigued by the question of how to situate this text by an African American within available genre distinctions and within the body of early black literature (Baepler 1999, 20–21). Adams's narrative defies easy generic classification, and the full title of his account, *The Narrative of Robert Adams, a Sailor, Who Was Wrecked on the Western Coast of Africa, in the Year 1810, Was Detained Three Years in Slavery by the Arabs of the Great Desert, and Resided Several Months in the City of Tombuctoo, with a Map, Notes, and an Appendix*, already suggests the transgeneric quality of the text. Although much of the text consists of geographic and ethnographic passages, it does not achieve the scientific objectivity found in the typical travel literature of professional exploration societies (Youngs 2002). Critics routinely situate Adams in the context of early American life writing and, more specifically, the popular Barbary captivity narrative, emphasizing the similarities between Adams's narrative and the texts of white Americans who experienced North African captivity and whose accounts contributed to an intensifying debate about slavery in the United States.[5] Modern scholars have paid further attention to the narrative's formal similarities with the slave narratives (Baepler 1999, 20), but these reflections on formal and generic aspects of the narrative stop short of entering into an analysis of its larger discursive implications. In fact, Adams's narrative raises intricate methodological questions about the availability of alternative subject positions in early African American personal narratives. A close examination of *The Narrative of Robert Adams* demonstrates that early black life writing does not lend itself to a mere application of established theories and discourses of subjectivity but requires new ways of thinking about African American self-fashioning and identity formation. The narrative's reliance on motifs familiar from travel writing, captivity stories, and slave narratives should not obscure the fact that Adams's articulation of a personal identity involves a challenge to fixed subject positions based on discourses of nationality and race.

Inventing and Developing Early African American Subjectivity

Although the close relationship between mobility and subversive subjectivities in African American travel writing is very often overlooked because of the genre's somewhat hybrid nature (Griffin and Fish 1998, xiv), it figures prominently in Adams's narrative. Like the protagonists of classical slave narratives, Adams relates the narrative trajectory from captivity/slavery to freedom to a change in place and location. Numerous studies have illustrated that in African American literature the representation of geographical mobility has been conducible to undermining essentialist notions of black subjectivity and that alternative identities dissociated from particular places, regions, or nations have been conceptualized in a transatlantic context.[6] Since Adams was exceptionally situated to argue for the instability of racially defined subject positions, his narrative offers alternatives to established strategies of subjectivization in life writing. Unlike the common display of a protagonist's thoughts and emotions in sensationalist accounts of travel, captivity, and slavery, Adams's narrative was not intent on evoking a readerly sympathy with a suffering and despondent subject (Baepler 1999, 21). Nor is his narrative primarily concerned with mediating between Western civilization and an Oriental other, as recent scholarship of travel writing so often suggests. Adams's narrative rather intervenes in the intensifying debate about slavery in the United States and the reverberations of that debate in African American attempts at alternative identities.

As a nonwhite captive, Adams's racial identity is not stabilized by the common white-black, civilized-uncivilized, and Christian-Muslim dichotomies that surface in the Barbary captivity accounts that were popular at the time. In his self-narration, Adams's subject position remains unstable in terms of race and nation, categories that scholars have repeatedly employed to describe the intercultural encounter of Americans and Arabs in this genre (Baepler 1999, 1–58). Prior to chronicling Adams's adventures in Africa, the narrative establishes the protagonist's identity as a free African American from Hudson, New York (R. Adams 1816, 5).[7] However, the narrative consciously obscures Adams's true identity; neither his upbringing nor his definitive motives and circumstances of leaving the United States are revealed. In a letter reprinted in the "Introductory Details," Joseph Dupuis, the British vice-consul who ransomed Adams, discloses that Adams had a mulatto mother, "which circumstance his features and complexion seemed to confirm." He firmly believes that the man in his custody is an American because of Adams's "involuntary exultation at the sight of the American flag" (xxviii). However, Dupuis initially mistakes Adams for an Arab due to his appearance, dress, and speech (xxiii–xxiv).

While the evidence leads Dupuis to conclude that Adams must be a black American, Adams challenges these delimitations of his racial and national selfhood throughout the narrative. He repeatedly refers to himself as a white man: "Adams could not hear that any white man but themselves [Adams and his Portuguese shipmate] had ever been seen in the place; and he believes, as well from what he was told by the Moors, as from the uncommon curiosity which he excited (though himself a very dark man, with short curly black hair), that they never had seen one before" (R. Adams 1816, 42). Recounting his time in Timbuktu, Adams provides us with a seemingly clear marker of his identity, speaking about himself as a white man—only to make a parenthetical qualification that compels the reader to identify him as an African American.[8] Adams also counts himself among the white men in the list documenting those men who left Timbuktu—"2 white men" (himself and the Portuguese) among the "10 Moorish traders," "14 Moorish prisoners," and "1 slave" (47). Similarly, Adams never appears with the label "black man" in any of the ship's crew lists in the narrative, whereas other shipmates are identified as "Swede" (6) or "black seaman" (160n) in the editor's concluding remarks. Adams's self-perception as a relatively privileged white captive in Timbuktu is substantially modified during the ensuing journey through the desert, when the daily misery of a captive's life and the hot climate are further "aggravated by despair of ever being released from slavery" (53). During the itinerant period of his captivity, Adams likens his state to that of a slave, intriguingly without pointing at his most obvious commonality with slaves: his race. Robert Adams's creation of a white identity as he moves through the different stages of his captivity reveals a practice that anticipates the instances of "passing" that are prominent in modern African American literature.[9]

Adams does not construct a consistent racial identity, nor is his nationality conceived as a fixed category in the narrative. He appears intermittently as an American or Englishman. In fact, there is an important discrepancy in the use of national designations between the editorial commentaries of the white editors and the voice of Robert Adams in the body of his narrative. Although the editorial compendium repeatedly presents Adams as an "American seaman" (R. Adams 1816, xi, xxvi), Adams introduces himself as "an Englishman" (80) to the Moroccan emperor, well knowing that the designation "Englishman" would place him on safer ground than "American." Certainly, Adams must have felt indebted to the British because he was ransomed by a member of the British consulate. As an Englishman, Adams would also be able to claim the protection of the British navy and receive the same kind of preferential treatment as British sailors.[10] After all, passing as an Englishman also reinforced Adams's status as a free man vis-à-vis his insecure status as a free black in America. The editor's use of the classification "American" as a marker to establish Adams's identity is significant as *The Narrative of Robert Adams* was part of the rich Barbary Coast literature of the time. The fact that

American citizens were captured by Barbary pirates and sold into slavery in the Barbary States became a source of national indignation, and Barbary captivity narratives documented the pervasive anxiety about the loss of the newly won national sovereignty and pride.[11] The nationalist overtones perceptible in the Barbary literature, however, do not adequately capture the pragmatic and strategic uses that captives like Adams made of claims to particular national identities while in North Africa. The account of Adams gestures at the possibility that the actual experience of captivity required extensive editorial interventions into the narrative in order to render original accounts conducible to the readerly expectations of Barbary captivity stories.[12]

In light of his volatile racial and national identity, it is not surprising that Adams also carries more than one name. Some of his acquaintances know Robert Adams as Benjamin Rose, conjecturing that fear of impressment by the British navy or fear of prosecution due to an illicit relationship in America could have prompted the name change (R. Adams 1816, xxvii–xxviii). Studies of maritime culture also suggest that black sailors frequently made use of the anonymity of the seafaring business to adopt new names (Bolster 1997, 216).[13] What the composite narrative emphatically documents time and again is that Adams redefined himself at decisive points in his life—as Benjamin Rose vs. Robert Adams, white vs. black, and American vs. Englishman. The similarities between Adams's narrative and the Barbary captivity narrative underline the (quite possibly unintentional) revisionary agenda of Adams's critique of Western liberalist discourse as a source of legitimizing slavery as a forced labor system. In view of texts by white Americans who experienced North African captivity, Adams's account destabilizes racially assigned identities. Adams offers to critique an inherent contradiction between the popular revolutionary promise of universal natural rights and the liberalist guarantee of individual property—the main obstacle against which the advocates of manumission and gradual emancipation in the early nineteenth century had to struggle.

Natural Rights and the Politics of Economic Resistance

Although Robert Adams redefines himself as he sees fit and thereby highlights the ineffectiveness of such concepts as race and nation in the black Atlantic, his identity is anything but arbitrary. The liberal discourses of natural rights and possessive individualism are fundamental to Adams's self-fashioning and understanding as a full human subject who exists outside the oppressive practice of enslavement and forced labor. His appeals and maneuvers during his captivity underline his demands to hold property and to be recognized as endowed with natural rights. Both principles form a stable framework for defining Robert Adams's identity throughout the narrative. A close reading of Adams's narrative in the context of an emergent political and economic liberal ideology thus contributes to our understanding of the black Atlantic as a transnational and transcultural space where black people perpetually moved, "not only as commodities but engaged in various struggles towards emancipation, autonomy, and citizenship" (Gilroy 1993, 16).[14]

That Adams was acutely aware of an Enlightenment discourse of natural rights shows in his depiction of the ruling king of Timbuktu, Woollo. Adams employs a decidedly political vocabulary when he describes the king as a "despotic" man who "could compel his subjects to take up arms when he required it" (R. Adams 1816, 40). In the first-person Cadiz narrative, Adams's rendering of the king's rule is delineated in even more rigorous terms, alluding to a specifically American revolutionary vocabulary. The king, Adams relates, is "absolute." He presides over both law and government:

> He is the sole dispenser of justice. He alone frames and executes the laws. I could never ascertain whether this rank and its privileges were elective or hereditary, though I was led to believe the former. He has power over the liberties and lives of his subjects, and directs their occupations as he pleases. The people seem formed, in fact, but for his purposes; to amuse, benefit, and aggrandize him. The greater part of his subjects are in his immediate service. . . . They are sometimes rewarded according to a previous stipulation, but more commonly according to his own pleasure and caprice. . . . [E]very individual in his dominions is at his disposal, whenever he chooses to deprive any one of liberty. (R. Adams [and Sparks] 1817, 18)

The king's "power over the liberties and lives of his subjects" and his control over their "occupations" preclude the people's obtaining "life, liberty, and the pursuit of happiness," the fundamental natural rights codified in the American Declaration of Independence. Adams makes it plain to his American amanuensis in Cadiz that he is aware of himself as a post-revolutionary subject who is familiar with such political dichotomies as monarchy vs. republic and hereditary vs. elective monarchy. Adams ultimately characterizes Timbuktu as a tyranny where natural rights are violated, and he is convinced that the absence of a government that protects the natural rights of individuals will result in monarchical relationships of dependency and involuntary servitude. The despotic character of the political system, where the king's subjects are "at his disposal," makes Adams acutely aware of an eerie proximity between political power and legal ownership structures. Read in the context of an early black Atlantic mode of life writing, Adams's enslavement entails not only the loss of his personal liberty but also a loss of his economic autonomy as a subject entitled to hold property and to determine his way of sustaining his livelihood. Adams's experience transforms him from a free black American into a captive/slave of an Oriental other, the reverse situation usually found in the classical slave narrative, in which the slave moves from being property to being the proprietor of his own body and labor (Kawash 1997, 23–84).[15]

Pondering Adams's options for terminating his precarious position as an enslaved subject, the narrative depicts a variety of primarily economic strategies, including flight, refusal to work, physical fighting, and buying his freedom. Adams probes what it means to be free in his attempts to withdraw from work by flight. When his master reclaims him, Adams appeals to the governor, contending that his master's broken promises of taking him to a town inhabited by other Westerners prompted him to flee. Adams asserts that he will not return to his master and, invoking the 1775 call of the American patriot Patrick Henry, declares that he will "either obtain his liberty or die" (1816, 57). The governor henceforth becomes his new master, but Adams is sold again after he has an affair with one of the man's wives. Adams initially justifies his flight by a broken contractual relationship that, in his reasoning, dissolves his ties to his master and thus restores him to his original state of freedom. But his being sold and resold among the desert Moors is expression enough that such laws were ineffective in his case. Like other slave narrators, Adams keeps track of his pecuniary value as a popular object of ransom. Although he invokes his right to freedom, he remains moveable property (the common definition of chattel) until he is finally ransomed—purchased again—by the British vice-consul.

As fleeing proves unsuccessful, Adams resorts to another form of resistance against his captivity: he refuses to work on the Sabbath, "urging that it was not the custom of any slaves to work on the Sabbath day, and that he was intitled to the same indulgence as the rest" (1816, 70). After a physical encounter with his master's son that is reminiscent of Frederick Douglass's famous fight with the overseer Covey, Adams refuses to kiss the man's feet and hands, citing "that it was 'contrary to his religion' . . . [and] that in his own country he had never been required to do it" (71–72). Here, he demands to be treated as if he were at home and a free American citizen. Adams rejects his shipmates' path of converting to Islam in order to become free and waits to be ransomed. When he is finally brought to Mogadore, Adams describes the moment of his imminent emancipation in terms of deliverance and rebirth familiar to readers of classical captivity narratives and their spiritual subtexts.

Adams's satisfaction "that his complete deliverance was at hand" is rendered not only in direct speech but in his use of personal pronouns: "I felt as if a new life had been given to me" (78). Linguistically, this episode signals Adams's shift from the third-person object into a full subject who expresses himself in the first person. But even this last transaction is economic, not a religious or spiritual transformation. The only way out of slavery that the narrative depicts as successful is being ransomed, by which the property rights of the slaveholders are not violated. The termination of Adams's captivity is politically delicate, as buying the freedom of American slaves was at the time one idea circulating among antislavery advocates, especially those favoring the colonization of blacks in Africa. Yet, by furnishing this ending, Adams does not solve the inherent contradictions between a rising liberalist discourse based on natural rights and property and the system of slavery in his narrative.

Conclusion: Liberal Ideologies in the Black Atlantic

The Narrative of Robert Adams ranks among a range of early African American texts that conceptualize the position of the black subject in terms of the nascent ideological formation of liberalism. Adams's narrative participates in the project of "early black Atlantic autobiography" when it exposes the incompatibility between an emergent liberalist discourse and the global reality of slavery and the slave trade. Liberalism's political emphasis on universal natural rights as well as its economic component (property privileges) becomes seminal for the proto-abolitionist argument of the narrative. Throughout his captivity, Adams acts according to his precarious position as a free African American, appropriating notions from a liberal discourse of natural rights to conceptualize his own experience of temporary enslavement. Thus, Adams narrativizes his experiences in terms of a liberal ideology whose political basis of universal natural rights allows him to criticize its global economic entanglement in the transatlantic slave trade.

The consistent adherence of Adams's narrative to the principles of an emergent liberal ideology demonstrates the usefulness of Philip Gould's suggestion to revise Paul Gilroy's notion of the black Atlantic in the light of early African American autobiographical writing. Gould is able to fill a terminological gap in the discussion of texts embracing revolutionary and post-revolutionary discourses of natural rights, liberty, and property as valuable rhetorical resources for the early antislavery literature of the black Atlantic. Gilroy's concept of the black Atlantic as an expression of the "desire to transcend both the structures of the nation state and the constraints of ethnicity and national particularity" (1993, 19) is enhanced by Gould, who allows for a "creative potential of individual rights discourse" as a means of articulating the experience of the transatlantic slave trade and slavery in the New World (Gould 2000, 660). The black Atlantic is a useful category that can provide the starting point for a compelling critique of the ideological and economic basis of this transnational space. Gould modifies Gilroy's critique of Enlightenment thought and emphasizes the adoption of a natural rights discourse that is directed against defining the African American subject as legal property.

Such a reconsideration of early African American life writing further elucidates the significance of marginalized figures such as Robert Adams. Gould's qualification of Gilroy's concept of the black Atlantic paves the way for a new interpretation of so far understudied early black texts, such as the personal narratives by John Marrant, Venture Smith, and Briton Hammon, and even of canonical texts such as Equiano's *Interesting Narrative*. A reconsideration of the African American canon and literary achievement prior to the antebellum slave narrative cannot ignore the subtle and manifold discursive implications or the volatile political interventions of texts like Adams's. The only surviving Barbary captivity narrative by a black American requires critics to bypass the heated transatlantic debate between commentators in Great Britain and the United States about the authenticity of the narrative in order to engage the revisionary challenge of Adams's narrative to established forms of expressing one's identity. As Adams moves along in the desert, he changes identities as he sees fit between black and white, free and slave, American and British, thus exposing the arbitrariness of racial and national designations in the world of the black Atlantic. Recovering marginalized texts will in the long run also allow for a reconsideration of and fresh look at what have been considered as the central literary achievements of African Americans in response to captivity and slavery. A close analysis of the sources on which African American authors draw to articulate their opposition to slavery and racism will challenge scholars to rethink the complex ways in which African American texts intersect with European intellectual traditions. Scholars now and in the future will continue to record the means by which African Americans define their identity, often according to the pragmatic requirements of a particular historical situation. The experience of being a captive in the Barbary States at the beginning of the nineteenth century has produced an early and important moment of African American creativity in *The Narrative of Robert Adams*.

Notes

1. Gould spearheads a host of scholars who argue for the inclusion of eighteenth-century texts in a transnational African American literary canon. The idea of "early

black Atlantic autobiography" has been most prominently laid out in Gould 2000 and Gould 2003, 122–51. In his effort to develop a conceptual framework in which to discuss those early texts, Gould undertakes a critical reconsideration of Paul Gilroy's notion of a "black Atlantic" as a substitute for race and nation as the key terms of Eurocentric metanarratives. He shows how Gilroy's notion of a black Atlantic can still serve as a useful heuristic category (Gould 2008). The notion of a black Atlantic has become an umbrella term in revisionist literary and historical scholarship for texts outside the fold of an established African American canon (Brooks and Saillant 2002; Carretta and Gould 2001; Rice 2003). The black Atlantic remains a guiding concept for a transnational approach to African American studies, besides similar categories such as "Atlantic creole," "transatlantic," and "circumatlantic." As Vincent Carretta has observed, "What all of these transnational categories usefully share is an emphasis on the roles geographical movements of people and culture play in the creation of identities" (2008, 100–101). For other critical assessments of the consequences of such revisionist interventions in the African American canon, see the essays in Drexler and White 2008.

2. Also see Helena Woodard's study on "[t]he politics of race and reason in Enlightenment English literature and its impact on colonial African-British writings," in which she argues that "the Enlightenment reasons race both through a complex, aesthetic language—typically didactic instructions about the function of literature and moral assertions about the human condition—and through concepts that obscure, displace, or absent race precisely where social practice dictates that it figures most prominently" (1999, xviii, xiii). As I will argue in the following, Adams's narrative validates Woodard's analysis in that it highlights the significance of enlightened natural rights discourse for configurations of racial difference.

3. Noting the substantial imbalance between Adams's narrative and the editorial apparatus, Hester Blum has pointed out "a remarkable resemblance to the prefatory and authenticating materials found in African American narratives of chattel slavery" (2008, 61). Beyond two London editions (1816) and a Boston release (1817), Adams's narrative was available in Paris (1817), Stockholm (1817), and Amsterdam (1818) (Baepler 1999, 306–7).

4. For a study of the myth surrounding Timbuktu and an outline of Western explorations, see Gardner 1968 and C. Adams 2005, xxxi–xlii. Contrary to earlier confirmations of Adams's Timbuktu episode as truthful, recent scholarship reassesses the Timbuktu section as probably inauthentic (C. Adams 2005, xvi–xxii).

5. The Barbary captivity narrative is generally seen as having coevolved with the Indian captivity narrative (Baepler 2004). The Indian captivity narrative, especially in the vein of Mary Rowlandson's archetypal example, has traditionally been read as an elongation of the spiritual autobiography and testifies to an individual's—and, by ex-

tension, the community's—redemption. The Barbary captivity narrative can be seen as a marker of the captivity genre's transition to a more secularized form. In its depiction of the encounter between a Christian American captive and his Muslim North African captors, Adams's report imitates the narrative development of a traditional Indian captivity narrative. However, for an American readership, Adams's narrative might lack the clear confrontation between a Western, civilized, and Christian subject and the savage, uncivilized, and unchristian captors that is constitutive of other captivity narratives.

6. However, African American travel to Africa was often futile in its endeavor to arrive at an African American identity by retracing the ancestral roots of the African diaspora to Africa. Hoping to come to terms with America as their country of birth, African Americans journeying to Africa rarely reached full identification with Africa (Campbell 2006, xix–xxii).

7. The narrative's title lacks a clear racial marker that would allude to Adams as African American. Although it is not unusual for texts published in the early Republic to avoid explicit racial designations, the title page is usually the place where racial attributes are prominently positioned. John Marrant, for instance, is silent on his racial identity in the narrative, but the title page carries the designation "John Marrant, a Black."

8. Similarly, in the first-person Cadiz narrative that Adams related to an American even before he told his story in England, Adams remarks: "[Y]et I could not understand that here was any tradition or remembrance that a white man had ever been seen among them before" (R. Adams [and Sparks] 1817, 22). In several other instances in the London narrative, Adams identifies himself or is identified as white (R. Adams 1816, 57). The narrative's editor suggests that not his race but his being "a Christian, and a *Christian slave*" was more likely what surprised the Negroes at Timbuktu (127n37).

9. As scholars of passing in African American literature have claimed, passing is a powerful means of identity formation. Elaine Ginsberg argues that "[i]n its interrogation of the essentialism that is the foundation of identity politics, passing has the potential to create a space for creative self-determination and agency: the opportunity to construct new identities, to experiment with multiple subject positions, and to cross social and economic boundaries that exclude or oppress" (1996, 16). The example of Robert Adams illustrates that marginalized early African American autobiographers challenged any form of essentialized identity.

10. Since the end of the Revolutionary War, American ships could no longer rely on the protection of the maritime power of the British Empire. Pirate attacks on American vessels in the Mediterranean region and along the Barbary Coast were prevented only by American tributes to the dey of Algiers and other potentates (Blum 2008, 48–

49). The security of American ships in the area depended on fragile diplomatic relations between the United States and the Barbary States, a situation that was exploited by the British government when it invited the Barbary pirates to renew their attacks on American ships on the eve of the War of 1812 (Baepler 1999, 1–20; Leiner 2006, 20–24).

11. The humiliating implications of this episode for an American audience were not lost on the nationalist and editor of the *North American Review,* Jared Sparks. In a slating review, he dismissed the veracity of the narrative on the basis of its scientific faults ([Sparks] 1817, 206), and he presented testimonials that denied Adams's credibility (223–24). While these commentaries mirror prevailing ideas of African American mental and intellectual inferiority, Sparks's primary intention might in fact have been to object against the British depiction of U.S. ineffectiveness to provide adequate protection to its citizens overseas.

12. For an extensive discussion of the overlap between the Barbary literature and American claims to liberty and independence in the late eighteenth century, see Rojas 2003.

13. The phenomenon of several names is of course familiar to scholars of early and especially mid-nineteenth century slave narratives. Frederick Douglass famously changes his name three times on his way to freedom, from Bailey (the name he was given by his mother) to Stanley (Baltimore), to Johnson (New York), and finally to Douglass (New Bedford) (1997, 71–72). Similarly, Equiano introduces himself as both Olaudah Equiano and Gustavus Vassa on the cover of his book, a "binomial author" with "a dual identity" that reflected his belonging to both African and European culture (Carretta 2000, 385; see also Carretta 2005, xix).

14. Gilroy further notes that "[t]he history of the black Atlantic . . . provides a means to reexamine the problems of nationality, location, identity, and historical memory. They all emerge from it with special clarity if we contrast the national, nationalistic, and ethnically absolute paradigms of cultural criticism to be found in England and America with those hidden expressions, both residual and emergent, that attempt to be global or outer-national in nature" (1993, 16).

15. The slave narrative tells us the story of a "slave [who] becomes a free subject when he or she is no longer the property of another," thus defining the former slave *ad negativum,* as not being property (Kawash 1997, 24).

References

Adams, Charles Hansford, ed. 2005. *The Narrative of Robert Adams, a Barbary Captive: A Critical Edition.* Cambridge: Cambridge University Press.

Adams, Robert. 1816. *The Narrative of Robert Adams, a Sailor, Who Was Wrecked on the Western Coast of Africa, in the Year 1810, Was Detained Three Years in Slavery by the Arabs of the Great Desert, and Resided Several Months in the City of Tombuctoo, with a Map, Notes, and an Appendix.* Edited by S. Cock. London: John Murray.

Adams, Robert, [and Jared Sparks]. 1817. "Interiour of Africa." *North American Review,* May, 11–26.

Baepler, Paul, ed. 1999. *White Slaves, African Masters: An Anthology of American Barbary Captivity Narratives.* Chicago: University of Chicago Press.

———. 2004. "The Barbary Captivity Narrative in American Culture." *Early American Literature* 39 (2): 217–46.

Blum, Hester. 2008. *The View from the Masthead: Maritime Imagination and Antebellum American Sea Narratives.* Chapel Hill: University of North Carolina Press.

Bolster, W. Jeffrey. 1997. *Black Jacks: African American Seamen in the Age of Sail.* Cambridge: Harvard University Press.

Brooks, Joanna, and John Saillant, eds. 2002. *"Face Zion Forward": First Writers of the Black Atlantic, 1785–1798.* Boston: Northeastern University Press.

Campbell, James T. 2006. *Middle Passages: African American Journeys to Africa, 1787–2005.* New York: Penguin.

Carretta, Vincent. 2000. "Defining a Gentleman: The Status of Olaudah Equiano or Gustavus Vassa." *Language Sciences* 22 (3): 385–99.

———. 2005. *Equiano, the African: Biography of a Self-Made Man.* Athens: University of Georgia Press.

———. 2008. "Early African-American Literature?" In *Beyond Douglass: New Perspectives on Early African-American Literature,* edited by Michael J. Drexler and Ed White, 91–106. Lewisburg: Bucknell University Press.

Carretta, Vincent, and Philip Gould, eds. 2001. *Genius in Bondage: Literature of the Early Black Atlantic.* Lexington: University Press of Kentucky.

Douglass, Frederick. 1997. *Narrative of the Life of Frederick Douglass, an American Slave, Written by Himself: Authoritative Text, Contexts, Criticism.* Edited by William L. Andrews and William S. McFeely. New York: Norton.

Drexler, Michael J., and Ed White, eds. 2008. *Beyond Douglass: New Perspectives on Early African-American Literature.* Lewisburg: Bucknell University Press.

Gardner, Brian. 1968. *The Quest for Timbuctoo.* London: Cassell.

Gilroy, Paul. 1993. *The Black Atlantic: Modernity and Double Consciousness.* Cambridge: Harvard University Press.

Ginsberg, Elaine K., ed. 1996. *Passing and the Fictions of Identity.* Durham: Duke University Press.

Gould, Philip. 2000. "Free Carpenter, Venture Capitalist: Reading the Lives of the Early Black Atlantic." *American Literary History* 12 (4): 659–84.

———. 2003. *Barbaric Traffic: Commerce and Antislavery in the Eighteenth-Century Atlantic World.* Cambridge: Harvard University Press.

———. 2008. "Early Black Atlantic Writing and the Cultures of Enlightenment." In *Beyond Douglass: New Perspectives on Early African-American Literature,* edited by Michael J. Drexler and Ed White, 107–21. Lewisburg: Bucknell University Press.

Griffin, Farah Jasmine, and Cheryl J. Fish, eds. 1998. *A Stranger in the Village: Two Centuries of African-American Travel Writing.* Boston: Beacon.

Kawash, Samira. 1997. *Dislocating the Color Line: Identity, Hybridity, and Singularity in African-American Narrative.* Stanford: Stanford University Press.

Leiner, Frederick C. 2006. *The End of Barbary Terror: America's 1815 War against the Pirates of North Africa.* New York: Oxford University Press.

Rice, Alan J. 2003. *Radical Narratives of the Black Atlantic.* London: Continuum.

Rojas, Martha Elena. 2003. "'Insults Unpunished': Barbary Captives, American Slaves, and the Negotiation of Liberty." *Early American Studies* 1 (2): 159–86.

[Sparks, Jared.] 1817. "Art. IX." Review of *The Narrative of Robert Adams* [Boston, 1817]. *North American Review,* July, 204–24.

Woodard, Helena. 1999. *African-British Writings in the Eighteenth Century: The Politics of Race and Reason.* Westport, Conn.: Greenwood.

Youngs, Tim. 2002. "Africa/The Congo: The Politics of Darkness." In *The Cambridge Companion to Travel Writing,* edited by Peter Hulme and Tim Youngs, 156–73. Cambridge: Cambridge University Press.

Upon the Public Highways

Travel and Race in Charles W. Chesnutt's *The Marrow of Tradition*

Walter Bosse

> [W]hen I hear the iron horse make the hills echo with his snort like thunder, shaking the earth with his feet, and breathing fire and smoke from his nostrils . . . it seems as if earth had got a race now worthy to inhabit it.
>
> —Henry David Thoreau, *Walden,* 1854

> Not only could you travel upward toward success but you could travel downward as well . . . meeting your old selves coming and going and perhaps all at the same time.
>
> —Ralph Ellison, *Invisible Man,* 1952

In "Traveling Cultures," anthropologist James Clifford articulates a methodological problem: "Twentieth-century ethnography—an evolving practice of modern travel—has become increasingly wary of certain localizing strategies in the construction and representation of 'cultures.'" By inquiring into "[w]ho determines where (and when) a community draws its lines, names its insiders and outsiders," Clifford asserts his intention "to open up the question of how cultural analysis constitutes its objects—societies, traditions, communities, identities—in *spatial* terms and through specific *spatial* practices of research" (1997, 19). Redefining the nature and purpose of fieldwork within anthropological practices, Clifford recognizes the importance of reading culture or community for internal or self-contained characteristics *in addition to* and *against* prevalent means of exchange—namely, via travel and the traveler. An ethnographer in his own right, Charles W. Chesnutt expresses a similar attitude toward the cultural, racial relevance of spatial mobility at the beginning of the twentieth century. As an indelibly influential writer of both race and region, Chesnutt develops travel as metaphor in a way that anticipates Clifford's anthropological focus on movement. Additionally, his use of travel exhibits "the tension between roots and routes" that Paul Gilroy recognizes in later black moderns like W. E. B. DuBois and James Weldon Johnson (1993, 133). The conditions of community and identity become spatialized and mobilized in Chesnutt's fiction as he works to expose and upend the constraints of both "black" and "white" in America.

He employs such localizing and mobilizing strategies in his 1901 novel, *The Marrow of Tradition,* which takes a historically specific incident as its launching point. As a response to the Wilmington, North Carolina, race riots of 1898, *Marrow* operates within a southern social milieu plagued by violent racial and political unrest. Though rooted in factual circumstance, Chesnutt's artful rendering of the occasion requires readings that go beyond recognizing its status and utility as a historical record. Furthermore, as a direct indictment of American racism, *Marrow* marks a significant aesthetic departure from his previously well-received *The Conjure Woman,* a short story collection with subtle rhetorical nuances that display what Houston Baker Jr. calls Chesnutt's "ability to give the trick to white expectations, securing publication for creative work that carries a deep-rooted African sound" (Baker 1987, 49). No such "tricks" confound expectations in *Marrow*; William Dean Howells's rather unforgiving critique of the novel as overly "bitter" reveals that the opposite ethos—that of outspoken invective—prevails in the text (Andrews 1980, 207). However, this is certainly *not* to say that Chesnutt's palpable censure of American race politics inhibits or detracts from the novel's aesthetic complexities. To be sure, the riots provided Chesnutt with the opportunity to articulate his political disillusionment, but *Marrow* also—and more importantly—contains significant commentary on the nature and construction of identity and community, commentary that complicates essentialist understandings of race.

Under the shadow of Jim Crow arbitration, the categorical and dualistic conceptions of race—particularly in the American South—greatly inform Chesnutt's social and artistic philosophy. Yet, his take on race in *Marrow* goes beyond breaking down political (mis)conceptions. Chesnutt sets race in motion at the turn of the century and emphasizes the fluidity of American identity. The dramatic element of travel within the novel directly relates to racial affiliation and identity construction. Chesnutt illustrates that identity is in a state of flux and that "race" is mobile, unfixed, insecure. He presents racial identity as a fluid construct and exposes the harmfully rigid nature of institutional regulations and social mores in the South at the turn of the century. In *Marrow,* travel functions as a metaphor for race, as a vehicle that allows Chesnutt to test and tear down dualistic categories and to explore the social possibilities that exist during the racial nadir. Ultimately, however, Chesnutt's level of commitment to travel as a socially progressive trope remains in question. Indeed, mobility offers a potentially liberating experience, but the threats of rootlessness and of a deferred sense of community remain part of the traveler's equipage.

Because my argument relies on topographical considerations—on the recognition that Chesnutt renders race via place and mobility—it is important to recognize the novel's interesting deployment of literary regionalism. Though Chesnutt is often classified as a writer with strictly regionalist proclivities, his innovative use of travel in *Marrow* defies the narrative and generic confines at work in most regionalist texts. Although the majority of the novel is concentrated within the borders of Wellington (Wilmington), the physical movement that occurs resists fixed containment and thereby subverts any attempt to reach essentialist conclusions about identity. In other words, this reconsideration of region and regionalism on a formal, generic level presages Chesnutt's subversion of essentialist, static conceptions of race on a more conceptual level. Furthermore, Chesnutt's use of the travel metaphor illustrates his awareness that movement and displacement represent defining and culturally pervasive features of the black experience in America. Indeed, travel pervades African American history and literature. From the Middle Passage to accounts of escape in nineteenth-century slave narratives, from postbellum migration north to the settling movements within cities in the twentieth century, issues of travel "are especially important in the history of the black Atlantic, where movement, relocation, displacement, and restlessness are the norms rather than the exceptions" (Gilroy 1993, 133). To be sure, Chesnutt's own lived experience of relocation from the South (Wilmington) to the North (Cleveland) further informs his employment of these cultural-geographic dynamics. What remains productively in question, then, is the degree to which Chesnutt uses his craft and imagination to signify on the promise of America. Writing from his own "tight spaces" as a black author, his project "is not only framed by the American South, but also is inextricable . . . from specific institutionalizations of human life below the Mason Dixon" (Baker 2001, 26).

After making his full debut on the literary scene with the publication of *The Conjure Woman,* Chesnutt devoted his subject matter almost exclusively to issues involving racially mixed individuals. In the series of essays collectively titled "The Future American"—published in the *Boston Evening Transcript* in 1900—Chesnutt both prophesies and endorses racial mixing in America. He maintains that the future ethnicity of all Americans "will be formed of a mingling, in a yet to be ascertained proportion, of the various racial varieties which make up the present population of the United States" (1999a, 122). His description of the racial makeup of "the present population" is purposefully ambiguous; he suggests that the collective whole is in a state of metamorphosis.[1]

Moreover, as "The Future American" continues, Chesnutt cites "conditions of trade and *ease of travel*" as environmental factors that will perpetuate the continued mixing of American ethnic groups (123; emphasis mine).

Chesnutt clearly foregrounds this "ease of travel" in *Marrow*'s narrative propulsion. Racial issues are embedded in each circumstance of dramatic movement. Travel functions as an overarching metaphor in which these social complexities take shape. While primarily set in the town of Wellington, North Carolina, the novel profoundly resists geographic restraint. There are various levels of transit that exist in *Marrow;* large-scale, interstate motion at the beginning gives way to more subtle—though extremely significant—traveling within the town at the end.

Crossing State Lines: Railroads, Race, and Large-Scale Movement

In his discussion of travel and culture, Clifford gives specific examples of liminal and often mobile sites that can lead to ripe anthropological exploration—"a hotel lobby, urban café, ship, or bus" (1997, 25). A train fits rather appropriately into this list. Chapter 5 in *Marrow*—"A Journey Southward"—contains a dramatic account of railroad travel. This first major occurrence of geographical movement confers an evident momentum to the novel and foregrounds Chesnutt's development of travel as a metaphor for issues of racial fluidity and for the permeable and porous boundary of race. The novel's protagonist, Dr. William Miller, is "returning from New York, where he had been in order to purchase equipment for his new hospital" (1901, 51). A successful black physician in Wellington, Miller is just one generation removed from slavery. However, his education and sense of professional success have fostered a self-image that has alienated him from the lower-class blacks of Wellington. Furthermore, his skin color has automatically prevented him from realizing full association with white intellectuals. This sense of rootlessness, of unfixed identity and identification, pervades the chapter as the train crosses the border from North to South, and as the color line is crossed and recrossed within the train car. Critic Dean McWilliams elaborates on the railroad's symbolism in Chesnutt's fiction by pointing to the fact that "the value of the north-south road . . . resides in the tension between seeming clarity and deep ambiguity in racial meanings" (2002, 148). This tension is central to Chesnutt's argument against racial essentialism: the coexistence of "seeming clarity" and "deep ambiguity" confounds any dualistic understanding of race. Travel itself enhances this tension as it dislocates certain characters in the novel and disrupts environmental singularity. By introducing the novel's protagonist at a significant geographical remove from his "home," Chesnutt exhibits an ethnographic concern that, again, anticipates Clifford's commentary on method: "Why not focus on any culture's farthest range of travel while *also* looking at its centers, its villages, its intensive fieldsites?" (1997, 25). Furthermore, Miller's education in Europe—"studying in the hospitals of Paris and Vienna, the two most delightful years of his life"—advances the inherent waywardness of his character (1901, 50). His enriching experiences in France and Austria bring the southbound train journey of the novel's present into relief, establishing a marked tension between liberating edification on the one hand and increasing social restrictions on the other.

Focusing primarily on the chance meeting between Miller and his onetime teacher and mentor, Dr. Burns, the chapter begins with a sequence of fluctuating identification. Upon recognizing his former student, Dr. Burns declares: "William Miller—Dr. Miller of course. Sit down, Miller, and tell me all about yourself" (1901, 48). In his excitement, Dr. Burns initially identifies his friend using his first and last name; he then employs his professional title; finally, he resorts to just "Miller." Taking Chesnutt's emphasis on names into consideration, this is a significant beginning to the interface between the two men. Burns's first impulse is to use his friend's first and last name, a rather personal way of engaging his acquaintance. However, he checks that, recognizing Miller's professional accomplishment as a medical doctor. Though this reveals an impulse grounded in respect, his ultimate decision to use just "Miller" as his operative method of address throughout the chapter shows a pulling back on Burns's part, a nominal distancing act that anticipates the literal segregation enforced by the conductor later in the chapter. Perhaps, as the former teacher, Burns would have been accustomed to saying "Miller" in the classroom. Nonetheless, the primary significance here lies in the changing nature of the address. While their interaction is completely benign, this inconsistency of nominal forms shows the difficulty involved in fixedly situating Miller.

At this point the train is still in the North, and Miller sits down to chat with his friend, unhindered by any legal interference. They have encountered each other on common (but moving) ground, sharing professional and class affiliation: "[B]oth seemed from their faces and their manners to be men of culture and accustomed to the society of cultivated people." Despite racial difference, Miller and Burns share each other's company freely, but the train is inevitably nearing the Mason-Dixon Line, where such differences are subject to rigidly enforced segregation. Chesnutt anticipates exposing the folly of this arbitration as the narrative voice assumes a cynical tone: "Looking at these two men with the *American eye,* the differences would perhaps be more striking, or at least the more immediately apparent, for the first was white and the second *black,* or, more correctly speaking, *brown;* it was even a *light brown,* but both his swarthy complexion and his curly hair revealed what has been described in the laws of some of our states as a 'visible admixture' of African blood" (1901, 49; emphasis mine).

The color progression in this passage is rather significant. This three-step sequence of colors attributed to Miller's skin tone parallels the nominal progression set forth in Dr. Burns's greeting a few paragraphs before. The narrator wants to begin by describing Miller's physical appearance in a formal way, as simply "black." However, this is revised as he attempts to be more specific, and the narrator recants on his initial statement and says Miller is "brown," ultimately deciding that he is "light brown." The indecision on the part of the narrator is artfully crafted. Chesnutt emphasizes the fluid movements through which Miller's identity passes as he travels south. He cannot simply be labeled under the all-inclusive term of "black." This sense of racial indeterminacy works to subvert the action later in the chapter when Miller is literally compartmentalized within the "black" car. Furthermore, Chesnutt's use of the phrase "the American eye" indicts the nation with a charge of racial and social superficiality, of prejudiced overreliance on what is "visible" as signifiers of race (1901, 53).

Throughout their conversation, Burns and Miller shed light on the subject of race relations. In expressing his desire to foster the advancement of blacks in Wellington, Miller admits that he is not sure how much good he alone can do, "but I'll do what I can . . . it will take a great deal of learning to leaven that lump." This statement is met with grave acknowledgment from Burns. He realistically understands the weight of the situation, but he reduces the scenario to a level of abstraction: "It is not only your problem, but ours. Your race must come *up* or drag ours *down*" (emphasis mine). Aligning himself with this equation between moral progress and vertical motion, Miller maintains that "[w]e shall come up" (1901, 51). The connotations of travel are explicitly stated in this discourse of coming and going. Though they advocate social progress, both men perpetuate a definite separatism in this dialogue. Miller's racially exclusive "we" echoes Burns's use of the terms "[y]our race" and "ours." Thus, Miller affirms Burns's separatist conception of race. The syntactical nuances of the dialogue expose the tendency to categorize race in America, and the attachment of those personal pronouns to vertical motion—"up" and "down"—reinforces the metaphoric operation of travel.

The latitudinal movement of the train south has direct bearing on the two doctors' sense of vertical, moral movement. In his seemingly sympathetic agreement with Miller, Burns betrays the view that whites are naturally on a higher plane of civilization than African Americans. Their interests are viewed as separate; Burns divides the racial communities into two distinct and unrelated categories. His primary fear lies in what he sees as the potential downfall of the white population as a result of the degeneracy of African Americans. At the same time, however, Miller's statement that "we shall come up," that African Americans should conform to the imaginary moral level of whites, places him in the camp of Booker T. Washington and his "campaign of reconciliation and accommodation" (Andrews 1976, 335). Though Miller is, in a way, Chesnutt's spokesman on a number of issues, his apparent moralizing in this chapter does not accord with Chesnutt's own sense that it is white Americans who need moral improvement. As Eric J. Sundquist points out, "Chesnutt's novel may be read as a critique of, among other things, the Washington ethos" (1993, 274). In the course of the Burns-Miller dialogue, the southbound motion of the train evokes a separatist vocabulary among its passengers.

The racial separatism discussed by Miller and Burns is made manifest in the second half of chapter 5. After the train has traversed far into Virginia, Miller is told by the conductor that he will have to leave his seat and move into the "colored" car. Chesnutt's essay "The White and the Black," published in the *Boston Evening Transcript* in March of 1901, details a scenario from his own experience that directly informs this episode. A commentary on the general ills of segregation, "The White and the Black" uses racially separated railway cars to express his view that "[t]he brunt of separation falls upon the Negro, but the white man does not escape" (1999b, 140). Dr. Burns echoes this proclamation when he is informed that he cannot sit with Miller in the colored car: "You are curtailing the rights, not only of the colored people, but *of white men as well*" (emphasis mine).[2] Miller, however, acquiesces to the conductor's demand and reassures Burns that they will both end up in the same place regardless: "I'll reach my destination just as surely in the other car" (1901, 55). Although the Jim Crow laws here rigidly imply a concrete set of standards by which race is determined, the direction of travel in both a literal and social sense is the same for both white and black Americans. The cars are linked; the races are connected; the destination of one is the destination of both. However, the fact of a shared destination hardly means equality in travel. He recognizes the intense conceptual clash between the fact that, metaphorically, travel affords an evident momentum and flux to individual identity at the same time that it recapitulates racist constraints. Chesnutt's employment of the travel metaphor is thus marked by this tension between positivistic commitment to the possibilities of the mobile experience and disappointment in the contingency of recurrent racism.[3]

The novel's subsequent description of the printed "black" and "white" signs in this chapter further exposes and complicates the prevalence of identity issues within the mobile American experience. During Burns's argument with the conductor, the narrator gestures toward the posted "color" sign, which is "neatly framed and hung at the end of the car, containing the legend, 'White,' in letters about a foot long, *painted in white upon a dark background,* typical, one might suppose, of the distinction thereby indicated" (1901, 54; emphasis mine). Chesnutt is quite straightforward about the implications of printed text and color definition. Unlike the physical text of the novel, the letters in the train are "painted in white upon a dark background." Unlike Chesnutt's indeterminate definition of race, these texts in the train demand categories. Thus, the compartmental construction of the train and the presence of actual texts within the cars reveal the direct link between travel and representation. As a metaphor for race in America, the train literally embodies the text and carries out Chesnutt's subversion of Jim Crow. *Marrow* continues with the narrator's description of the signs in the "colored car": they are "similar to those in the other car, except they bore the word, 'Colored' in *black letters upon a white background*" (56; emphasis mine).

Ultimately, by the end of chapter 5, Miller is left feeling even more alienated in the colored car than he felt among the white passengers. Sitting in a car with rural African Americans who pass the time with music and dancing, "[f]or a while Miller was pleased," but this feeling soon fades (1901, 60). The uncertainty of his rootless identity compels him to leave the car and move out to the platform alone because "these people were just as offensive to him as the whites in the other end of the train" (61). Here, the divider between Miller and the other black passengers is class based. By providing this moment of intraracial difference between Dr. Miller and the other black passengers, Chesnutt accentuates the impossibility of maintaining a dualistic conception of race. Like Clifford's traveler figures, "[h]e is and is not of the local culture" (1997, 27). Though Robert Stepto deals specifically with DuBois' *The Souls of Black Folk,* his establishment of "ascent" and "immersion" as coexisting tendencies in the African American postbellum experience correspond with Miller's conflicted position at the end of the chapter. Miller's education and professional standing place him on the axis of cultural "ascent"—"a quest for literacy as well as for freedom" (Stepto 1979, 67). At the same time, however, his commitment to the social progress of blacks in the South immerses him within the community from which he has "risen." By allowing for Miller's complete alienation at the end of the chapter, Chesnutt recognizes the psychological stress incurred by any "heroic" attempt to navigate the dual movements of ascent and immersion.

The southbound movement of the train—coupled with the dynamics that occur within and between the cars—ultimately leaves Miller in a state of isolation. In a larger sense he is not alone in his rootlessness, but the static institutions of the South demand affiliation with one of two "races." The doctor's solitary musings in this chapter rest on scenes of developing civilizations. In his thoughts he trumps the whites by alluding to the early advancements of the Egyptians: "The negro was here before the Anglo-Saxon was evolved, and his thick lips and heavy-lidded eyes looked out from the inscrutable face of the Sphinx across the sands of Egypt while yet the ancestors of those who now oppress him were living in caves, practicing human sacrifice, and painting themselves with woad—and the negro is here yet" (1901, 62).

While the reference to body painting in this passage foreshadows the manipulation of identity performed by Tom Delamere when he puts on blackface later in the novel, the more important symbol here is the Sphinx. Left in a state of isolation, Miller travels in his imagination to the wonders of Africa. Not only does the figure of the Sphinx parallel Miller's mixed biological heritage, it works as an allegory for the entire dilemma of race relations in America. The first definition of Sphinx in the *Oxford English Dictionary* is "a hybrid monster," but the second expands the metaphor: "one who propounds or presents a difficult question or problem." By traveling in his imagination to Africa, Miller evokes not only the sense of amalgamated, indefinite identity, but also the fact that the static regulations under Jim Crow are the antagonistic forces that prevent a fuller understanding of an ethnically diverse culture. Perhaps the novel performs a Sphinx-like role as it presents the problem of racism to a mystified readership.

Furthermore, the evocation of the Sphinx in Miller's imagination provides an alternate topos to the American landscape, a place that signifies geographical origins for Miller and his fellow travelers in the black car. Indeed, Miller's musings here can be read as an escape of sorts, a mental creation of a past locale that ostensibly serves to remind Miller that he is indeed linked to the other black passengers in the car, if only by way of heritage. However, even this imagined level of travel is touched by conflict. As Anthony Appiah points out, "[S]haring a common group history cannot be a criterion for being members of the same group, for we would have to be able to identify the group in order to identify *its* history" (1985, 27). Because of his feeling of alienation, we cannot read Miller as truly a member of "the group" in the black car. Moreover, Egypt signifies for Miller a "symbolic geography"; Stepto asserts that "a landscape becomes symbolic in literature when it is a region in time and space offering spatial expressions of social structures and ritual grounds on the one hand, and of *communitas* and *genius loci* on the other" (1979, 67). Egypt brings the issue of cultural heritage to the forefront, but group identity—via shared history—remains unrealized. A locale defined by a wavering between mobility and constraints, the moving train presents Miller with an enigma of Sphinx-like proportions.

This large-scale, north-south interstate travel at the novel's beginning allows Chesnutt to mobilize the problems of identity construction. Formally, this larger sense of travel gradually narrows as the novel continues. Subsequently, travel occurs in a more localized arena: racial issues play out in the quick but significant movements within Wellington. In this way, Chesnutt establishes a more internalized depiction of mobility. The railroad in *Marrow* allows these issues to play out on the interstate, on a common American stage. Thus, by moving into the city limits of Wellington, he enacts a topographical and narrative focus that emphasizes the problematic import of travel in a more specifically local arena.

Local Motion: Intraregional Travel and Racial Dynamics

One of the most widely scrutinized chapters in the novel, chapter 13—"The Cakewalk"—is saturated with role reversals and fabrications of identity. Characters not only mask race and self, they also perform versions of *other* characters that ultimately undermine the static conception of identity under Jim Crow. Employing a cultural phenomenon that is nominally bound up in notions of movement and travel, the cake*walk* serves as a metaphorical device with a variety of social and racial implications.

Sundquist contextualizes the cakewalk as it applies to the artistic and social purposes of Chesnutt. Historically, the cakewalk allowed southern plantation owners "to entertain, and to instruct visitors that the region's blacks were under control." However, as the black "entertainers" would cavort in the masters' clothing and speak in high and domineering tones, the cakewalk assumed a more subversive element and allowed the slaves to mock the controlling personae of their white masters. Because it takes on these underlying social and psychological components, the cakewalk "evokes the complex dialectical process by which African American culture defined itself in relation to the paradigm of white mastery that lingered . . . in the aftermath of Reconstruction" (Sundquist 1993, 273).

Notwithstanding the connection to locomotion that is implied in the name of this performance, the fact of its exhibition is in response to regional tourism: it is conducted in front of white people visiting the town who are unfamiliar with local race relations and customs. It is exactly a consequence of travel and of the need to create a façade of contentment and good health among southern blacks; of the "party of Northern visitors . . . the ladies were much interested in the study of social conditions, and especially in the negro problem" (Chesnutt 1901, 115). Developed under tourist impulses, the delusive performance of the cakewalk is subject to the detached, voyeuristic gaze of the northern visitors. Thus, the function of the cakewalk in *Marrow* is twofold: it perpetuates Chesnutt's use of travel as a metaphor for racial mobility, *and* it frustrates certain regional preconceptions about race that condescendingly reduce complex social and political issues to racist clichés—that is, "the negro problem."

The cakewalk, an assumption of another's identity (the slave mocking the master), is complicated in this chapter as Tom Delamere blackens his face and enters the festivities as his grandfather's trusted servant Sandy. The "archetype of the New South in the dress of a dissolute southern aristocrat," Tom represents the moral and economic degeneration of upper-class white southern society (Sundquist 1993, 431). Participating in a performance that is rooted in subversive parody, Tom ultimately caricatures not Sandy, but rather the upper-class white society from which he himself is descended. In donning blackface and Sandy's attire, Tom engages in a multiple act of identity (de)-construction. He mimics Sandy's movements in a performance that historically has been centered on mocking the dominant white class—it is the ultimate form of self-parody. It is significant that Tom succeeds at constructing a self-contradicting identity under the gaze of traveling visitors. The detached gaze from outside precipitates behavior on the part of the local aristocracy that is wrought with self-caricature. Moreover, Tom uses Sandy's black identity as a vehicle by which he exposes the inherent connection between blacks and whites in the sphere of southern society. Sundquist takes this association even further: "Tom and Sandy are doubles; they resemble each other to the degree that Tom's cakewalk charades can be successful, and given old Delamere's fondness for Sandy and Sandy's apparent devotion to him, there is more than a hint that there may be a blood relation between them" (432).

Ellis, the only spectator with any inkling that Tom is the winner of the cakewalk, expresses a reserved awareness about the event. He thinks that there "was a vague suggestion of unreality about his performance" (Chesnutt 1901, 119). The *un*reality lies in the very self-contradiction of the masquerade. By negating the notion of "reality" as it applies to matters of racial identity, Chesnutt undermines objective and categorical distinctions. Furthermore, because this negation of racial "reality" occurs within a performance motivated by travel and consisting of movement, it gives preference to mobility, fluidity, and flux.

Taking place under the tourist gaze of the northern visitors, Tom's performance in blackface during the cakewalk directly foreshadows his donning of Sandy's identity in chapter 18—"Sandy Sees His Own Ha'nt"—and as indirectly recorded in the next chapter—"A Midnight Walk." This second instance of reverse passing is occasioned by a much more insidious motive.[4] Tom, to alleviate the burden of his gambling debts, disguises himself as Sandy, breaks into Polly Ochiltree's house, steals her money, and kills her. It is during his journey from Polly's house back to his grandfather's that the narrator reveals Tom's literal and figurative mobility, as well as the connectedness between Tom and Sandy in their mirroring travel.

After seeing Tom in blackface wearing his clothes, Sandy is convinced that he is seeing his own ghost. Accordingly, he begins to follow Tom. A repeated phrase appears in both chapters and describes the movement of the two men—"*equal* distance" (Chesnutt 1901,167, 172; emphasis mine). This language of equality is crucial, especially in light of the fact that neither traveler is aware of the presence of his counterpart. From the perspective of Ellis, it appears as if two identical Sandys simultaneously move along the street: "[T]he two were as much alike as twin brothers" (173). In conjuring this fraternal imagery, Ellis's thoughts express Sundquist's observation that the two may very well have blood ties, that Sandy may be a product of old Mr. Delamere's illicit sexual exploits during antebellum days on his plantation.

Chesnutt carefully renders the action in this chapter. Within the nuances of Sandy and Tom's local sojourn, *Marrow* develops the uncertainty of racial identification. Ellis cannot successfully determine who they are. As Tom consciously and deviously assumes Sandy's identity, his doing so raises questions about his own racial subjectivity. In passing for black—and doing so quite successfully—Tom undermines the rigid boundaries of the South. In Ellis's estimation, Tom *is* Sandy. The identities of the two men are conflated to such an extent that Ellis is absolutely certain that Tom is Sandy, and that the man following him (who actually *is* Sandy), is "some younger negro, taking Sandy for a model" (Chesnutt 1901, 173).

These theatrics of travel and misidentification stage an intersubjectivity in which the prescribed racial binaries under Jim Crow cannot cohere. Both on the train and in the town, Chesnutt's travel metaphor performs a distinct sociopolitical commentary in advance of critics like Houston Baker Jr., who recognizes that "mobility in public" is central to a "United States Black Modernism" that ensures political participation and fullness of citizenship (2001, 83). However, the figural device of travel within Chesnutt's novel sustains a necessary tension. As Miller's isolation on the train suggests, and as Tom's cakewalk confirms, movement, flux, and instability fall short of providing completely efficacious alternatives to rigid racial constraints. Although Chesnutt embraces fluidity as a conceptual model for understanding race as a lived experience, the dramatic movement of characters often results in physical, social, or psychological damage. It is this sustained contradiction within the travel metaphor that suggests the real potentiality and prescience within Chesnutt's aesthetic project. The novel's end refuses to settle the racial conflict in Wellington; its cliffhanger ending defies absolute meaning and repudiates formal coherence. *Marrow* derives its energy from riots and, in turn, explodes the conventions of regional literature as it urgently signifies the racial tension between freedom and rootlessness inherent in the nation's new forms of mobility.

Notes

1. The problem of defining "race" is central to his argument in "The Future American." There, he describes race in nonbiological terms and asserts that external forces explain differences in skin color and other physical features. However, he carefully maintains a level of ambivalence in his employment of the word, a move that anticipates many contemporary ethnographic perspectives. See Appiah 1985, 21.

2. This critique of segregation that Burns vocalizes also echoes Albion Tourgée's rhetoric in the *Plessy v. Ferguson* case of 1896. Interestingly, Burns's inability to win the argument parallels Tourgée's unsuccessful attempt to prevent the Supreme Court from ruling that "separate but equal" facilities were constitutional. For more on the language of the case, see Elliott 2006.

3. The historical experience of the black Pullman porter reveals an analogous tension: "The Pullman porter who benefits from the enhanced mobility provided by technology but does so in a subordinate role . . . [constitutes] an important symbol of the new opportunities and new constraints that fell upon blacks in the late nineteenth century" (Gilroy 1993, 133).

4. It is worth noting that the act of passing for white was typically predicated upon physical displacement, as "the individual had to leave an environment where his or her 'true identity' . . . was known to find a place where it was unknown" (Ginsberg 1996, 3).

References

Andrews, William L. 1976. "William Dean Howells and Charles W. Chesnutt: Criticism and Race Fiction in the Age of Booker T. Washington." *American Literature* 48 (November): 327–39.

———. 1980. *The Literary Career of Charles W. Chesnutt.* Baton Rouge: Louisiana State University Press.

Appiah, Anthony. 1985. "The Uncompleted Argument: DuBois and the Illusion of Race." *Critical Inquiry* 12 (Autumn): 21–37.

Baker, Houston A., Jr. 1987. *Modernism and the Harlem Renaissance.* Chicago: University of Chicago Press.

———. 2001. *Turning South Again: Re-thinking Modernism / Re-reading Booker T.* Durham: Duke University Press.

Chesnutt, Charles W. 1901. *The Marrow of Tradition.* Ann Arbor: University of Michigan Press, 1969.

———. 1999a. "The Future American." In *Charles W. Chesnutt: Essays and Speeches,* edited by Joseph R. McElrath Jr., Robert C. Leitz III, and Jesse S. Crisler, 121–35. Stanford: Stanford University Press.

———. 1999b. "The White and the Black." In *Charles W. Chesnutt: Essays and Speeches,* edited by Joseph R. McElrath Jr., Robert C. Leitz III, and Jesse S. Crisler, 139–44. Stanford: Stanford University Press.

Clifford, James. 1997. *Routes.* Cambridge: Harvard University Press.

Elliott, Mark. 2006. *Color-blind Justice: Albion Tourgée and the Quest for Racial Equality from the Civil War to* Plessy v. Ferguson. Oxford: Oxford University Press.

Gilroy, Paul. 1993. *The Black Atlantic: Modernity and Double Consciousness.* Cambridge: Harvard University Press.

Ginsberg, Elaine K. 1996. "The Politics of Passing." In *Passing and the Fictions of Identity,* edited by Elaine K. Ginsberg, 1–18. Durham: Duke University Press.

McWilliams, Dean. 2002. *Charles W. Chesnutt and the Fictions of Race.* Athens: University of Georgia Press.

"Sphinx." *OED Online.* http://dictionary.oed.com (accessed November 12, 2005).

Stepto, Robert B. 1979. *From Behind the Veil: A Study of Afro-American Narrative.* Urbana: University of Illinois Press.

Sundquist, Eric J. 1993. *To Wake the Nations: Race in the Making of American Literature.* Cambridge: Harvard University Press.

III
RACE *and* NATION

Washing the Ethiop Red

Sir Francis Drake and the Cimarrons of Panama

Cassander L. Smith

In 1572, England's Sir Francis Drake and a motley crew of pirates landed on the Panama Isthmus, intending to rob a Spanish mule train—or caravan of mules—loaded with tons of gold and silver farmed out of mines along the west coast of South America. As mule trains had done on so many occasions before, this caravan intended to travel north to Panama, then cut across the isthmus, traveling east to the port city of Nombre de Dios, where a treasure fleet would be waiting to transport the riches across the Atlantic Ocean to Spain. This particular caravan, however, fell victim to a calculating seaman. For more than five months, Drake and his men stalked the isthmus, planning and awaiting the arrival of that caravan.

Due to a series of serendipitous events, Drake encountered and formed an alliance with a band of black African Cimarrons—ex-slaves who had run away from their Spanish masters and built settlements in the Panamanian mountains and jungles. Cimarrons had been waging guerilla warfare against the Spanish for some forty years before Drake arrived. They themselves had attacked Spain on more than one occasion in the very manner Drake proposed. It seemed only natural that Drake and the Cimarrons would join forces. When the caravan finally arrived in April of 1573, a mixture of Englishmen, Cimarrons, and a few Frenchmen who had stumbled onto the scene some months earlier all descended upon an outmatched envoy of Spanish commissaries and slaves, quickly ridding the caravan of nearly all it carried. Sir Francis Drake walked away with enough loot to fill the holds of two frigates.

In the narrative of that raid, *Sir Francis Drake Revived* (Nichols 1626), Drake explains the specific role of the Cimarrons as guides through Panamanian forestry, as spies at Nombre de Dios, and as servants performing manual labor for Drake and his men. Historians have led the way in discussing Drake's interactions with the Cimarrons. Discussions, however, replicate his perspective of the alliance, assigning him agency as the author of the collaboration and relegating the Cimarrons to servants.[1] From a literary perspective, there has been little discussion of the rhetorical and discursive relationship between the two parties. This critical silence persists even in discussions of the Cimarrons' representations in those masques and epic poems published in the century following Drake's death that commemorated his exploits. Edmund Morgan (1975) is one of the few to consider the rhetorical work the Cimarrons perform for Drake, arguing that Drake positions the Cimarrons as victims of Spanish tyranny in need of English liberation.[2] There was only one problem with Drake's rhetorical intent. As Morgan points out, the Cimarrons had liberated themselves long before he arrived. Morgan, a historian, stops short of contemplating what this rhetorical conflict does for the narrative Drake creates.[3]

In constructing himself as a national hero, Drake revels in an English, Protestant identity.[4] Importantly, that identity gains its meaning from the presence of that group of Cimarrons, through whom Drake renders himself in opposition as a liberator come to free them and weaken Spain's hold in the Caribbean. In this regard, Drake's text extends Toni Morrison's (1992) argument about the ways in which nineteenth- and twentieth-century American literature employed a symbolic "Africanist presence" designed to more clearly delineate racial constructions of whiteness and monitor certain social, political, and cultural structures.

I do recognize the potential drawbacks in linking Drake's sixteenth-century English narrative to Morrison's argument. Morrison, for example, focuses only on Anglo-American writers and mostly fiction, primarily in the nineteenth and twentieth centuries. A larger issue is the very notion of race, central to the lens through which Morrison examines American literature. The term *race* in sixteenth-century England did not articulate human difference in quite the same manner that it would after the eighteenth century.[5] For Drake and his contemporaries, racial classification was determined by cultural factors such as dress, religion, and language, not biological, scientific categories. However, regardless of what Europeans meant when they deployed the term *race* in the early modern period, it remains true that black Africans were—even then—set aside for uniquely denigrative treatment, which made them especially vulnerable to the horrors of enslavement and other discriminatory practices. Morrison's approach offers us one method for understanding how race prejudice influenced the literature constructed in America in the later period. I offer an approach that allows us to examine race in the earliest narratives chronicling cultural encounters in the Americas.

The black Africans who populate Drake's narrative, then, serve a symbolic function very much in line with Morrison's theory—but with one key distinction. The Africanist presence for Drake had an actual, historical referent, whose actions in the material world outside the text conflicted with Drake's rhetorical goals.[6] This conflict manifests in a set of competing impulses that frame Drake's representation of the Cimarrons. His first and more dominant impulse, made all the more credible by the Cimarrons' hostility toward their former Spanish masters, is to situate them into a "Black Legend" discourse, portraying them as victims suffering under the cruel hand of Spain. In this regard, his narrative fell in line with a steady flow of political tracts, travel narratives, pamphlets, and poetry circulating through England in the sixteenth and seventeenth centuries that criticized Spain's actions in the Americas. Although American Indians most often occupied the position of victim in a Black Legend discourse, Drake inserted those black African slaves and former slaves who sought refuge in the Panama jungle and then, upon his arrival, with Drake. In a sense, he remakes the Cimarrons as suffering Indians in his narrative. He can never fully render them as such, though, for the reasons I mentioned earlier—they are not Indians and they are not passive victims. In addition, this impulse to re-create the Cimarrons is undermined by his second impulse to render them as tropes of blackness. He participates in a racial discourse that does not render them victims but inhuman. This discourse encroaches upon the text through his references to their savagism, bestiality, and servile state. It, too, however, is inconsistent because the Cimarrons established free-governing settlements in the Panama jungle that were civilized and organized, a fact Drake himself concedes at one point in the text. What we have, then, is a narrative that vacillates between discourses, neither fully able to articulate the Cimarrons' interactions with Drake.

In this essay, I argue that the Cimarrons occupy a problematic, unstable space in Drake's narrative. That instability, resulting from a conflict between Drake's rhetorical ambitions and the actual, material details of his exploits, undermines Drake's very project of self-creation. My discussion begins with an overview of the political energies and racial ideology guiding Drake's rhetoric. I then examine the challenges Drake encounters in his efforts to represent the Cimarrons within established discourses, especially when the Cimarrons' actions outside the text do not translate into discourse. Lastly, I offer a discussion of a key encounter between Drake and one of those Cimarrons named Pedro. That encounter is crucial because it contradicts the representation Drake constructs of the black Africans who populate his text, illustrating the struggle European-descended authors faced in attempting to construct what Toni Morrison has famously called an Africanist Presence.

Propelled by Politics

To write the Cimarrons as victims of Spanish cruelty allowed Drake to participate in a wider European political discourse that discredited Spain; the country was viewed as brutal, savage in its pursuit of New World riches and power. Although there is disagreement about how, why, where, and when the Black Legend began, most scholars agree that Spanish Dominican friar Bartolomé de Las Casas inadvertently played a role in the propagation of the image. He was one of the harshest critics of conquistadors' treatment of Indians in the Americas and often complained to the crown of their actions. In his 1552 seminal treatise, *Breuissima relacion de la destruycíon de las Indias*, Las Casas describes what was essentially genocide, explaining that some 15 million Indians were slaughtered during a forty-year period.[7] He characterizes the Indians as noble savages. In a direct address to Prince Phillip, he describes the Indians as "naturally so gentle, so peace-loving, so humble and so docile" (1992, 6). Las Casas catalogued the violence not to showcase Spanish brutality and savagery but to illustrate the severity of the problem. He sought reform. Although Las Casas imagined his work addressing a national crisis, the text soon took center stage in a continental debate about empire and conquest. The Dutch were the first to translate Las Casas's narrative, in 1578. They used the text to illustrate their own experiences of tyranny as a Spanish colony. In 1583 the French and the English also translated and manipulated the text.[8]

England's Richard Hakluyt, in his *Principal Navigations,* and Samuel Purchas, in *Purchas His Pilgrimes,* included versions of Las Casas's text in their collections of travel narratives. Over the next few centuries, the account would be seminal in England's war of words with Spain. But it wasn't the only text fueling anti-Spanish sentiment in sixteenth-century England. Las Casas's narrative joined a bevy of pamphlets, epistles, political tracts, travel narratives, and the like being published in London.[9] All of this is to say that by the time Drake conceived of his narrative and wrote the epistolary preface in 1592, it was an established rhetorical convention to represent indigenous populations in America as oppressed, victims of Spanish tyranny.

Although the Cimarrons were largely transplanted people, uprooted from various sub-Saharan regions in Africa, Drake still characterizes them as indigenous by careful attention to how well adapted they are to the land. Consider his description of all the Cimarrons did to help him raid Spanish gold: "These Cimaroons, during all the time that we were with them, did us continually very good service, being unto us, purveyors, to provide victuals for us; of house-wrights, to build our lodgings; and had indeed able and strong bodies, carrying all our necessaries" (Nichols 1626, 72). Drake portrays them as sons and daughters of the forest who can erect and tear down houses in a matter of hours. They navigate dense jungles and hunt with deadly efficiency. They know which plants are edible and where to get fresh water. In short, they move around and master the land like Panama natives rather than African immigrants.

Drake's efforts to distance the Cimarrons from their African heritage is evident in the concise description he offers of who the Cimarrons are: "a black people which about 80 years past fled from the Spaniards their masters, by reason of their cruelty, and are since grown to a nation, under two kings of their own. The one inhabiteth to the west, the other to the east of the way from Nombre de Dios to Panama" (Nichols 1626, 8). In this description Drake clearly casts the Spanish as the Black Legend by referencing "their cruelty." He also portrays the Cimarrons as refugees who "fled," which also connotes passivity and victimization. The final point here regards the diction. Throughout the narrative, Drake refers to black Africans as Negro. In the above passage, though, he refers to the Cimarrons as a "black people." There is a subtle shift in diction. According to the *Oxford English Dictionary,* "Negro" was the standard terminology for denoting a person of sub-Saharan ancestry up through the seventeenth century. Indeed, Drake seems to adhere to this usage in his text—mostly. The term clearly locates its referent within a specific geographical lineage—sub-Saharan Africa. "Black," on the other hand, though loaded with social and political connotations, carried no such geographical restrictions. As Kim Hall notes in *Things of Darkness,* "The trope of blackness had a broad arsenal of effects in the early modern period, meaning that it is applied not only to dark-skinned Africans but to Native Americans, Indians, Spanish, and even Irish and Welsh as groups that needed to be marked as 'other'" (1995, 7). It would seem that Drake employs "black" to mark the Cimarrons as other without restricting them to an African birthplace, a necessary move to re-create the Cimarrons as suffering Indians, not Africans.

Drake's use of the term *black* appears even more a conscious choice if we consider that his contemporaries writing about those same Cimarrons described them as Negro and/or referenced their African heritage. Richard Hakluyt published a shortened version of the raid in *Principal Navigations,* and he referenced the Cimarrons as Negroes. William D'Avenant, in a masque inspired by Drake's raid published in 1659 describes the Cimarrons as a "Moorish people brought formerly to Peru by the Spaniards, as their slaves" (9). Although he changes the location of their arrival from Panama to Peru—for political purposes of his own—he makes it clear that they were not just held captive by the Spanish but also transplanted from a "Moorish"—an African—homeland. Hakluyt—in another text—also makes reference to the Cimarron's Moorish identity. In his *Discourse of Western Planting,* published in 1584, Hakluyt describes them as "moores and suche as the Spaniardes have broughte thither for the mynes and for slavery" (43). Although the reference to a Moorish identity is a bit ambiguous, suggesting either a Muslim North African culture or a sub-Saharan culture, both Hakluyt's and D'Avenant's descriptions remind readers that the Cimarrons are forced immigrants to the Americas. Drake de-emphasizes this aspect of the Cimarron's history and cultural identity. His semantics ploy, however, falls short of sustaining the Cimarrons' image as suffering Indians, as a close reading of the text illustrates.

Constructing the Ethiop

Complicating Drake's participation in a Black Legend discourse is the link between that discourse and African-based slavery. In his defense of Indians, Las Casas advocated the use of slaves from sub-Saharan Africa to alleviate their suffering. It was believed that black Africans could better withstand the hard work and the heat. There was a pervasive belief among Europeans that sub-Saharan Africans were inferior, inhuman.[10] Drake's text perpetuates this belief, digressing at times into a discourse of blackness, which was being formulated in England at the same time as the Black Legend.

Alden and Virginia Mason Vaughan (1997) and Kim Hall (1995) agree that the Elizabethan era was a crucial time in the development of a racial discourse in England.[11] Vaughan and Vaughan argue that before the mid-sixteenth century there were few representations of sub-Saharan Africans in English literature. The second half of the century, however, saw a dramatic increase. They point out that during this time, "English representations of sub-Saharan Africans in print and performance were increasingly . . . critical of the Africans' bodies and beliefs, customs and character. With few exceptions, the emerging composite picture portrayed African skin as unattractive and, in some texts as the stigma of divine punishment" (44). Kim Hall suggests that the increased focus on racial difference was a consequence of an economic expansion that was also a "linguistic and ultimately an ideological expansion in which writers and travelers grappled with ways of making use of the foreign *materia* 'produced' by colonialism" (4). To stabilize an English identity in an ever-expanding world, a problem Drake faced, racial discourse became a useful means for ordering those foreign encounters. That order, according to Hall, was achieved through what she calls a binary of light and dark, which manifested physically as a relationship between fair, English bodies and dark, African bodies. Hall maintains it was the "conduit through which the English began to formulate the notions of 'self' and 'other' so well known in Anglo-American racial discourses" (2). Black African bodies were tropes connoting inferiority, savagery, bestiality.[12] Although there are few explicit references to the Cimarrons' skin color or their African heritage, Drake often describes their behavior as savage and bestial—in opposition to his own civilized demeanor.

Discursive Fluctuations

To understand how central—and problematic—the Cimarrons are in Drake's construction of himself, we need only examine his deployment of a Black Legend discourse. Narrative dissonance occurs as early as the opening scene where Drake first encounters a group of black African slaves off the coast of Panama working on a frigate bound for Nombre de Dios. Drake steals the ship, and sets down the slaves on the mainland in an undisclosed location farther away from Nombre de Dios—to ensure they won't reach the port city first and betray Drake's plan for a raid. This is before the Cimarrons and Drake join forces. Drake imagines that he has done the slaves a great favor by steering them away from the city, which would allow them to "perhaps join themselves to their countrymen the Cimarrons and gain their liberty" (Nichols 1626, 25). Here Drake dons that liberator persona, suggesting that he himself is the means of their freedom, their deliverance from Spanish cruelty. It is a much tougher sell, though, to convince readers that he is a liberator once he reaches Nombre de Dios several nights later, where his breach of the city is made all the more difficult by past Cimarron attacks. Drake explains that when his men began the assault, "[t]he town took alarm (being very ready thereto, by reason of their often disquieting by their near neighbours the Symerons) as we perceived, not only by the noise and cries of the people, but by the bell ringing out and drums running up and down the town" (11). Soldiers and citizens quickly armed themselves. Needless to say, this attack is a dismal failure because past Cimarron raids have left the town in a perpetual state of readiness. In this opening scene, we see how Drake intends to represent himself as a liberator. We see just as clearly, however, the problem inherent in such a rhetorical move: the situation at Nombre de Dios shows clearly that the Spanish and Cimarrons have a contentious history, suggesting that the Cimarrons don't need rescue.

Furthermore, the Black Legend discourse is difficult to maintain because Drake indulges in certain blackness tropes designed to highlight his own grandeur. In those instances, however, when Drake reverts to tropes of blackness, he contradicts images of the Cimarrons as victims. After the failure of Drake's initial raid attempt on Nombre de Dios, he and his men retreat to an area he calls Port Plenty. They hide out in this location for some months upon the recommendation of the Cimarrons, who by now have started advising them. The Cimarrons explain that the mule trains travel during the dry season, and if Drake wants to capture them, he must wait until the cargoes begin traveling again. They wait some five months. At one point during this time, Drake and his crew capture a Spanish ship loaded with food provisions as it sails near their hideout. Drake takes as hostages thirteen Spaniards. He makes it clear that he intends to treat the hostages humanely, which means holding back a band of bloodthirsty Cimarrons. He says: "[The Spaniards] we used very courteously, keeping them diligently guarded from the deadly hatred of the Symerons, who sought daily by all means they could to get them of our Captain, that they might cut their throats, to revenge their wrongs and injuries which the Spanish nation had done them; but our Captain persuaded them not to touch them or give them ill countenance, while they were in his charge, and took order for their safety, not only in his presence but also in his absence" (Nichols 1626, 52). This moment is a character-elevating move for Drake. He is able to revel in that light/dark binary of which Hall speaks as he places the Cimarrons into a blackness discourse. No longer are they helpless, suffering Indians. Rather, they are bestial black Africans, the polar opposite of Drake, who is determined to treat the Spanish captives "very courteously," civilly. While the moment defines and elevates Drake's character, it is also another example of Spain's own savagism. Drake explains the Cimarrons' fury as a reaction to the brutality they themselves encountered from the Spanish. In a sense, their savagism is mimetic, a learned behavior. Both the Cimarrons and the Spanish are blackened at once. But here the moment turns ironic as well because Drake, still recognizing himself as the great liberator, is no longer protecting the Cimarrons. The victims needing protection are suddenly the Spanish, which completely disrupts the narrative's propagandistic intent. We get a scene in which the English and the Spanish unite, European protecting European, while the Cimarrons are cast as the outsiders. Drake, then, becomes the liberator and protector not of a native population but of England's chief European rival.

Perhaps the most vivid example of Drake's struggles to discursively relegate the Cimarrons involves a figure in the narrative named Pedro, a Cimarron leader. At the end of the narrative, when Drake's frigates are loaded with gold and silver and they are ready to leave for England, the English and the Cimarrons say their good-byes at the departing port. In a final grand gesture, Drake opens the cargo holds of his frigates and invites four of the Cimarron leaders aboard, including Chief Pedro, to claim a prize from among the valuables. It is a patronizing gesture, a show of generosity such as a lord might bestow on a faithful tenant—or more precisely what Queen Elizabeth will do for Drake when he returns home. It perhaps comes as a surprise, then, for Drake when Pedro refuses the gold and silver. Pedro's eyes instead fall on a sword Drake had received earlier in the narrative from a Frenchmen. The sword had at one point belonged to France's King Henri II. Drake values the weapon, which is not among the loot from which he invites Pedro to choose. With hesitation and some regret, Drake hands it over, but Pedro refuses it as a gift. He insists on paying Drake with gold nuggets. In purchasing the sword, Pedro transforms a potentially patronizing moment into an exchange between equals, made all the more so because Drake himself prizes the sword so highly. He explains that he "could have been content to have made no such exchange, but yet desirous to content him that had deserved so well, he gave it him with many good words; who received it with no little joy, affirming that if he should give his wife and children (which he loved dearly) in lieu of it, he could not sufficiently recompense it (for he would present his king with it, who he knew would make him a great man, even for this very gift's sake); yet in gratuity and stead of other requital of this jewel, he desired our Captain to accept these four pieces of gold, as a token of his thankfulness to him and a pawn of his faithfulness during life" (Nichols 1626, 92).

Ostensibly, Drake's diction continues to characterize Pedro as a faithful servant who "deserved so well." By focusing on the chief's profuse gratitude, his vow of "faithfulness during life," Drake attempts to undermine the chief's own motives. This perspective of the exchange, though, contradicts the "four pieces of gold" Drake accepts for the sword and Pedro's apparent expectation that the sword will "make him a great man." Pedro reveals that the gold he offers to Drake is a stash "he had hidden, intending to have reserved . . . until another voyage" (Nichols 1626, 91). It becomes apparent that Pedro speaks a commercial English. He understands the value of gold to the English and attempts to convert it into power, revealing certain political ambitions for which he uses Drake. Pedro's own calculated moves complicate Drake's rhetorical intentions as the monarchy/subject paradigm Drake attempts to construct by opening up the ships' coffers mutates into a mercantile paradigm, in which Pedro recognizes his own leverage. Granted, Drake is not impressed by the gold, given that he already has two ships full of it. He is locked into this exchange, though, a reluctant peddler who understands he must negotiate; part of what is at stake is his future relationship with these Cimarrons and further raids on the Spanish. In a sense Drake's and Pedro's ambitions mirror each other. Drake will present the queen with boatloads of gold and silver and in return receive acclaim; Pedro will present his king with a fancy French sword and in return will become a "great man."

This moment clearly suggests that Pedro, more than a rhetorical tool for Drake, worked his own motives through the encounter, motives that register ever so slightly on the page. More important, this moment helps unsettle the representation Drake attempts to create of the Cimarrons. Pedro is a clear reminder that the Cimarrons who collaborated with Drake to steal gold and silver from the Spanish were not victims. They were not Indians. They did not see themselves as inferior. These are the facts that complicate and hinder Drake's efforts to police the Cimarrons' racial identity to construct his own.

Whether Pedro actually became a great man among the Cimarrons we don't know. We do know that the Spanish were forced to broker peace with the three main palenques of Cimarrons in Panama several years later. Their truce recognized Cimarron liberation and granted them the land on which they had built their settlements. In exchange, the Cimarrons agreed to stop their raids and signed a fugitive slave act that promised they would return future runaway slaves to their Spanish masters. As for the English, Drake's was the first and last successful collaboration with Cimarrons. The next year, John Oxenham, one of Drake's subordinates, returned to Nombre de Dios, expecting to find similar success. He did collaborate with a band of Cimarrons, but they were mostly captured by the Spanish. Oxenham was executed five years later in Peru. When Drake returned to the region in 1585, he sought to restore his alliance with the Cimarrons, but by that time they had already secured their self-interest with the Spanish and they rejected Drake's offer. In Drake's last trip to the Spanish Main in 1595, the Cimarrons actually took up arms alongside the Spanish to fight him off. Whatever common mission the Cimarrons and Drake might have shared in 1572 had vanished by 1595.

Drake's narrative relates the degree to which he and the Cimarrons forged an alliance based on accommodation and negotiation. This alliance occurred precisely because Drake recognized—even if he did not always admit it—the limit of his own power. Together, they wreaked havoc on a common foe. As the saying goes: *The enemy of my enemy is my friend.* That mantra fueled the negotiation of power between Sir Francis Drake and the Cimarrons of Panama.

Notes

1. For examples, see Dudley 2003; Cummins 1995; Andrews 1978; and Mackie 2005. Price's understanding of the collaboration is an exception. He deems it an "alliance of convenience . . . based on opportunism by both sides" (1996, 14).

2. Morgan discusses Drake's participation in a Black Legend discourse, the maligning of Spain as a cruel, brutal empire victimizing Indian populations in the New World. By condemning Spain's imperial project, England was able to justify its own.

3. Indeed, *Sir Francis Drake Revived* is a difficult text to approach as a literary document given its complex writing and publication history. This full-length account of the 1573 raid at Nombre de Dios was not published until 1626, by Drake's nephew of the same name. This was more than thirty years after Drake's death. That the narrative was written during Drake's lifetime, though, is evidenced by an epistolary preface accompanying the narrative, which Drake signs and dates in 1592. According to the title page, Philip Nichols, a minister, compiled the narrative proper from the notes of Drake and those who accompanied him on the voyage. The title page does suggest, however, that Drake was involved in the writing process throughout, claiming the text was "enlarged by divers Notes with [Drake's] owne hand here and there Inserted." Although it's difficult to determine how much of the text might have been written by Drake, what is essential for my purposes here is that Drake takes credit for having written the entire narrative, saying it is "the first fruites" of his pen (Nichols 1626, sig. A4, verso).

4. For more on Drake's Protestant identity and England's imperial activity in the Americas, see Hodgkin 2002.

5. Recently, historians and literary scholars have pointed out the anachronism of applying the term *race* to systems of human classification in earlier periods of American and European history. They argue that the notion of race as we know it today—a taxonomy based on biological, scientific classification—is a relatively modern construction, arising in the late eighteenth and early nineteenth centuries. See Wheeler 2000; Hill 2005; Banton 2000; and Hudson 1996.

6. Here I channel Myra Jehlen's argument (2002). She argues for a way of reading early American texts that considers not only the discursive life of the text but also the material world beyond it. She reminds us that what occurs outside the text is crucial to understanding what happens in the text.

7. Some scholars, like Anthony Pagden (1992), characterize Las Casas's text as hyperbole, arguing that his numbers are exaggerated for rhetorical effect.

8. For a concise discussion of how England and other Protestant nations manipulated Spanish texts to justify Spain's image in the Black Legend, see Bumas 2000.

9. See Maltby 1971 for a concise survey and discussion of such primary documents circulating in England during the later sixteenth century.

10. See Jordan 1977. See also Fryer 1984; and Lowe 2005.

11. For further discussion regarding the development of racism in early modern England, see Benjamin Braude's "Michelangelo and the Curse of Ham: From a Typology of Jew-Hatred to a Genealogy of Racism" and Francesca Royster's "'Working Like a Dog': African Labor and Racing the Human-Animal Divide in Early Modern England" both in Beidler and Taylor 2005. See also Iyengar 2005.

12. Winthrop Jordan, who has conducted one of the most extensive studies to date examining cultural perceptions of black Africans in England and America, maintains, “In England perhaps more than in southern Europe, the concept of blackness was loaded with intense meaning. . . . No other color except white conveyed so much emotional impact. Black was an emotionally partisan color, the handmaid and symbol of baseness and evil, a sign of danger and repulsion” (1977, 7).

References

Andrews, Kenneth R. 1978. *The Spanish Caribbean: Trade and Plunder, 1530–1630.* New Haven: Yale University Press, 1978.

Banton, Michael. 2000. “The Idiom of Race: A Critique of Presentism.” In *Theories of Race and Racism: A Reader,* edited by Les Back and John Solomos, 51–63. New York: Routledge.

Beidler, Philip, and Gary Taylor, eds. 2005. *Writing Race across the Atlantic World: Medieval to Modern.* New York: Palgrave Macmillan.

Bumas, E. Shaskan. 2000. “The Cannibal Butcher Shop: Protestant Uses of Las Casas’s Brevisima relacion in Europe and the American Colonies.” *Early American Literature* 35 (2): 107–36.

Cummins, John. 1995. *Francis Drake: The Lives of a Hero.* New York: St. Martin’s.

D’Avenant, William. 1659. *The history of Sr Francis Drake. The first part: exprest by instrumentall and vocall musick, and by art of perspective in scenes, &c.* London. Early English Books Online. http://eebo.chadwyck.com .

Dudley, Wade G. 2003. *Drake: For God, Queen and Plunder.* Washington, D.C.: Brassey’s.

Fryer, Peter. 1984. *Staying Power: The History of Black People in Britain since 1504.* Atlantic Highlands, N.J.: Humanities.

Hakluyt, Richard. 1584. *Discourse of Western Planting.* Early English Books Online. http://eebo.chadwyck.com.

———. 1599–1600. *The principal nauigations, voyages, traffiques and discoueries of the English nation made by sea or ouer-land, to the remote and farthest distant quarters of the earth, at any time within the compasse of these 1600. yeres: deuided into three seuerall volumes, according to the positions of the regions, whereunto they were directed. The first volume containeth the worthy discoueries, &c. of the English . . . The second volume comprehendeth the principall nauigations . . . to the south and south-east parts of the world.* Early English Books Online. http://eebo.chadwyck.com.

Hall, Kim. 1995. *Things of Darkness: Economies of Race and Gender in Early Modern England.* Ithaca: Cornell University Press.

Hill, Ruth. 2005. *Hierarchy, Commerce, and Fraud in Bourbon Spanish America: A Postal Inspector’s Expose.* Nashville: Vanderbilt University Press.

Hodgkin, Christopher. 2002. *Reforming Empire: Protestant Colonialism and Conscience in British Literature.* Columbia: University of Missouri Press.

Hudson, Nicholas. 1996. "From 'Nation' to 'Race': The Origin of Racial Classification in Eighteenth-Century Thought." *Eighteenth-Century Studies* 29 (3): 247–64.

Iyengar, Sujata. 2005. *Shades of Difference: Mythologies of Skin Color in Early Modern England.* Philadelphia: University of Pennsylvania Press.

Jehlen, Myra. 2002. *Readings at the Edge of Literature.* Chicago: University of Chicago Press.

Jordan, Winthrop. 1977. *White over Black: American Attitudes toward the Negro, 1550–1812.* New York: Norton.

Las Casas, Bartolomé de. 1552. *Breuissima relacion de la destruycíon de las Indias.* Seville.

——. 1992. *A Short Account of the Destruction of the Indies.* Translated by Nigel Griffin. New York: Penguin.

Lowe, Kate. 2005. "The Stereotyping of Black Africans in Renaissance Europe." In *Black Africans in Renaissance Europe,* edited by T. F. Earle and K. J. P. Lowe, 17–47. Cambridge: Cambridge University Press.

Mackie, Erin. 2005. "Welcome the Outlaw: Pirates, Marrons, and Caribbean Countercultures." *Cultural Critique* 59 (Spring): 24–62.

Maltby, William S. 1971. *The Black Legend in England.* Durham: Duke University Press.

Morgan, Edmund. 1975. *American Slavery, American Freedom: The Ordeal of Colonial Virginia.* New York: Norton.

Morrison, Toni. 1992. *Playing in the Dark: Whiteness and the Literary Imagination.* Cambridge: Harvard University Press.

Nichols, Philip. 1626. *Sir Francis Drake reuiued calling vpon this dull or effeminate age, to folowe his noble steps for golde & siluer, by this memorable relation, of the rare occurrances (neuer yet declared to the world) in a third voyage, made by him into the West-Indies, in the yeares 72. & 73. when Nombre de Dios was by him and 52. others only in his company, surprised. Faithfully taken out of the reporte of M. Christofer Ceely, Ellis Hixon, and others, who were in the same voyage with him. By Philip Nichols, preacher. Reviewed also by Sr. Francis Drake himselfe before his death, & much holpen and enlarged, by diuers notes, with his owne hand here and there inserted. Set forth by Sr Francis Drake Baronet (his nephew) now liuing. London.* Early English Books Online. http://eebo.chadwyck.com .

Pagden, Anthony. 1992. Introduction to *A Short Account of the Destruction of the Indies,* by Bartolomé de Las Casas. Translated by Nigel Griffin, xiii–xliii. New York: Penguin.

Price, Richard. 1996. Introduction to *Maroon Societies: Rebel Slave Communities in the Americas,* 1–32. Baltimore: Johns Hopkins University Press.

Purchas, Samuel. 1625. "Voyages to and Land-Travels in Florida, Virginia, and other Parts of the Northerne America." In *Purchas his pilgrimes In fiue books,* vol 1. London.

Vaughan, Alden T., and Virginia Mason Vaughan. 1997. "Before Othello: Elizabethan Representation of Sub-Saharan Africans." *William and Mary Quarterly*, 3rd ser., 54 (1): 19–44.

Wheeler, Roxann. 2000. *The Complexion of Race: Categories of Difference in Eighteenth-Century British Culture.* Philadelphia: University of Pennsylvania Press.

Nations, Migration, and Métis Subsistence, 1860–1940

Delia Hagen

After 1860, Canada and the United States invaded the northern Great Plains. A stream of non-Indian agricultural settlers inundated the region's indigenous societies. Among the affected indigenous groups were the Métis, a racially and ethnically mixed nation produced by the intercultural contact of the fur trade. The Métis relied on a highly mobile trapping and trading lifestyle to take advantage of seasonal resources from the Great Lakes into the Rocky Mountains. Imperial occupation transformed the possibilities for moving through and using this territory.

Settler colonization and the expansion of market capitalism reworked the prairie landscape and decimated crucial native flora and fauna populations. At the same time, new governmental forms engulfed the Great Plains. Mobile populations like the Métis contended with myriad changes over a vast region comprising many jurisdictions. Local, state, provincial, and federal regulations increasingly forbade Métis use of critical resources. These legal limitations stemmed from how colonizing societies categorized Métis people: colonial authorities often refused to grant Métis people membership in any of the spatial, racial, or tribal categories into which they divided their populations. Because membership in official categories conveyed rights to resources, exclusion undermined Métis people's material well-being, and colonial codes criminalized their commonplace survival activities.

In the early 1870s, surveyors plotted the U.S.-Canadian border across the Great Plains. The southern core of Métis territory became the American states of Montana and North Dakota. American authorities, and the non-Indian populace, defined Métis people as Canadian, non-Indian, and nonwhite. They focused especially on the mobile, interracial, and intertribal aspects of Métis society in order to discursively displace the Métis, that is, to define them as foreign. Discursive displacement underwrote a simultaneous refusal to recognize Métis rights to American-claimed resources. These processes left many Métis in a legal and social limbo: they could claim neither the rights of (white) American citizens nor the rights of (federally recognized) American Indians nor the rights of immigrants to America. The history of the U.S. Métis thus illuminates important and enduring conflicts over territory, people, and resources in the context of North American colonialism. In examining that history, this essay contributes to a growing literature on the complex ways settler colonialism used social and legal categories to allocate rights in and to imperial nation-states. It explores this question through an explicit focus on how the interaction of these categories produced, in the case of many Métis, a layered statelessness. Statelessness is garnering increased attention among historians, but indigenous peoples rarely figure into recent discussions. A focus on Métis statelessness not only expands our understanding of how populations were excluded from rights-bearing colonial categories but also calls attention to the political ecology of such categories, shedding light on the lived material consequences of the colonial production of power.[1]

Before proceeding, a discussion of language is in order. The people who are the focus of this essay were a mixed group. Historians have emphasized especially the Chippewa, Cree, and French ancestries of Métis people, but Métis groups and individuals claimed innumerable combinations of Native American and European lineages. Métis people moved often and far, and groups broke apart, reformed, and mixed with other groups throughout the border region. In doing so, they connected communities across what became the North American West. To emphasize these connections, I use the word *Métis* to refer to the people in this essay. I do not mean that every single person was of mixed European and Indian ancestry. As used here, *Métis* is intended to suggest not only individuals of mixed ancestry but also a mixed and amorphous group composed of people of a variety of backgrounds.

My choice of language is, in part, an attempt to call attention to persistent deficiencies in our understanding of Métis history. In the United States, much of this history has been misinterpreted, or missed entirely, by historians who write about populations that were inextricably intertwined as though they were separate. Although sources explicitly affirm the entangled, inseparable nature of the ancestries within Métis groups and the confusion of observers about individual and group identities, historians adopt the simplistic labels in sources ("Canadian," "Cree," "Chippewa," and so on) as though they are accurate. By writing about intertwined populations as though they are separate, scholars replicate the inaccurate and destructive social simplifications employed by states as tools of colonialism. We must recognize and respect the racial, spatial, and tribal complexity of Métis people or we perpetuate the colonial epistemes that underlay the persecution of the Métis explored in this essay.

Making the Métis Canadian

Large-scale immigration onto the northern Plains began in the 1860s. Thereafter, south of the U.S.-Canada boundary, the Métis found themselves treated "as foreigners in the territory [they] had always called, 'home'" (Rivard and Littlejohn 2003, 196). American government officials and other contemporaries defined the Métis in such a way as to refuse them recognized membership in any of the communities and population categories understood to have legitimate claims in and to U.S. territory. This entailed constructing the Métis as neither American, Indian, or white.

Government agencies, and non-Indian settlers, routinely labeled Métis people Canadian. They did so based on their ideas about Métis nativity, ancestry, and mobility. Discursive constructions of the Métis as Canadians relied on both their real and alleged place of birth. The United States legislated birthright citizenship in 1868, and a few years later surveyors plotted the international border across the Great Plains. The line they marked bisected the Métis homeland. The United States used this fact to argue that Métis were not American. Many, probably most, U.S. Métis families included members who had been born on both sides of the international border (Hagen 2008). Métis people had been highly mobile for generations, and continued to be so after the U.S. and Canadian empires marked their common border and implemented their respective sedentarization schemes. Chance often determined where Métis women were when they bore children. Colonial authorities nonetheless used the locations of those chance moments as a basis for denying Métis "American" status: when it suited their needs, colonial agents and settlers viewed birthplace as the sole determinant in ascribing Métis nationality. When adhering to the birthplace standard interfered with their efforts, authorities often violated it, labeling as "Canadian" Métis people who were born in the United States to what they called "Canadian parents" or "Canadian families."[2] The nature of nativity documentation abetted the discursive displacement of the Métis. Colonial agents privileged written records, but the Métis documentary record was minute and unreliable. Moreover, for the most part, the fur-trading posts that became Métis administrative centers stood north of the international boundary, and parents often recorded births only upon return to these centers. Written records were therefore predominantly Canadian in provenance and undermined claims to recognition as Americans.

Some colonial authorities recognized the absurdity of applying nativity criteria to the Métis community. In 1890, commissioners charged with making a census at North Dakota's Turtle Mountain Reservation "for the purposes of determining who should participate in negotiations" protested the futility of distinguishing between "Canadian" and "American" Métis at Turtle Mountain. As the commissioners explained, during much of the 1800s the Turtle Mountain people moved throughout the region

> without any reference to an [unsurveyed and unmarked] international boundary line, their nearest church was at St. Boniface, and the nearest important trading post was at Winnipeg. Their children were in most cases baptized at St. Boniface, and nothing suggested at the time the importance of distinguishing between American nativity and British allegiance. Indeed, through the Hudson Bay Company, Great Britain had pushed her claims far south of the present boundary line. . . . In view of these facts it must seem superogatory to draw attention to the extreme difficulty of preparing at Turtle Mountain a census of only genuinely American Indians—Indians to whom British affiliations may not by some record or other means be ascribed, as, for example, the baptismal record at St. Boniface.[3]

The commissioners' efforts to introduce into the census proceedings some responsiveness to the complexity of historical conditions proved fruitless. Such an approach ill served the goals of the Congress that had appointed them. They were supposed to minimize the tribal rolls, remove the people, and conclusively settle the community's claims in order to open lands for unfettered non-Indian settler colonization. When they instead called attention to the misguided nature of the assignment, they were ignored and then replaced.

Many Métis couldn't even identify, much less document, where they were born. On the northern Plains, the international boundary was "based on an astronomical concept instead of 'natural features'" like rivers, canyons, or mountain ranges (MacManus 2005, 7). Prior to the 1872 boundary survey, "there was no telling where the precise line lay" (Stegner 1962, 85). As iconic western author Wallace Stegner pointed out, "[W]olfers and traders did not carry astronomical instruments" (1962, 85). Even colonizing governments couldn't pinpoint the limits of the territory they claimed: when surveyors reached the Red River, they discovered that the Canadian customhouse stood south of the line (88). Once survey crews completed their work in 1874, piles of rocks or earth marked the borderline only every three miles. The region's famed winds, as well as its irreverent inhabitants, quickly diminished these minimal markings.

Nativity information remained elusive for decades. Even fifty years after the Office of Indian Affairs (OIA) began keeping records on the region's indigenous inhabitants, many Métis remained uncertain about the details of their birth. When asked in 1929 where they were born, respondents offered such vague answers as "[R]ight around here, my father told me," or "[M]y father told me in this country some place, but I don't know where. It was on the line some place" (U.S. Congress 1932, 12509, 12511). According to the Turtle Mountain superintendent, in 1942 "many of the enrolled as well as the non-enrolled people here [were] not even able to tell whether they were born on the north or the south side of the Canadian line."[4]

In order to categorize U.S. Métis as Canadians, American authorities also seized on their ancestries and cultural attributes. Officials linked both the European and Native American ancestries of Métis communities to Canada. They emphasized especially the French and Cree aspects of Métis groups, both of which they construed as Canadian. Métis groups and individuals boasted a dizzying array of backgrounds that defied any single ethnic label. Many Métis people considered themselves neither Cree nor French. But Métis communities contained lots of people of Cree and/or French ancestry, and many Métis lived in so-called Cree communities. Michif, the Métis language, incorporates words from Chippewa, English, Gaelic, Assiniboine, and other languages, but it draws predominantly on Cree verbs and French nouns (Laverdure, Allard, and Crawford 1983). In the United States, observers equated Cree and French with Canadian. Although Cree people lived in and used areas south of the 49th parallel before and after widespread non-Indian settlement, "the charge was ever present—[the Cree] are Canadian Indians with no claim to protection from the United States government" (Dusenberry 1962, 28). Likewise, at the time it colonized the Great Plains, the United States was officially and emphatically Anglophone. Many Francophone people lived in American-claimed territory after the retreat of the French Empire, but those who sought to displace the Métis disregarded this. They also disregarded the other European ancestries in Métis communities: equating Métis with French rendered them foreign. "French" or "French half-breed" meant Canadian. As an ethnic description in the northern Great Plains, "French Canadian" had no American counterpart. In 1931, Charles Gordon, justice of the peace for Wolf Point,

Montana, illustrated this when he described the "non-reservation" Indians in his area. As he put it, "[M]any of the families talk French. It is white men's opinion that these are 'Canadian Breed French.'"[5]

The argument that the U.S. Métis belonged in Canada also drew on specific historical events. Foremost among these were armed conflicts between Métis groups and Canadian armies in 1869–70 and 1885. The Red River conflict and North West conflict that followed are the most-discussed events of Canadian history. They linked the Métis irrevocably to Canada. The aftermath of the rebellions also shaped American ideas about Métis nationality. Persecution by Canadian authorities and settlers led Métis participants and civilians alike to retreat southward into the United States. This movement relied on and reflected long-standing, well-established spatial and social networks, but the fame of the rebellions obscured this more mundane historic context. Earlier, ongoing movements were effectively erased in the eyes of American colonizers, who recast the Métis as refugees in their ancestral territory. Contemporaries and historians also recast subsequent U.S. migrations. These migrations were modern examples of long-established, purposeful Métis practices. Americans interpreted them as the aimless wanderings of foreigners in an unfamiliar land (Foster 2006, 177; Ens 1998, 2006; Peterson 1978; Dusenberry 1954, 3, 11–12; 1998, 33–34, 43; Wessel 1975, 26–42; Burt 1986, 48, 50; Burt 1987; Ryan 1998; River 1990).

Refusing to Enroll Métis in American Indian Tribes

The aftermath of the 1885 rebellion coincided with increasing efforts in the United States to formalize and police racial categories. The end of Reconstruction and the rise of Jim Crow laws in the American South, the influx of southern European immigrants, and the ascendance of scientific racism, among other phenomena, played into and bespoke a shifting racialism in America. On the Great Plains, the United States tried to police both the social and spatial boundaries of the racial categories it constructed. The mixed, mobile Métis vexed these efforts. Their inseparability from Indians, the region's largest nonwhite population, aggravated colonial authorities to no end.

In 1887, Congress passed the Dawes Allotment Act to open reservations to white settlement by allotting collectively held tribal lands to individual Indians. The act spawned racial and tribal classification commissions charged with making official tribal membership lists. On the Great Plains, these commissions tried to separate the Métis from other Indians and from Indian reservations. As in the efforts to equate Métis people with Canada, the attempts to purge Métis people from the Indian communities of which they were a part used the mobility and mixed ancestry of the Métis as grounds for exclusion. The proceedings of the 1892 McCumber Commission at North Dakota's Turtle Mountain Reservation exemplified this effort. The commission refused to enroll over 45 percent of community members. The rhetorical tools with which it carved the Turtle Mountain community were by then well honed. The commissioners employed every trope of racial, cultural, and national citizenship at their disposal when they dismissed some applicants as Canadian (either Indian or white); some as white (either by "blood" or, especially in the case of females married to "white" men, by social status or life choice); some as American Indian but belonging, in the commissioners' opinion, to other bands or tribes; and some as Indians of proper tribal or band affiliation but lacking proper spatial affiliation (that is, inarguably bound to a 9-million-acre tract delineated in Turtle Mountain treaties) (Hagen 2003).

Withholding Whiteness from the Métis

By purging tribal rolls as they did at Turtle Mountain, authorities formally defined many Métis as non-Indian. At the same time, authorities often considered Métis people nonwhite indigenes and thereby denied them the possibility of citizenship regardless of where they were born. In the myriad documents discussing people purged from the Turtle Mountain roll, OIA officials usually referred to them as Indians. Through the 1930s, statistical reports formally counted many Métis as "non-enrolled Indians." In the eyes of government officials, Métis were Indians, either American (and therefore ineligible for birthright citizenship), or Canadian (and therefore ineligible for legal immigration and naturalization).[6] Many non-Indian people in the private sector shared this belief, withholding social whiteness from the Métis in a range of interactions.

No Safe Place: Consequences of Discursive Displacement

All of the categories from which Métis were excluded conveyed rights. Discursive displacement thus left many Métis in a legal and social limbo in which they could claim neither the rights of (non-Indian) American citizens nor the rights of (federally recognized) American Indians nor the rights of immigrants to America. Foremost among these rights was the right to inhabit places that the American Empire assigned to each group. In 1895, when members of Montana Métis communities traveled east with "Montana's Wildest West Show," promoters billed them as "the only people in the United States without a country" (Gray 1942, 32). Lacking rights to any one place, the Métis made do by moving between many: refusing to ascribe Métis people a stable and secure national, tribal, or racial status perpetuated the very mobility that colonial authorities sought to minimize.

Since Americans categorized the Métis as Canadians, authorities persecuted them for the ostensible crime of being south of the international boundary. U.S. government persecution of American Métis on the grounds of their alleged Canadianness began in the nineteenth century, with the advent of a federal presence in the northern Plains, and endured into the mid-twentieth century. The most spectacular episodes of persecution centered on the right to occupy American-claimed space. At times, authorities responded ferociously to Métis peoples' alleged national trespass. Late in the fall of 1867, five years *before* the international boundary survey, U.S. marshals descended on a Métis camp on the Milk River in northern Montana, ostensibly "having heard that Canadian traders were transacting business" there. Ben Kline, a camp resident, recalled that the marshals "went among them, confiscated their complete stock of goods, valued at not less than $15,000," set fire to their cabins, and ordered two traders in the camp to leave American territory.[7] Their actions left the Métis facing the coming winter with neither supplies nor shelter. The marshals also seized their ammunition so they couldn't hunt for furs to trade, for hides to make shelter and clothing, or for food. Few Métis could have felt safe during this period, as army officials issued repeated calls "to break up" what they called "trading parties from the British possessions and execute summary justice on the principals engaged."[8]

In the 1880s, sporadic attacks on Montana Métis gave way to more systematic efforts. Although previous attempts to expel Métis groups had failed to oust them, newspapers around the state clamored for their expulsion. In this they were joined by many individuals, like rancher and attorney Thomas Miles, himself an immigrant from New Brunswick, Canada. In 1892, Miles campaigned for the "permanent removal" to Canada of "Cree Indian . . . pests." He wrote to newspapers and state officials and met with Montana's U.S. attorney and with U.S. senator T. C. Power.[9] The demands of Miles and others among the newly arrived non-Indian population met with apparent success four years later, when Congress appropriated $5,000 to "deport from the State of Montana and deliver at the international boundary line to the Canadian authorities, all refugee Cree Indians in said State" (U.S. Congress 1896; Gray 1942, 34). In the months that followed, the Canadian government collaborated in rounding up and expelling "Cree" people from Montana (Canada Department of Interior 1896, 23, 342–43; Gray 1942, 47; *Choteau Acantha* 1905).

The 1896 deportation events proved to be the most high profile of many instances of the U.S. government persecuting the Montana Métis on the basis of supposed Canadian status. They were not the last. For at least the next fifty years, similar but less widespread and well-orchestrated deportation efforts plagued the Métis. In 1942, Métis attorney Raymond Gray claimed that his people "dread[ed] the menace of deportation more than any evil that can befall the victims of exploitation." This menace lurked even as Gray wrote: in 1941–42, authorities deported "Cree Indians" George Red Thunder and Charles Kennedy (22).

The American refusal to grant Métis formal Indian status also undermined Métis rights to specific places in the United States. By categorizing Métis as Canadian, the United States denied their right to occupy American-claimed space in general. By purging them from the rolls of tribes of which they were a part, the United States denied their right to live on American Indian reservations in particular. American (and Canadian) Indian policy during this period focused on separating "Indian" people from "non-Indian" people. Authorities operated as though there were some clear line between "races" that could be mapped and then enforced, which in turn would maintain separation between ostensibly distinct races. The fact that racial and spatial realities were not that simple seldom prompted policy makers to question their goals. Reservations were for enrolled Indians, not for their unenrolled spouses, siblings, parents, offspring, and other assorted kin and companions. Likewise, off-reservation places were forbidden to Indians, who were supposed to stay within the perimeter of the reservation on which they were enrolled. As with the efforts to deport Métis people from the United States, the attempts to keep enrolled Indians on reservations, and to keep unenrolled people off enjoyed some level of international collaboration but little success. In 1889, Canada and the United States explored developing a joint international Indian pass system. They ultimately instituted separate similar systems that required enrolled Indians to obtain written permission to leave their reservation. On both sides of the border agents also tried to limit reservation visitors to Indians or whites with official permission to be there (Samek 1987, 154–56).

Government attempts to create distinct populations and enforce a corresponding physical separation perpetually plagued the Métis. Under Canadian and American racial and tribal categorization policies, many reservations and reserves included Métis people on their rolls. At the same time, many Métis people were on no official tribal roll, either in Canada or the United States (Hagen 2008). This placed families in a position in which some family members were prohibited from being on the reservations where other family members were enrolled. Such situations abounded. The Magee family typified this dilemma: after moving around for years, Emma Minesinger Magee and her husband tried to settle on western Montana's Flathead Reservation in 1896.

This proved fruitless. As Emma recalled, "Flathead blood gave me the right to live on the Reserve. Not so, my husband." The Magees resumed a nomadic existence that took them back and forth across the international border.[10]

Although American authorities controlled Indian lands more intensely than other spaces, attempts to create, and then physically separate, distinct races also complicated Métis claims to places outside of the OIA's jurisdiction. Even while the OIA refused to enroll Métis in federally recognized tribes, government officials (and many in the general public) considered them Indian. This complicated Métis efforts to live outside of reservations. On the basis that Métis were Indian, and therefore ineligible for citizenship, federal authorities rejected Métis homestead applications and thereby foreclosed a primary option for families to secure a home. Métis attempts to live in cities often met with failure as well. Even in winter, police in places like Devil's Lake, North Dakota, "ordered them to leave." Urban officials were so intent on ridding their jurisdictions of Indians that they sometimes paid to transport Métis people to distant reservations where they had no residence rights.[11]

"No help no place": Resources and Opportunities Denied the Métis

Clearly, exclusion from the United States' national, racial, and tribal categories made it difficult for Métis to find a place, literally, in their homeland. The fact that official categories conveyed rights to resources compounded their dilemma. Under U.S. rule, enrolled members of federally recognized Indian tribes retained rights to use certain natural resources. They also could access services and opportunities intended exclusively for their use. The same was true for white Americans. When the United States excluded them from both of these demographic categories, Métis lost legal access to a wide range of critical resources.

In the United States, enrolled Indians usually had rights to resources on their reservations and sometimes had hunting, fishing, trapping and harvesting rights to lands ceded during treaty negotiations.[12] In contrast, regulations barred unenrolled Métis from cutting firewood for winter warmth or felling larger timbers for building. Laws also forbade the unenrolled from hunting and trapping for hides, furs, and meat, or from digging and harvesting plants, like snakeroot, that contributed to their survival. Because the products of these flora and fauna resources could be sold as well as consumed, regulations barring Métis access impaired not only their subsistence but also their market economy.

Métis people who were excluded from tribal rolls lost access to other goods as well. Enrolled Indians sometimes received a variety of items aimed at contributing to their survival. The most (in)famous of these were rations of food and clothing. But in different times and places, material assistance included housing or construction materials; household implements like cook and heat stoves (and coal to fuel them); seed for planting cash and food crops; animals to raise for sale or consumption; and farm implements and draft animals with which to work their lands.

Other services available to enrolled Indians, many of which had material benefits, also eluded unenrolled Métis. Although many Indian people detested the OIA and Christian schools designed to eradicate their native cultures, these schools could provide a Western education that might help students survive in the society surrounding them. Métis people often wanted to attend Indian schools. Material incentives contributed to this desire: as Sister Genevieve of Turtle Mountain's St. Mary's Industrial Boarding School observed, "[T]he people here, being very poor, send their children to be clothed and fed" (U.S. Department of Interior 1890, 29). U.S. Indian agents, however, tried to limit OIA schools to children on tribal rolls.[13]

Métis people also had trouble accessing Indian medical services. OIA and Christian hospitals tried to exclude unenrolled patients, and doctors elsewhere learned that the OIA paid medical bills only for services to people on tribal rolls. Other opportunities with obvious material outcomes, like OIA employment or use of tribal flour and timber mills, also remained off-limits to many Métis. The scarcity of jobs and infrastructure in the rural northern Plains exacerbated the impact of such prohibitions.

Even enrolled Métis experienced difficulty accessing resources that were ostensibly available to them. Religious and secular officials who managed Indian infrastructure preferred to provide the services under their control to those tribal members they considered properly American, or more Indian, or tribally pure. Using a system of national, racial, and tribal triage, authorities allocated school desks, hospital beds, jobs, and other resources to applicants they deemed most worthy. The tribally and racially mixed Métis, besmirched by the taint of Canadian association, suffered accordingly.

Métis people found few opportunities on non-Indian lands to offset those denied to them on the basis of their tribally unenrolled status. Government authorities and the general public still considered most Métis to be Indian and discriminated against them as such. In this regard their unenrolled status left the Métis particularly vulnerable, for they lacked even the guise of federal protection or Indian-specific rights that might moderate the impacts of anti-Indian racism. Being Indian in the eyes of non-Indians inflicted serious material consequences on the Métis community. The general public, and U.S. law, understood Indians to be wards of the federal government. Contemporaries thus deemed Indian assistance to be the responsibility of the nation, not of the state, county, or city. On this basis, public officials consistently denied services to Métis people. School administrators barred or dismissed Métis pupils. Hospitals and clinics refused them medical care and referred them to the same Indian Health Service that sent them away to non-Indian facilities. Local and state service organizations withheld food, clothing, and other aid from Métis families.

In 1932, Patrick Lizotte, a Montana Métis, wrote in desperation to the Fort Peck Indian Reservation. He implored the superintendent for help. The Great Depression had deepened his community's crisis: as the need for aid spread throughout society, public and private agencies formalized their policies and became ever more adamant that the Métis were somebody else's responsibility. The result, according to Lizotte, was that they could get "no help no place."[14] The colonizing society's ideas about the spatially, racially, and tribally mixed Métis had radically altered Métis people's ability to survive.

Colonial policies that ascribed national, racial, and tribal statuses to the residents of the northern Plains left many Métis people with no secure legal status. Over the course of the late nineteenth and early twentieth centuries, state-ascribed status increasingly conveyed specific rights to land, natural resources, and a variety of services. Lacking rights in and to any one place, Métis people had to make do by moving between many. Ultimately, by refusing to ascribe the Métis a secure spatial, racial, or tribal status, colonial authorities perpetuated the very mobility and intermixture that they despised.

Notes

1. This essay focuses on the interaction of legal and social categories of race, place, nation, tribe, and band with one another and with rights to land and other resources under U.S. colonialism in the North American West. Most recent literature examines the interplay of some, but not all, of these factors. For discussions of Indianness, land, and settler colonialism, see, for instance, Banner 2005; Ford 2010; and Weaver 2003. Some examinations of indigenous people and official rights-bearing legal categories include Harmon 2001, 1998; and Rosen 2007. For an excellent broad overview of the dynamics of colonial power among northern Plains indigenes, see Ostler 2004. Key recent works on statelessness include Kerber 2005, 2007.

2. Tilda R. Lefort application file, box 190 (Turtle Mountain); Mrs. Lewis Langie application file, box 190 (Turtle Mountain)); C. H. Asbury, Superintendent, to Addiea

Brooks, Superintendent, Florence Crittendon Home, February 1, 1932, Social Relations, 1932 file, box 73 (Turtle Mountain); James Hyde, Superintendent, Turtle Mountain Agency, to Commissioner of Indian Affairs (CIA), July 26, 1928, Enrollment of Citizenship, Degree of Blood, 1918–27 file, box 58 (Turtle Mountain).

3. CIA D. M. Browning to Secretary of Interior, July 6, 1893 (U.S. Congress 1900, 95).

4. F. W. Boyd, Superintendent, Turtle Mountain Agency, to CIA, enclosing a "list of Canadian Indians on the reservation," Indian Reorganization Enrollment, 1936–40 file, box 58 (Turtle Mountain).

5. Charles Gordon, Secretary, Commercial Club of Wolf Point, to Superintendent McCullough, Fort Peck Agency, July 14, 1931, Poplar, Montana, Tribal Relations, 1948 file, box 58 (Turtle Mountain); Superintendent, Turtle Mountain Agency, to CIA, April 27, 1923, Mixed-bloods, 1923 file, box 150 (Turtle Mountain).

6. Not until the Nationality Act of 1940 were "Indians from Canada and elsewhere" permitted to become naturalized citizens of the United States. F. W. Boyd, Superintendent, Turtle Mountain Agency, to CIA, February 26, 1941, enclosing a "list of Canadian Indians on the reservation," Indian Reorganization Enrollment, 1936–1940, box 58 (Turtle Mountain).

7. Father Van Den Broeck. December 2, 1931. "Sketch of Ben Kline's Life," unpublished manuscript, November 14, 1925, and Oscar Mueller, notes, interview with Ben Kline, Small Collection 942, Ben Kline Reminiscence, Montana Historical Society.

8. Father Van Den Broeck. December 2, 1931. "Sketch of Ben Kline's Life," unpublished manuscript, November 14, 1925 and Oscar Mueller, notes, interview with Ben Kline, Small Collection 942, Ben Kline Reminiscence, Montana Historical Society; C. A. R. Dimon, Colonel First U.S. Volunteer Infantry, Fort Rice, Dakota Territory, to Lieut. Col. Edward P. Ten Broeck, January 24, 1865, Small Collection 927, U.S. War Department, Department of the Platte, Montana Historical Society.

9. Thomas O. Miles Papers, 1892–1908, Small Collection 475, Montana Historical Society. See also Gray 1942, 16–17, 147–55.

10. James Hyde, Superintendent, Turtle Mountain Agency, to James Ryder, Superintendent, Hayward Indian School, Enrollment of Citizenship, Degree of Blood, 1918–27 file, box 58 (Turtle Mountain); Emma Minesinger Magee, "Montana Memories," K. Ross Toole Archives, University of Montana.

11. Superintendent, Turtle Mountain Agency, to Peter Timboe, Chief of Police, Devils Lake, North Dakota, December 22, 1922, Law and Order file, box 157 (Turtle Mountain).

12. Even for enrolled Indians, these rights existed more in law than in fact, as government policies, the non-Indian public, and ecological changes often interfered with their access to resources.

13. Superintendent, Turtle Mountain Agency, to CIA, April 27, 1923, Mixed-bloods, 1923 file, box 150 (Turtle Mountain).

14. Patrick Lizotte to H. D. McCullough, Superintendent, Fort Peck Agency, January 5, 1932, Drouth Relief, 1931–32 file, box 113 (Turtle Mountain).

References

Banner, Stuart. 2005. *How the Indians Lost Their Land: Law and Power on the Frontier.* Cambridge: Harvard University Press.

Burt, Larry. 1986. "In a Crooked Piece of Time: The Dilemma of the Montana Cree and the Métis." *Journal of American Culture* 9 (1): 45–51.

———. 1987. "Nowhere Left to Go: Montana's Crees, Métis, and Chippewa and the Creation of the Rocky Boy Indian Reservation." *Great Plains Quarterly* 7 (Summer): 195–209.

Canada Department of Interior. 1896. *Annual Report of the Department of Indian Affairs.* Ottawa. http://www.rootsweb.ancestry.com/~mtteton/Métisridgeproposal.html.

Choteau Acantha. 1905. October 5. http://www.rootsweb.ancestry.com/~mtteton/Métisridgeproposal.html.

Dusenberry, Verne. 1954. "The Rocky Boy Indians, Montana's Displaced Persons." *Montana Magazine of History* 4 (Winter): 1–15.

———. 1998. *The Montana Cree: A Study in Religious Persistence.* Norman: University of Oklahoma Press.

Ens, Gerhard. 1998. "The Reformulation of the Turtle Mountain Métis Community, 1879–1905." In *New Faces of the Fur Trade: Selected Papers of the Seventh North American Fur Trade Conference, Halifax, Nova Scotia, 1995,* edited by Jo-Anne Fiske, Susan Sleeper-Smith, and William Wicken, 139–51. East Lansing: Michigan State University Press.

———. 2006. "The Border, the Buffalo, and the Métis of Montana." In *The Borderlands of the American and Canadian Wests: Essays on Regional History of the Forty-ninth Parallel,* edited by Sterling Evans, 139–54. Lincoln: University of Nebraska Press.

Ford, Lisa. 2010. *Settler Sovereignty: Jurisdiction and Indigenous People in America and Australia, 1788–1936.* Cambridge: Harvard University Press.

Foster, Martha. 2006. *We Know Who We Are: Métis Identity in a Montana Community.* Norman: University of Oklahoma Press.

Gray, Raymond. 1942. "The Cree Indians" (U.S. Federal Writers Project, photocopy) University of Montana Libraries.

Hagen, Delia. 2003. "The Process and Consequences of Creating the Turtle Mountain Tribal Roll of 1892." Paper presented at "Immigration and Ethnicity," University of California–Berkeley.

———. 2008. "'The Territory We Had Always Called Home': Nations, Migration, and the Northern Plains Métis, 1880–1930." Paper presented at "Writing New Histories of Indigineity and Imperialism: A Workshop," University of Manitoba, May 21–23.

Harmon, Alexandra. 1998. *Indians in the Making: Ethnic Relations and Indian Identities around Puget Sound.* Berkeley: University of California Press.

———. 2001. "Tribal Enrollment Councils: Lessons on Law and Indian Identity." *Western Historical Quarterly* 32 (2): 175–200.

Kerber, Linda K. 2005. "Toward a History of Statelessness in America." *American Quarterly* 57 (3): 727–57.

———. 2007. "The Stateless as the Citizen's Other: A View from the United States." *American Historical Review* 112 (1): 1–34.

Laverdure, Pauline, Ida Allard, and John Crawford, eds. 1983. *The Michif Dictionary: Turtle Mountain Chippewa Cree.* Winnipeg: Pemmican.

MacManus, Sheila. 2005. *The Line Which Separates: Race, Gender, and the Making of the Alberta-Montana Borderlands.* Lincoln: University of Nebraska Press.

Montana Historical Society. Helena, Montana.

Ostler, Jeffrey. 2004. *The Plains Sioux and U.S. Colonialism from Lewis and Clark to Wounded Knee.* Cambridge: Cambridge University Press.

Peterson, Hans. 1978. "Imasees and His Band: Canadian Refugees After the North-West Rebellion." *Western Canadian Journal of Anthropology* 8 (1): 21–36.

Rivard, Ron, and Catherine Littlejohn. 2003. *History of the Metis of Willow Bunch.* N.p.: Saskatchewan.

River, Celeste. 1990. "A Mountain in His Memory: Frank Bird Linderman, His Role in Acquiring the Rocky Boy Indian Reservation for the Montana Chippewa and Cree." Master's thesis, University of Montana.

Rosen, Deborah. 2007. *American Indians and State Law: Sovereignty, Race, and Citizenship, 1790–1880.* Lincoln: University of Nebraska Press.

Ryan, Luke. 1998. "Freedom, Fear, and the American Periphery: The Chippewa and Cree in Montana, 1885–1923." Master's thesis, University of Montana.

Samek, Hana. 1987. *The Blackfoot Confederacy, 1880–1920: A Comparative Study of Canadian and U.S. Indian Policy.* Albuquerque: University of New Mexico Press.

Stegner, Wallace. 1962. *Wolf Willow: A History, a Story, a Memory of the Last Plains Frontier.* New York: Viking.

Turtle Mountain. National Archives Branch Depository, RG 75. Kansas City, Mo. U.S. Congress. Senate. 1896. 54th Cong., 1st sess. Report no. 821.

———. 1900. Turtle Mountain Band of Chippewa Indians. 56th Cong., 1st sess. S. Doc. 444.

———. 1932. Committee on Indian Affairs. *Survey of Conditions of the Indians in the United States,* part 23, *Montana.* 72nd Cong. 1st sess.

U.S. Department of Interior. 1890. *Annual Report of the Commissioner of Indian Affairs*. Washington, D.C.

Weaver, John. 2003. *The Great Land Rush and the Making of the Modern World, 1650–1900*. Ithaca: McGill-Queen's University Press.

Wessel, Thomas. 1975. *A History of the Rocky Boy's Indian Reservation*. Bozeman: Thomas Wessel.

Disorientation in Julie Otsuka's *When the Emperor Was Divine*

The Imprisoned Spaces of Japanese Americans during World War II

Abigail G. H. Manzella

"[A] Jap is a Jap," the commander of the Western Defense, Lieutenant General John L. DeWitt, stated in the midst of World War II, but this statement was not made against the Japanese who had attacked Pearl Harbor. Instead, it directly questioned the loyalty of Japanese American soldiers. DeWitt had explained this ideology when he spoke before a congressional committee the day before: "You don't need to worry about the Italians at all except in certain cases. Also, the same for Germans except in individual cases. But we must worry about the Japanese all the time until he is wiped off the map" (U.S. Commission 1997, 66). This hateful language against American citizens who were fighting for the United States connects racist ideology to a geographic context: white U.S. citizens would not be safe until these "invading" Japanese, a scant 2 percent of the California population (Daniels 2004, 8), had been effaced. Using this rhetoric, the U.S. government justified the mandatory evacuation of people of Japanese descent from the West Coast—over 110,000 people. This essay investigates the effects of that displacement. By looking at history and its literary representation in Julie Otsuka's *When the Emperor Was Divine,* I argue that this dislocation was not temporary but instead had long-term effects on those imprisoned, breaking down families and altering individuals, who lost a sense of place and self.

When the Emperor Was Divine (2002) tells the story of a family of Japanese descent that endures a forced migration from their home in Berkeley, California, in a convoluted path both to and from U.S. concentration camps during World War II.[1] Readers follow the unnamed mother, sister, and brother to the Topaz Relocation Center in Utah and hear indirectly about the father's imprisonment as an enemy alien. Told from the shifting perspectives of different family members, this minimalist novel subtly revisits the psychological and cultural effects of a racist government policy on a group of people.

The government emptied people of Japanese ancestry from the West Coast and tried to change the people themselves, "depleting" them so that they would have no effect on the "mainstream": the Anglo-American United States. The removal was an attempt to change the people themselves. As Michel Foucault has noted, "[P]enal imprisonment, from the beginning of the nineteenth century, covered both the deprivation of liberty and the technical transformation of individuals" (1995, 233). Otsuka's novel shows that evacuation becomes not just the movement of people but also the attempted alteration of them through the emptying of their self-worth, their individuality, and their connection not only to Japanese culture but to the United States as well. This targeted "emptying" of Japanese immigrants and citizens has continued consequences for Japanese Americans negotiating the legal and political aspects of their heritage.

Internment Narratives

This governmental approach has a literary parallel. While the initial impetus of complete "evacuation" of Asian American literature by the Anglo-American mainstream has been replaced by a "multicultural" acceptance, some Asian American literature is still sold through its focus on the individual's need to change before being accepted and feeling acceptable.[2] David Palumbo-Liu has noted this trend of marketing Asian American literature as "the literature of an assimilated group now at peace after a 'phase' of adjustment" (1999, 410). The adjustment is an inward assimilation that he labels a "model minority discourse" (397). By embracing this discourse the reader experiences a sense of resolution that neatly wraps up the problem and blends Japanese American characters into whitewashed "Americans" (410).

Internment narratives in particular attempt to escape this model minority discourse because their subject matter addresses such imposed alterations of self. As Lisa Lowe has pointed out when looking at some interment narratives, they "refuse, in different manners, to develop, reconcile, and resolve" (1996, 48). In contrast, scholars Fu-Jen Chen and Su-Lin Yu argue that many of these narratives are written with a linear structure, enabling readers to conclude that there were few long-term repercussions to those interned merely because the narrative creates a sense of "finality about 'returning' and 'being free'" (2005, 552). Admittedly, the first memoir about the camps, Miné Okubo's *Citizen 13600* (1946), possesses a strict linearity and decisive resolution: it ends with Okubo's release and her statement "I was finally free. . . . I turned my thoughts from the past to the future" (208–9), as though separating those times were that simple. It is reasonable, however, that a narrative published immediately after the experience could not give a long view on the subject.[3] Narratives written with any distance from World War II reveal that the internment experience continues to haunt the story and its subjects. For instance, Yoshiko Uchida's chronicle *Desert Exile: The Uprooting of a Japanese-American Family* (1982), while following a narrative structure similar to Okubo's account, adds an epilogue discussing the history beyond the camps, giving the *longue durée* view. Also, in Jeanne Wakatsuki Houston's memoir about her experiences at camp, *Farewell to Manzanar* (Houston and Houston 1973), the story extends beyond her time at the camp and even includes nonlinear segments, such as a proleptic chapter delaying the expected release from camp and again showing how the effects of internment continue after their expected end date. Finally, Hisaye Yamamoto's short story "The Legend of Miss Sasagawara" (1950) and John Okada's novel *No-No Boy* (1957) frame their narratives with outside observers, thus upsetting strict linearity. Therefore, internment narratives generally break up narrative expectations so that the stories cannot be neatly contained. Specifically, the camps disrupt the stories' progression through time and space, leaving characters of Japanese descent, whether interned or not, dwelling on these events long after their conclusion.

The works discussed thus far were composed by those who lived through the experience of the camps, but now the narratives of the next generation (most often the Sansei—the third generation of Japanese Americans) are appearing, such as Otsuka's novel. With these additions to the canon, we should consider how the new authors draw upon or depart from earlier texts. Otsuka is certainly indebted to those who came before her in content and approach, but her work shows crucial distinctions. Structurally, Otsuka follows Houston's lead by including what happens to the characters after their return from the camps, and many of the details that she relates are based on her close reading of earlier works. However, what separates her work is that each chapter is narrated by a different character so that perspective affects the experience of time and space. Her motivations for writing also differ from those who came before her. Otsuka's purpose is not to relate her own experience, nor is she writing to advance the political goal of reparations for those interned, since that goal has already been reached. Instead Otsuka's novel raises generational questions about the ramifications of the camps and the continued threat of state-sponsored racism.

Otsuka's mother, uncle, and grandmother had been interned, but she was born years after their release. The novel's existence underscores that the next generation continues to be affected by the trauma their parents and grandparents experienced; they experience "postmemory," Marianne Hirsch's term for an "experience of those who grow up dominated by narratives that preceded their birth, whose own belated stories are evacuated by the stories of the previous generation shaped by traumatic events that can be neither understood nor recreated" (1997, 22). Therefore, this generation may suffer a "spatial and temporal exile" (Chu 2008, 97), not the exile of their parents in the concentration camps, but the exile *from* the camps, the site of the trauma.[4] Part of the next generation's writing, then, becomes an attempt to understand what they can never fully grasp and yet still feel, showing that there has not been an easy resolution to the story and the history.[5] Or, as Yamamoto explains about the different generations' views of the camps: "[W]e find the Nisei [second-generation] writer choosing not to dwell on his camp experience. . . . Perhaps it was because the Nisei, in the years after the war, was preoccupied with survival. Whatever, it is more often the Sansei writer who goes back to the subject of evacuation again and again, sometimes to the point of obsession[,] . . . in this age of self-examination" (1994, 70). While the Nisei have obviously not been completely silent on the subject since a substantial earlier canon exists, the next generation continues to write about the concentration camps, showing that people of Japanese descent are still sorting through the forced movements that affected their community and themselves.[6]

Significant identity issues resulted from the forced migration of Japanese people in the United States because, as I show, the cultural identities of people are inextricably tied to migration and space. I use the general term *commutatory practices* to describe how the movement of people, whether forced or voluntary, results in a change of perception of space, community, and self. In the specific instance of the 1940s U.S concentration camps, the government adopted a particular commutatory practice that I term *disorientation* because it resulted in the migrants' loss of a sense of place and self through a complex pattern of movement and alienation from space.[7] They have lost their bearing. The government's policy attempts to "dis-orient" by compelling the internees to turn away from the East—here it is not the compass direction but any Japanese cultural connections—and to instead adopt an imagined communal binary view of "us vs. them," opposing Americanness to Japaneseness.[8] *When the Emperor Was Divine* shows how this practice of disorientation dissociated physiognomy, cultural practices and objects, and cultural/national identities from one another at a particular point in U.S. racial history, resulting in an alteration of identity with effects into the present day for those who were interned and their descendents. As this essay illustrates, the alteration of self based on movement, community, and government shows that external oppression can easily slip into internal oppression when the environment is so unforgiving that the individual cannot maintain a separation between the oppressors' tactics and his or her own internal thoughts. When characters lose their sense of place they also lose their sense of self, resulting in self-hatred, disappearance, or vengeance, all of which weaken both individuals and the communities in which they reside.

Orientation

In the beginning of the novel, the mother is clearly oriented in her world. Although Pearl Harbor had occurred months before the novel starts, she and her children still live in their home, enabling them to maintain a sense of stability. She is grounded in space and time and has positive interactions with her neighbors while being able to incorporate Western and Eastern ideologies into her everyday life. Once the government begins to move them, this grounding is lost. This enforced movement demonstrates the power of the United States over the places people occupy, a fact that bears out Foucault's statement, "Space is fundamental in any form of communal life, space is fundamental in any exercise of power" (1984, 252). In this case, for people of Japanese descent, the government "shattered their sense of community and replaced it with another one, a somewhat prisonlike existence where they lived under Caucasian domination" (Taylor 1993, xviii). In this new space the military ruled and the inhabitants needed to submit to the authority of the government; the path of the journey itself further accentuates their disempowered position.

After the mother and children begin their physical journey, the details of the father's journey, already under way, are more fully articulated. Unlike the rest of his family, the father is arrested and tried, although the details of his treatment remain vague. What is explained is that the father has already made several moves, including four states, since his arrest on December 7, 1941. The father's zigzagging forced migration functions to keep him unsettled and his family uncertain about his whereabouts. Taken in the middle of the night while he was still wearing his pajamas and slippers, he is not given the time to put on his shoes or his hat before they push him into the back of a police car (Otsuka 2002b, 83). (Seven hundred Japanese resident aliens were arrested the day of Pearl Harbor [Levine 1995, 231].) The government, functioning as one of Althusser's repressive state apparatuses, was rounding up the perceived heads of the Japanese American community who, officials publicly stated, they believed would lead acts of sabotage and espionage (even though the Munson Report, written just prior to Pearl Harbor, showed "there is no Japanese 'problem' on the Coast"), but they were also rounding up the heads of Japanese American families.[9] By removing these patriarchs, the government quickly forced its own patriarchy onto fatherless/husbandless families.[10] The government appeared to believe that without the fathers, these families would be more easily maneuvered—a reversal of earlier immigration policies that kept wives from their husbands as a means to bring in workers from abroad while controlling the population of immigrants. Supposedly, without the "Japanese" fathers, these families would renounce what the United States viewed as the truly threatening father figure—the emperor. The United States wanted people to turn away from Hirohito and metonymically from Japan.[11]

The camp instead becomes the-father-that-sees-all from the watch towers, Foucault's panopticon, with the family almost fully replaced by the military culture, in which people sleep in "barracks" and go to the bathroom in "latrines." Otsuka's characters live in a military space as the enemy within. The armed guards on the towers stare at them with binoculars and searchlights just as they surveilled the enemy during their recent "tour of the Pacific" (Otsuka 2002b, 52). The U.S. patriarchy can attack those living under its gaze, but for the interned it stands as the only acceptable father figure. The separation of the father from his family and his constant movement isolate him and make it more difficult for his family to clearly identify him. By making the physical body impossible to locate in a specific place, the cultural body is undermined. Under the policies of the government, space and movement become weapons against identity.

Dislocation and Disorientation

The mother and the two children, like the father, feel fully displaced because they are moved more than once. In the novel, we learn (the information, given out of linear order, adds to the disorientation) that they are first taken by bus to the Tanforan racetrack near San Francisco, where they are housed in horse stalls and treated like animals. From there they are moved by train to Utah, with the final leg of the journey by bus to the Topaz Relocation Center. None of these characters is merely relocated. Each is taken on a convoluted ride that promotes confusion through indirect paths and different means of transportation. This constant movement is part of the disorientation process. They can never be completely certain where they are going or when they will be moved next.

While the train to Utah has windows that allow the family members to see the country they are traversing, each time they pass a town the soldiers who "guard" them tell them to pull down their shades. This separation between the external and internal space is supposed to protect them because so many people see them as enemies. On two separate occasions, however, a stone and then a brick are thrown through the window regardless of whether the shades are up or down (Otsuka 2002b, 29, 43). These physical attacks highlight that the threat comes not just from the government (here represented by the soldiers who, although they carry weapons, appear kind) but from the county at large—it is this that allows the government to take such actions against an entire group of people in the first place. The danger is from both inside and outside the train.

Looking at one attack, this moment is the first time in the text when a character is fully disoriented. The girl wakes up to the crashing glass:

> She was sweating and her throat was dry and sore and she wanted a glass of cold milk but *she could not remember where she was.* At first she thought she was in her yellow bedroom in the white stucco house in Berkeley but she could not see the shadow of the elm tree on the yellow wall or even the yellow wall itself so she knew she was not there, she was back in the stalls at Tanforan. But at Tanforan there were gnats and fleas and the awful smell of the horses and the sound of the neighbors on either side fighting until late in the night. At Tanforan the partitions between the stalls did not reach all the way up to the ceiling and it was impossible to sleep. The girl had slept. Just now she had slept. She had slept and dreamed about her father again so she knew she was not at Tanforan, either. (Otsuka 2002b, 43–44; emphasis mine)

The attack causes her not to know where she is, a type of confusion that has been historically noted at the camps: "[W]henever the community was racked by a disturbing event the younger children became disoriented" (Taylor 1993, 126). In the girl's case, she wakes to being threatened, which makes no sense to her; therefore, her surroundings make no sense either. She works logically through her environment to try to ascertain her location using sight, sound, and smell. Her continued inability to uncover her current location turns her to the past and a positive memory of her father. She recedes from the current place and time because of its hostility and instead returns to a better place and time—one where her father was more dominant than the attacking community. Her disorientation on the way to the camp is only an early signal that these characters are being individually altered by their physical movement.

Once at Topaz, all of the major characters experience disorientation. This confusion is brought on by the destabilizing movement that makes them unable to resituate themselves and by the clear inhospitableness of the environment. As though their first stop at the racetrack was not bad enough, the concentration camp where these characters have been brought differs vastly from their West Coast home, which had moderate temperatures, easy access to the ocean, and an urban community. Space in this novel is not romanticized, as scholars Fu-Jen Chen and Su-Lin Yu state, which often occurs in literature depicting the Southwest as "something sublime, spiritual, or therapeutic" (2005, 553). Underlining this removal of the romantic, the boy comments on how his previous knowledge of the desert does not match the reality he experiences: "It was not like any desert he had read about in books. There were no palm trees here, no oases, no caravans of camels slowly winding across the dunes. There was only the wind and the dust and the hot burning sand" (Otsuka 2002b, 53). The family members find themselves in a barren desert that not only lacks the basic elements of their former lives but physically affects them as well. The glare off the sand is so bright it leaves them unable to see (48), and the dust storms take their breath away, leaving them no means to avoid the environment. The way that the dust permeates their space shows that while they are being contained, their space is still being invaded, leaving them no sense of privacy:

> The dust got into your shoes. Your hair. Your pants. Your mouth. Your bed. Your dreams.
>
> It seeped under doors and around the edges of windows and through the cracks in the walls.

The dust is invasive, but also violent. It "made your skin burn. It made your nose bleed. It made your eyes sting. It took your voice away" (64). The harsh environment parallels the harsh treatment of these interned people. Historically, people recalled: "The dust storms were the worst. Everyone would become white" (Levine 1995, 50). Ironically, the alkaline ground speaks to the underlying desires of those who put them in the camp. Either they would be attacked and destroyed or they would become "white" through assimilation.

The bleak desert climate surrounds them, yet the space accessible to them is even more strictly confined, from the small size of their rooms to the borders of the camp—the barbed-wire fences: "The rules about the fence were simple: You could not go over it, you could not go under it, you could not go around it, you could not go through it" (Otsuka 2002b, 61). These rules show how clearly imprisoned the characters are by the boundaries of their physical world and the rules imposed on them. Even the few times they are allowed outside the camp they are reminded again of their place: "They said they'd been shot at. Spat on. Refused entrance to the local diner. The movie theater. The dry goods store. They said the signs in the windows were the same wherever they went: no japs allowed. Life was easier, they said, on this side of the fence" (66–67). They are being trained to stay within their confines through both physical and psychological means; they are being taught to know their place.

Turning Away from the East

The family members are not just disoriented in their sense of their specific location and time, they are disoriented in the sense of being turned from the East. They quickly learn that they are threatened because of their physiognomy and their cultural connections to Asia. The day after the father is taken, the mother "lit a bonfire in the yard and burned all of the letters from Kagoshima. She burned the family photographs and the three silk kimonos she had brought over with her nineteen years ago from Japan. She burned the records of Japanese opera. She ripped up the flag of the red rising sun. She smashed the tea set and the Imari dishes and the framed portrait of the boy's uncle, who had once been a general in the Emperor's army. She smashed the abacus and tossed it into the flames. 'From now on,' she said, 'we're counting on our fingers'" (Otsuka 2002b, 75). The mother's immediate response to the attack on her family is to destroy the material objects that connect her family to Japan. This destruction of Eastern material objects was a response noted several times in the historical record.[12] She then goes on to alter the food she makes for the children, giving them peanut butter and jelly sandwiches instead of rice balls in order to show that the children are "American," which is ironic since of course they are U.S. citizens.

At the camp, the boy adheres to the new rules while also resisting them. Although his mother tells him, "[N]ever say the Emperor's name out loud" (Otsuka 2002b, 52), sometimes as he passes the guard tower he whispers "Hirohito" over and over again. This moment of resistance is a small act of defiance that shows a shift in the boy's self-worth but not a total erasure of it. His action supports Foucault's claim: "There are a certain number of things that one can say with some certainty about a concentration camp to the effect that it is not an instrument of liberation, but one should still take into account—and this is not generally acknowledged—that, aside from torture and execution, which preclude any resistance, no matter how terrifying a given system may be, there always remain the possibilities of resistance, disobedience, and oppositional groupings" (1984, 245). While the boy's small act of resistance demonstrates the attempts of the characters to remain intact, they are also tied to magical thinking which, like dreams, is the withdrawal from logical causation to the symbolic when faced with a situation over which one has no control. Therefore, the boy's belief in the power of repeated phrases illustrates both his attempts to control his environment and his inability to do so.[13] Although the boy resists more often than the girl, much of his resistance is tied to irrational thinking.

The boy also has to deal with the confusion that surrounds him at the camp. He learns to play war, shouting, "*Kill the Japs!*" (Otsuka 2002b, 54), showing his internalization of the Japanese as the enemy that he needs to destroy. Additionally, the clothes given to the internees are U.S. Army surplus from World War I, and when the boy puts on the uniform and looks in the mirror, he "narrow[s] his eyes and [sticks] out his two front teeth," speaking in imitation of stereotypical Japanese pronunciation: "*I predge arregiance to the frag. . . . Solly. So so solly*" (87). This painful reversal of identification shows the complexity of vilifying the enemy and then seeing the enemy as yourself. He both wants to kill the enemy and sees himself as that enemy wearing a bullet-ridden, military peacoat.

The mirror then acts as the place where his internal self and external perceptions collide, spatializing the collapse of the boy's interiority. He looks into the glass and sees an image that resembles that of the Japanese enemy: the dark hair, the brown skin. Once he sees that image he wants to heighten it into a stereotype through his altering of its eyes, teeth, and voice. The problem of course is that the image he mocks is his own. He is no longer shouting to kill the Japanese who are over there somewhere, because in the case of the mirror, the over there is Foucault's classic example of a utopia, a no-where, that merely reflects the physical self here (1986, 24). Therefore, his external perception of the enemy in the mirror collapses into his perception of himself. The spatial distance deceives him into an altered perception of himself in a "broken mirror" that is rooted in external racist perceptions he has heard.

The use of the mirror reveals how the boy sees himself and his body through the eyes of the oppressors that stereotype his body. As Young states, "When the dominant culture defines some groups as different, as the Other, the members of these groups are imprisoned in their bodies. Dominant discourse defines them in terms of bodily characteristics and constructs those bodies as ugly, dirty, defiled, impure, contaminated or sick" (1990, 126). The boy and the girl, who is sometimes the source of information for the boy, recognize certain speech patterns, skin color, narrow eyes, bulging teeth, and dark straight hair as markers of the enemy, and they are trained to see the ugliness in those stereotypical phenotypes and then in themselves. It begins with the repetition of racist statements like "For it was true, they all look alike" (Otsuka 2002b, 49) when the boy sees the men in the camp. Although he sees his father in their bodies, he still separates himself from them. Eventually, though, the children become so repulsed by themselves that they pronounce, "We looked at ourselves in the mirror and did not like what we saw: black hair, yellow skin, slanted eyes. The cruel face of the enemy. . . . [W]e tried to avoid our own reflections whenever we could" (119–20). They have fully incorporated the racism aimed at them.

The Return Home

When the family finally returns home to Berkeley, it returns with a changed sense of self. In the traditional narrative form of internment stories that Chen and Yu analyze, the return home resolves the tale, but for this family that return does not create a sense of positive closure. Instead, the characters realize that their dream that "the world would be ours again" (Otsuka 2002b, 126) cannot exist as they imagined it. Their dreams were delusions. Because of the commutatory practice of disorientation that they have endured, their sense of place, self, and community has been altered, even though the place and the people outwardly appear very much the same as they did before the family's internment. The novel is unwilling to acquiesce to the idea that the return home brings resolution. This homecoming shows only more clearly the racism that this family has endured—the characters are now outside the prison walls but the prison persists.

Even though "[t]he town seemed much the same as before [and] Grove Street was still Grove, and Tyler Street still Tyler" (Otsuka 2002b, 114), the family home is only a shell of its former self. Many people had lived in the house while they were gone, and they had stolen most of the belongings and destroyed everything else. While the family members had dreamed that on their return their "phone would ring off the hook" (126), instead, silence greets them, and they observe that the community is no longer to be trusted because they might have taken some of their property. Distrust leads to such disconnection that even a neighbor who nods to the mother is ignored because who knows the possible intention of a nod? The family members feel isolated from their neighbors because of the physical change to their home, their space.

They have also learned direct lessons from the government prior to their reentry—telling them how they are supposed to relate among themselves, their neighborhood, and their neighbors: "*Keep your head down and don't cause any trouble,* we'd been told, weeks before, in a mess hall lecture on 'How to Behave in the Outside World.' *Speak only English. Do not walk down the street in groups of more than three, or gather in restaurants in groups of more than five. Do not draw attention to yourselves in anyway*" (Otsuka 2002b, 122). The children follow the rules they are taught by the government and their parents. They are told not to be individual and to turn away from being Japanese through their language and associations. Obeying these rules, the children beg for acceptance: "We would join their clubs, after school, if they let us. We would listen to their music. We would dress just like they did. We would change our names to sound more like theirs. And if our mother called out to us on the street by our real names we would turn away and pretend not to know her" (114). Here acceptance becomes directly tied to disavowal. They use the language from the mess hall lectures to negate themselves. Assimilation becomes a direct disorientation. The mother advises her children that this type of assimilation is to their advantage, while she, too, disappears into her new role as a servant, the only job she can find. When she first returns home, she attempts to reacclimate herself by reading newspapers again, but she reads about the symbols of mindless amusement and white acculturation, such as Shirley Temple.[14]

Still, the family members all continue to hope that things will return to normal, but interconnected changes in place, self, and community will not allow that type of homecoming. Two climactic scenes play out this disjunction. The first is the return home of the mother, girl, and boy. They tell the reader, "We were free now, free to go wherever we wanted to go, whenever we pleased. There were no more armed guards, no more searchlights, no more barbed-wire fences" (Otsuka 2002b, 113). Yet although the symbols and realities of imprisonment have been removed, they continue to act as though they are imprisoned. Specifically, they reconfigure the home space into the barracks space because they have become so acclimatized to their prison. The home has become their prison: "Without thinking, we had sought out the room whose dimensions—long and narrow, with two windows on one end and a door at the other—most closely resembled those of the room in the barracks in the desert where we had lived during the war" (111–12). At this point, to borrow Henri Lefebvre's (1991) spatial terms, they "perceive" the space of their home as the "conceived space" of the internment camp. In other words, the abstract purpose of the concentration camp, to confine and sequester, has filtered into the way they experience the space around them. They have incorporated these elements of imprisonment in the spatial practices of their home, replacing guards and barbed wire with figurative barriers around themselves.

This self-vigilance, however, does not imply that outside threats have vanished for this family. Even though they reconfigured the home into a barracks, the community continues to harass them with late-night phone calls and by throwing a whiskey bottle through the window. This physical breaking of the barrier between private and public space forces the mother, boy, and girl to even further sequester themselves because the separation has been broken down, with the dangerous "outside word" able to intrude on their private space. The symbolic boundary of their house has been broken, just as the barrier to their own internal and external perceptions has been besieged.[15]

The house has lost its connection to the symbolic American Dream even though the white picket fence still stands. As Amy Iwasaki Mass states from her position as someone who lived through the camps, "Our ideals about America were . . . shattered. We had believed the American dream of freedom in a democratic nation. We had been socialized to believe that by working hard and being good citizens we, too, could realize the American dream" (1986, 160). With a lost respect for this aspiration, the characters experience how the house loses its positive symbolism and the fence of dreams begins to take on the containing elements of prison walls.

The walls and fences keep them in and yet are penetrable to attack. With this knowledge, after the whiskey-bottle attack, the family moves upstairs to a room that does not have windows that face the street. Then the mother puts rice sacks on the windows "so no one could see in," and at night she turns out all the inside lights "so no one would know we were home" (Otsuka 2002b, 118). The mother reacts by enacting the advice of the soldiers on the train—"shades down." She maintains a separation that the girl first noted on the train: "Now she could not see anyone at all and no one outside the train could see her. There were the people inside the train and the people outside the train and in between them there were the shades" (28). The division between the outside world and this family continues even though the characters have supposedly returned to the "outside world." In addition to this repetition of the oppressor's spatial solution to a racist "problem" invented by the U.S. government, the room to which they retreat had been vandalized before their return home. While we are not told the words that are scrawled on the walls, the text implies that these words are racial slurs because of the family's inability to forget them: "[F]or years we could not get those words out of our heads" (111). The family is trapped inside a space filled with racism. The house literalizes a racism that has now been internalized. The self-negating lesson of the train has been fully learned—the characters need to hide themselves and expect anti-Asian attacks.

These lessons are also learned by the father, who had been separated from his family, building in the historically appropriate gendered separation that occurred for many adults. This separation created additional distinctions between how men and women responded to the end of their incarceration. Unlike the mother, the father cannot get a job anywhere, and he has been physically harmed at the government camp (now walking with a cane and missing all his teeth). His response, then, is not even the temporary reacclimation that the mother makes; instead, his identity continues to disintegrate after his return. Specifically, for the father, the space between dream and reality has become confused; he has become disoriented even in his dreams so that the internal and external spaces of perception cannot be separated even while he is asleep. In his recurring dream,

> [i]t was five minutes past curfew and he was trapped outside, in the world, on the wrong side of the fence. "I've got to get back," he'd wake up shouting.
>
> "You're home now," our mother would remind him. "It's all right. You can stay." (Otsuka 2002b, 137)

His wife, misunderstanding his dream, tries to comfort him with the knowledge that he has returned home, but his internment has upended his personality: he is so fearful of punishment that he desires to return to his imprisonment. For the father, there is no return home; he remains in prison. Even in his thoughts at the end of the novel, we see that he remains trapped, asking his captors, "Now can I go?" (144). He wants to leave the confinement the government created for him, but that prison has long extended beyond the internment fences into the community's space and into the characters' own minds. Nonetheless, the rage he demonstrates in his final soliloquy—"Who am I? You know who I am. Or you think you do" (142)—shows that his submission is not total, although the alterations to his personality are extreme and almost certainly irrevocable.

The family returns to a home that remains the same structure it was four years earlier, but because of the characters' journey, their feeling about that space and therefore how they feel about their community and themselves is fundamentally changed. Although the family does eventually move back into separate sleeping quarters, the damage is done, and although the children might be able to partially recover from their incarceration because of their youth,[16] the parents have slipped into their new invisibility and now self-inflicted imprisonment.

This essay has demonstrated that the four-year journey that finally returns the characters to their initial physical starting point is not a simple circle. And it most certainly does not end with a "final synthesis which denies the damage of the internment or which reconciles the Japanese American subject divided by the 'enemy/not enemy' logic of the state" (Lowe 1996, 50). Agreeing with Lowe's idea of this disjunction for the characters, I have added to it the idea of disorientation and its effects on how they see the space around them, in their community, and within themselves. With this knowledge, we can better understand the continuing ramifications of this displacement. As Mass details, "[T]he psychological impact of the forced evacuation and detention was deep and devastating" because people felt betrayed by their country to the point where it not only affected their trust in their environment but also damaged their own sense of self-worth (1986, 160). This Japanese American journey has not ended on the last page of this book written by the child of an internee. Instead, it is "a continuing project of suspicion and survival" (Lowe 1996, 49) that lasts to this day for many Japanese Americans who underwent this trauma, and, as *When the Emperor Was Divine* shows, for their children as well.

Notes

1. The nomenclature for the camps has been long discussed, and I recognize that there is no unproblematic name for these places. As Roger Daniels states, the government most commonly called the camps "relocation centers" as a palliative but that even Roosevelt himself called them "concentration camps" (2004, 46). Although camps did not become death camps like the German concentration camps, their goal was to concentrate these people in these locations, so I will often use this label. While I also acknowledge the limitations of "internment camp," I will occasionally refer to Japanese Americans' situation as internment since people were imprisoned against their will, although that imprisonment occurred without a legal trial preceding it.

2. This denial of Asian American literature was fought against most famously by the editors of *Aiiieeeee!* (Chin et al. 1974).

3. Instead, Okubo's work, through its use of medium, resists resolution through narrative dissonance. Okubo tells the facts plainly, accompanied by illustrations as in a children's book, yet the content remains very adult.

4. Rea Tajiri, the Sansei director and narrator of *History and Memory: For Akiko and Takashige* (1991) states her own sense of generational displacement in a voice-over: "I was haunted by this feeling that I had growing up that I was haunted by something, that I was haunted by this family full of ghosts. That there was this place they knew about. I had never been there, yet I had a memory for it. . . . I could remember a time of great sadness before I was born . . . we had lived with a lot of pain. I had no idea where these memories came from, yet I knew the place."

5. Otsuka, for instance, was partly trying to expand the one-sided story she discovered in a box of letters her grandfather had written to her grandmother while he was incarcerated (Otsuka 2002a).

6. Sansei author Perry Miyake's *21st Century Manzanar* (2002) tells the story of a dystopian near future where Japanese Americans are again interned (ReVac) when the

United States engages in an "economic war" with Japan. For this next generation both the past and the future remain haunted by the camps.

7. Using the base of "oriental" in *disorientation* is of course loaded since this term has a history of racist usage as a means to dehumanize people from Asia. For a discussion of this topic, see Edward Said's classic *Orientalism* (1978). I call upon this term precisely to point to the racist implications of the actions toward Japanese immigrants and Japanese Americans during internment.

8. This idea of disorientation can be tied to Palumbo-Liu's literary perception about the "model minority discourse" (1999, 397), but here the government and not the literary agent or audience is the one forcing the discourse.

9. Though written in 1941, the government did not publish the report until after the war in 1946. For further analysis of the Munson Report, see Weglyn 1996.

10. Removing the men also furthers stereotypical gendered perceptions of Asians as feminine and submissive since the camps included mostly women, children, and the elderly. Men in the camps were already disempowered because the males who were seen as "powerful" had been arrested and imprisoned separately. David Eng (2001) might even add that this feminization leads to sexualization that marks these men as homosexual. Lisa Lowe ties this gendered perception to the foundational laws of the United States that first granted citizenship only to white males, inextricably connecting gender and race, but "as the state extended citizenship to nonwhite male persons, it formally designated these subjects as 'male,' as well" (1996, 11), leaving Asian immigrants in an alien and feminine position until after World War II. Susan Koshy also points out that at the start of the twentieth century gendering Japan had separated male and female into two pieces with "'the color and poetry that is Japan' . . . associated with the feminine subject and the political and economic power of Japan . . . associated with the masculine subject," the "object of desire and object of threat" (2004, 43).

11. The characters' dreams reflect the government's own preoccupation with the father figure; they are filled with references to the absent father. The boy dreams that his father will return to sit next to him on his cot and put on a pair of regular shoes—therefore regaining his dignity, including his masculinity. The daughter dreams that her father will come and sweep them away on a boat in an amalgamated European space, and the mother dreams of her own father in Japan. Literally they hope for the return of the father, but from the U.S. governmental perspective this desire also contains a threat. That connection among father, country, and power actually plays out in one of the boy's dreams. He dreams he is trying to see a picture of the emperor, whom he labels as a god, but something always goes wrong. These repeated failures blend in his dream with the idea that "he was miles from home, and his father was not there" (Otsuka 2002b, 73). His father and his emperor are unreachable while he is far from his home—in his disempowered position he cannot hold onto these standard patri-

archal figures for himself. It is not just the government that recognizes an established connection between power and patriarchy.

12. For examples see Sone 1953, 155; Levine 1995, 24; and King-Kok Cheung's "Interview with Hisaye Yamamoto" in Yamamoto 1994, 80.

13. Other instances of the boy using magical thinking include when he thinks that if he does not look at a lock of his father's hair, "his father will be all right" (Otsuka 2002b, 79) or that if his mother takes the key off her neck, their house "would fall down, or go up in flames, or simply disappear. The war would last forever. Our mother would cease to be" (108).

14. Shirley Temple as a symbol of a desire to attain whiteness is an often-used allusion, from Toni Morrison's *The Bluest Eye* (1970) to Mitsuke Yamada's poem "American Son" in *Desert Run* where the narrator states, "When I was ten / I rolled my hair in rags for Shirley Temple ringlets / polished my teeth white / for a pepsodent smile / clattered about in slick / tap shoes / so my father / sent me away / to his mother in Japan" (1988, 17).

15. For more on this breaking down of the boundaries of the home, see Kawash 2000.

16. As Jeanne Wakatsuki Houston states about her own experience, "That hollow ache I carried during the early months of internment had shrunk, over the years, to a tiny sliver of suspicion about the very person I was. It had grown so small sometimes I'd forget it was there. Months might pass before something would remind me" (Houston and Houston 1973, 195–96).

References

Chen, Fu-Jen, and Su-Lin Yu. 2005. "Reclaiming the Southwest: A Traumatic Space in the Japanese American Internment Narrative." *Journal of the Southwest* 47 (4): 551–70.

Chin, Frank, et al., eds. 1974. *Aiiieeeee! An Anthology of Asian-American Writers.* Washington, D.C.: Howard University Press.

Chu, Seo-Young. 2008. "Science Fiction and Postmemory Han in Contemporary Korean American Literature." *MELUS* 33 (4): 97–121.

Daniels, Roger. 2004. *Prisoners without Trial: Japanese Americans in World War II.* Rev. ed. New York: Hill & Wang.

Eng, David L. 2001. *Racial Castration: Managing Masculinity in Asian America.* Durham: Duke University Press.

Foucault, Michel. 1984. "Space, Knowledge, and Power." Interview with Paul Rabinow. In *The Foucault Reader,* edited by Paul Rabinow, 239–56. New York: Pantheon.

———. 1986. "Of Other Spaces." Translated by Jay Miskowiec. *Diacritics* 16 (1): 22–27.

——. 1995. *Discipline and Punishment: The Birth of the Prison.* Translated by Alan Sheridan. New York: Random House.

Hirsch, Marianne. 1997. *Family Frames: Photography, Narrative, and Postmemory.* Cambridge: Harvard University Press.

History and Memory: For Akiko and Takashige. 1991. Dir. Rea Tajiri. Women Make Movies.

Houston, Jeanne Wakatsuki, and James D. Houston. 1973. *Farewell to Manzanar: A True Story of Japanese American Experience during and after the World War II Internment.* Boston: Houghton Mifflin.

Kawash, Samira. 2000. "Safe House? Body, Building, and the Question of Security." *Cultural Critique* 45:185–221.

Koshy, Susan. 2004. *Sexual Naturalization: Asian Americans and Miscegenation.* Palo Alto: Stanford University Press.

Lefebvre, Henri. 1991. *The Production of Space.* Translated by Donald Nicholson-Smith. Oxford: Blackwell.

Levine, Ellen. 1995. *A Fence Away from Freedom.* New York: G. P. Putnam's Sons.

Lowe, Lisa. 1996. *Immigrant Acts: On Asian American Cultural Politics.* Durham: Duke University Press.

Mass, Amy Iwasaki. 1986. "Psychological Effects of the Camps on the Japanese Americans." In *Japanese Americans: From Relocation to Redress,* edited by Roger Daniel, Harry H. L. Kitano, and Sandra C. Miller, 159–62. Salt Lake City: University of Utah Press.

Miyake, Perry. 2002. *21st Century Manzanar.* Los Angeles: Really Great Book.

Morrison, Toni. 1970. *The Bluest Eye.* New York: Knopf, 1993.

Munson, Curtis B. 1946. "Report on Japanese on the West Coast of the United States." Joint Committee on the Investigation of the Pearl Harbor Attack. *Hearings,* 79th Congress, 1st sess. Washington, D.C.: Government Printing Office.

Okada, John. 1957. *No-No Boy.* Seattle: University of Washington Press, 1979.

Okubo, Miné. 1946. *Citizen 13600.* Seattle: University of Washington Press. 2001.

Otsuka, Julie. 2002a. "A Conversation with Julie Otsuka." Interview with Kelley Kawano. *Bold Type.* (accessed February 27, 2011). http://www.randomhouse.com/boldtype/0902/otsuka/interview.html

——. 2002b. *When the Emperor Was Divine.* New York: Anchor.

Palumbo-Liu, David. 1999. *Asian/American: Historical Crossings of a Racial Frontier.* Palo Alto: Stanford University Press.

Said, Edward. 1978. *Orientalism.* New York: Pantheon.

Sone, Monica. 1953. *Nisei Daughter.* Boston: Atlantic Little, Brown.

Taylor, Sandra C. 1993. *Jewel of the Desert: Japanese American Internment at Topaz.* Berkeley: University of California Press.

Uchida, Yoshiko. 1982. *Desert Exile: The Uprooting of a Japanese-American Family.* Seattle: University of Washington Press.

U.S. Commission on Wartime Relocation and Internment of Civilians. 1997. *Personal Justice Denied: Report of the Commission on Wartime Relocation and Internment of Civilians.* Seattle: University of Washington Press.

Weglyn, Michi Nishiura. 1996. *Years of Infamy: The Untold Story of America's Concentration Camps.* Seattle: University of Washington Press.

Yamada, Mitsuke. 1988. *Desert Run.* Latham, N.Y.: Kitchen Table/Women of Color.

Yamamoto, Hisaye. 1994. *Seventeen Syllables.* Edited by King-Kok Cheung. New Brunswick: Rutgers University Press.

Young, Iris. 1990. *Justice and the Politics of Difference.* Princeton: Princeton University Press.

IV
RACE *and* IMAGINATION

Moreau avec Cuvier, Kant avec Sade

Saint Domingue, Sara Baartman, and the Technologies of Imperial Desire

Jonathan Glover

Bodies of Knowledge

In his essay "Kant avec Sade," Lacan posits equivalency between two philosophical extremes, noting that Sade's "*Philosophy in the Bedroom* comes eight years after [Kant's] *Critique of Practical Reason*. . . . [T]he one accords with the other. . . . [*Philosophy in the Bedroom*] gives the truth of the *Critique*" (1963, 55); both Kant's categorical imperative and Sade's primary nature demonstrate a formula for the possession of total knowledge. Kant, the ethicist of duty, equals Sade, the theoretician of desire. This pairing has since yielded much speculation, but as Joan Dayan notes, the place where these issues played out on living humans, the French Caribbean, has been left out of the discussion: "The one living model for *The Hundred and Twenty Days of Sodom* [another of Sade's masterworks] was slavery in the French Antilles. . . . [H]e revealed the truth at the heart of the traffic in slaves: not only economic gain, but the tempting and pleasurable reduction of human into thing" (1995, 212). Dayan brings Sade into the colonies but leaves Kant behind. Instead, she brings Descartes, thereby illuminating the Sadistic reality of Enlightenment thinking as manifested in the plantation system. Descartes' mind/body split posits "man" as that-which-thinks. This premise allows chattel slaves to become enlightened man's opposite, pure unthinking objects logically subject to all the tortures and dismemberments catalogued in the literature of Sade. Dayan's intervention reveals the erotic and Sadistic desire to turn "human into thing" that found ample space for expression in the colonies. But what happens if we bring Kant, the formalist of duty, back into the equation?

Beyond the planter class of the colonies, whose desire to brutalize slaves found everyday gratification under the protection of the Code Noir (Dayan 1995, 215), another class firmly associated with the disinterested duty to serve nation, colony, and empire supported colonialism through intellectual/scientific work for the public good. The concept of a disinterested scientific duty separated Enlightenment empiricism from the baser realms of human experience: politics, superstition, manual labor and, most important, sex. But scientific duty and sexual desire, like Kant and Sade, share a possession of knowledge as their ultimate pursuit, an affinity inscribed in certain figures of speech: thirst/lust for knowledge, carnal/intimate knowledge. The convergence of sexual desire and scientific duty manifested saliently in the figures of Moreau de St. Méry, late eighteenth-century Saint Domingue's "rigorous codifier of colonial law" (179), and Georges Cuvier, early nineteenth-century France's pioneer of comparative anatomy. Moreau and Cuvier brought the tools of Enlightenment thought to their respective vocations. Their crowning achievements—Moreau's *Description topographique* (translated as *A Civilization That Perished*), a mammoth ethnohistoriography of Saint Domingue, and Cuvier's dissection of Sara Baartman, the "Hottentot Venus"—create scientific bodies of knowledge through the "reduction of human into thing." *Description topographique* exemplifies a colonial discourse obsessed with containing its own racial-sexual chaos through scientific dichotomization and categorization, while Cuvier's dissection of Sara Baartman elucidates the other end of a scientific conversation between colony and metropole. This "circuitous imperial route" (Stoler 2002, 144) emerges as a polyvalent locus of sexuality, science, and Enlightenment discourse, where Moreau's and Cuvier's labors reveal a mutual investment in colonial fantasies of race and sex. The use of scientific principles legitimates these obsessive sexual and colonial endeavors as part of an Enlightenment-style classificatory enterprise, sanctifying them under the aegis of objectivity. In Moreau and Cuvier, the distinction between duty and desire, between Kant and Sade, dissolves, as a collective, national desire for white supremacy and a personal desire for the sexual ownership of slave bodies are both slaked by the same scientific operations. At the fundamental level of method, Enlightenment philosophy supports rather than refutes a colonial "scientific sadism," wherein humans are reduced to objects that meet the needs of an empirical and sexual pursuit of total knowledge.

Enlightened Sadists

As a member of national and colonial assemblies, Moreau de Saint Méry bridged the worlds of colonial Saint Domingue and metropolitan France. On July 29, 1789, fourteen days after the storming of the Bastille, he addressed the

Assembly of the Electors of Paris, describing the Revolution as a teleological journey out of bondage and darkness and into glory and liberty, a progression that secures the "rights of mankind" (1790, 3–4). Moreau commits a masterful maneuver of elision when he declares, "The abominable and inhuman engine of unrelenting despotism is destroyed" (4), since for years before his revolutionary activities in France, he had observed some of the harshest conditions in colonial history as a magistrate and statesman in Saint Domingue. In effect, Moreau sees the conditions of monarchical France as oppressive and tyrannical, while seeing something entirely different from his perch of colonial administration in Saint Domingue. What are the conceptual conditions necessary for this mental partitioning of brutalities?

The delineating factor between what Moreau sees as despotic monarchy in France and benevolent plantocracy in Saint Domingue is the concept of just rule. The establishment of just rule hinges on service to the public good. According to Moreau, "*Kings are only respectable as they are useful;* if they reign but for themselves, or sacrifice the public good to their private gratifications, they are to be considered as destructive monsters, and are only fit to be extirpated. A monarch possesses a fictitious, but no natural superiority whatever" (1790, 4–5). Dislodging the "natural superiority," the divine right of kings, Moreau posits legitimate monarchism as a social contract wherein a ruler's exercise of power must benefit public rather than personal "gratifications." Granting moral primacy to public gratification, Moreau creates a political hierarchy of desire: the satisfaction of collective needs, wants, and desires outranks the satisfaction of the individual. Through the political theory of republicanism, Moreau asserts the existence of a collective desire that must be gratified by just governance. The French Revolution becomes a national libidinal investment in the construction of a republic, the veritable overthrow of a government that has obstructed rather than gratified the public's collective desire. Following Moreau's political logic of public over private gratification, French colonial rule in Saint Domingue must obtain legitimacy through its value to the (metropolitan) public good, its collective gratification. The black slave masses in Saint Domingue do not constitute a public but rather serve as the foundation for the material growth of both the French metropolitan public and the colonial Creole public. In Moreau's speech to the assembly, the link between these colonial and metropolitan publics remains submerged (even though his career was nurtured in both settings), as his enthusiastic, exclamatory account of France's unique developmental status elides the fact that the "finest and most fertile country in the world" derives its wealth from colonial labor (8). Moreau makes himself spokesman for a national desire, that of a hyperproductive, hyperdeveloped France. But individual and collective desire cannot be libidinally separated from one another any more than France can be economically separated from Saint Domingue.

In *Description topographique,* Moreau reveals the inextricability of a public desire for colonial cultural and financial wealth and a personal desire for sexual mastery over Saint Domingue's slaves. The jewel of French imperialism, no other colony could produce as much profit for its metropolitan masters as Saint Domingue at its apogee of "development." But the future was cloaked in darkness, as French colonial practice yielded a critical mass of black slaves, many of whom practiced odd rites, such as *Vaudoux,*[1] or fled to maroon communities beyond the purview of the plantocrats. Against the nightmarish impenetrability of the interior, Moreau turned to documentation, a technology of capture and stasis, creating in writing a body of knowledge, a Saint Domingue with no dark spots, nothing hidden from his (in)sights. He attempted to write the most thorough and realistic account of any society in history, but the brutal realities of slavery are absent from his text—his ethnography is really a fantasy. The first nine chapters of *Description topographique* focus on the people of Saint Domingue, articulating the differences between the Europeans, white Creoles, African slaves, Creole slaves, mulattoes, and free people of color inhabiting the colony. This emphasis on character traits eclipses the contradictions inherent in a colonial project predicated on Enlightenment principles and glorifies Creole society as the thriving bedrock of "New World" civilization. Unlike the early New World explorers, Moreau was not a European proper; he was a Martinican Creole, born of European parents. In addition to his participation in continental French affairs, Moreau took great pride in the Creole cultures of Martinique and Saint Domingue, espousing a Creolist cultural nationalism (Garraway 2005, 246). As the foundation of Moreau's ethnographic fantasy, Creole nationalism eclipses not only the brutality of colonialism but also the mounting political tensions in prerevolutionary France and Saint Domingue. While continental and colonial political strife increases, Moreau's gaze lingers elsewhere—on the sexual and racial conundrum of miscegenation. Predicated on a black/white color divide, the slave system hierarchy had created its own problematic, the mixed-race person—the category-breaking figure of the hybrid. Subsequently, an ambivalence marks Moreau's descriptions of Saint Domingue's mixed-race people, as he is forced to justify their worth while still upholding the colonialism-justifying thesis of white racial supremacy. Hence, the mulatto is both a sterile mule and "the one who derives the greatest physical advantages" from "the blendings of the races": long life (1796, 79), "the strongest constitution," and a body "best fitted to the climate of Saint-Domingue" (76).

When Moreau turns to the mixed-race women of Saint Domingue, his ambivalence resides in a different register, one oscillating between insatiable lust and sanctimonious repulsion. A mulattress saunters through Moreau's pages, each movement a sign of seduction. Hips, arms, teeth—Moreau observes all features, declaring her "one of those priestesses of Venus beside whom a Laïs or a Phryné would have seen all her celebrity vanish." Moreau symbolizes the mesmerizing beauty of the mulattresses as a fire of love. This unbridled sensualism of "delicious ecstasies" and "seductive raptures" is "her whole study." Perhaps sensing a betrayal of his own tastes in these lines, Moreau begins tempering his description with negativity. He notes that the mulattress engages in "love-making" so early in life that the "period which separates childhood from puberty . . . is hardly respected," leading to "the inability to reproduce . . . or the coming of offspring who are feeble and weak" (1796, 81). Despite these improprieties, mulattresses are irresistible: "[T]hey have an attribute much more favorable to beauty than the white women . . . knowing full well that their perfume arouses sexual feelings" (88). The mulattress is a goddess of pleasure, a temptress as beautiful as she is dangerous to the man falling for her charms. Moreau salvages the taboo of miscegenation by giving it a colonial use-value: the creation of exquisite and unique beauty in mixed-race women, and the creation of bodies bred for the rigors of plantation work in mixed-race men. Moreau effectively conceals the harshness of slave labor, obscures the impropriety of mixed-race sex, and replaces the turmoil of the color caste system with a harmonious race-labor hierarchy. The demarcations between white and nonwhite must remain clear for the plantation system to continue operating, so Moreau chastises both those who "yield blindly to prejudice" against mulattoes and those "who want them to be considered superior to whites" (89). However, the mulatto, comprised in the *Description*'s racial mathematics of equal parts black and white blood, does not satiate Moreau's descriptive impulse. From the quadroon, *métif,* and *mameluke* to the *sacatra, griffe,* and *marabou,* Moreau continues—in expansive mathematical charts—classifying every mixed-race phantom imaginable, finally arriving at the terminal fraction of "one five-hundred-and-twelfth part of negro blood" (76–77). When we speak of the Enlightenment, we speak of a project whose goal is the obliteration of ambiguity; hence, Moreau turns to the tools of the Enlightenment—taxonomy, mathematics, categorization—to contain and define the racial "misalliances" produced by colonial sexuality.

The subsequent colonial fixation on racial categorization produced a number of eighteenth-century writings like Moreau's *Description topographique.* "At its origin," Garraway argues, "Moreau's classificatory system presupposes a fantasy: that of a white male coupling with a black female, whose offspring begins a chain of successive couplings, always with the same white male factor crossing with the mixed-race female product of his prior union, to the *n*th degree" (2005, 262), displaying a pornographic interest in contemplating and analyzing all conceivable products of interracial sex. Moreau takes these sexual combinations to the "*n*th degree," harkening to Deleuze's analysis of Sadism as a "demonstrat[ion] that reasoning itself is a form of violence" (1967, 18), a "mechanistic approach" of "endless repetitions" (20). Logic as a form of violence—this is what Lacan uncovers in joining Kant to Sade, the perverse underside of Enlightenment thinking: Kant's categorical imperative and Sade's primary nature both demonstrate a formula for acquiring total knowledge. Where Kant delivers a sermon in moral absolutism, a mechanism for cataloguing human action in a hierarchy of transcendent morality, Sade delivers a sermon in immoral absolutism, where all possible perversions are catalogued to affirm knowledge of all probability. What the Enlightenment can never admit, however, is that, in Lacanian terms, "the real" is the impossible because it resists symbolic/linguistic ordering, rejecting status/stasis as an object of knowledge. Colonial contact disrupts the symbolic culturo-linguistic order of the colonizer, but this reality/trauma is disavowed, displaced by technologies of fantasy: confronted with the hybrid other, the mixed-race person who upsets the binary categories of the plantocracy, Moreau traces all possible spermatic permutations, thereby capturing/knowing the miscegenational temptresses who haunt the periphery of his rational/rationalized civilization.

In "Kant and Sade: The Ideal Couple," Slavoj Žižek returns to this uncanny intellectual pairing and rebukes the typical misreading of Lacan's essay, that sadism is the hidden truth of Kantian ethics: "[I]t is not Kant who was a closet sadist, it is Sade who is a closet Kantian. . . . Lacan's interest . . . resides in the paradoxical reversal by means of which desire itself . . . can no longer be grounded in any 'pathological' interests or motivations and thus meets the criteria of the Kantian ethical act, so that 'following one's desire' overlaps with 'doing one's duty'" (1998, 12). The pairing of Kant and Sade, then, challenges the antagonism of desire to duty, positing instead a complementarity. This complementarity is postulated as duty subsuming desire and thereby depathologizing it. Žižek turns in his conclusion to finally dismantle the relationship of Kant and Sade, stating, "[T]he main effort of Lacan's seminar . . . is precisely to break up the vicious cycle of Kant *avec Sade*. How is this possible? Only if—in contrast with Kant—one asserts that the faculty of desiring is not in itself 'pathological'" (25). However, in the case of Moreau and Cuvier, a different relationship appears (regardless of whether we deem desire pathological), wherein duty and desire constitute and saturate one another via the complex nexus of sexuality—duty (whether national, colonial, political, or scientific) does not subsume desire or take its place but rather constructs and is constructed by desire. In Moreau, the circuitous pattern emerges thusly: French colonial desire for the possession and subjection of colonized peoples informs Moreau's desire for sexual ownership of their bodies as well as the bodies of their mixed-race progeny. Conversely, the desire of colonial officials to know and possess the bodies they colonize throughout the French Empire refracts and informs the colonial policies emanating from the metropole. Enlightenment philosophy and science purify this slippery relationship between duty and desire by asserting disinterested methodology and analysis as a sanctified service to the public good. Desire and duty, then, can be seen as two aspects of the same thing, a libidinal investment at individual and national levels in bodies of knowledge, sexual, scientific, and otherwise.

Moreau's chart serves as a scientific and sexual fantasy; knowledge and ownership are the impetus and the objective. But the slave rebellion disrupts Moreau's fantasy beyond all tenability. His book becomes a cheap piece of taxidermy which, though published after the Revolution, makes no mention of that signal event—the abolition of slavery and establishment of a black state—because to do so would flood the enshrined fantasy of Moreau's Saint Domingue with its nightmarish excess, Haiti, a black republic with no room for sexual or governmental white masters. Just as Moreau tries to preserve and own his fantasy of Saint Domingue, France, now under Napoleon Bonaparte's regime, continues to try to reinstate and preserve its colonial ownership of the former colony. The distinctions between personal and public desire, fantasy and duty, dissipate, as individual men (Moreau, Napoleon) and the collectivity of an empire fantasize about the former colony that spurned their advances with the unequivocal violence of revolution. But there are other colonies to lust after, other fantasies to indulge, and Georges Cuvier will use his comparative anatomy to grant scientific realism to the ur-fantasy of racial inequality as the French Empire turns its gaze to Egypt, using science to recast world history and achievement in the guise of whiteness.

Materiality of the Scalpel

At the dawning of the French Revolution, Moreau supplied weaponry to the Parisian militias and empowering oratory to the assembly, while Cuvier, much younger than Moreau, sought refuge from the chaos in the countryside. This fact has yielded a critical tendency to read Cuvier as a royalist, or as simply fearful of the Revolution, but as Martin Rudwick notes, Cuvier's views were more complicated, changing throughout the Revolution's different phases: "The outbreak of the French Revolution in 1789 hardly affected him at first. . . . [H]e was enthusiastic about the fall of the absolutist Old Regime. Later, however, as the Revolution lurched into its most radical phase, Cuvier witnessed scenes of atrocity that reinforced his profound horror of violence and social unrest" (1998, 3). Even Moreau, initially a revolutionary hero, had to retreat for his moderate politics, exiled in Philadelphia, as Robespierre's terror took control of France (Dayan 1995, 154). Here we see the implicit congruity between Moreau's and Cuvier's political thought: the Revolution offered hopes of secure and productive republicanism, but those hopes were eclipsed by a new form of tyranny more horrific, especially for the privileged classes Moreau and Cuvier represented, than the Old Regime itself. With the ascendancy of Napoleon Bonaparte, however, a series of survivals (intellectual and material) was allowed to occur, despite the disruption of the Revolution. Enlightenment science remained largely intact, as its ideals became reconfigured by the new regime and scientific specimens and artifacts were retrieved from "the cabinets of the wealthy who fled the conflict, as well as those from territories that France invaded" (Fausto-Sterling 2002, 71). These cabinets, much like the one Cuvier kept in the national museum, housed flora and fauna specimens from around the world. Their passing into the hands of Napoleon's revitalized museum system is a concrete example of how scientific knowledge is preserved and authorized. While historical records of ownership for the cabinets are scarce, many of them would have undoubtedly come from the estates of French Caribbean Creoles like Moreau, who traveled often between colony and metropole and were forced to flee during the Revolution. In his preface to *Le règne animal* (translated as *The Animal Kingdom*), Cuvier notes comparative anatomy's debt to such specimen collections: "This science has made immense progress, not only from the acquisitions of numerous travelers . . . who have explored every region of the globe, but by the rich collections which various governments have formed and rendered public" (1797, 11). Under the new regime, which supported the sciences with zeal, Cuvier rose to prominence quickly, benefiting from full access to these cabinets filled with the bounties of colonialism.

While Moreau performed his experiments in the laboratory of the mind, inscribing his scientific-sexual fantasies in writing only, Georges Cuvier, celebrated "father of comparative anatomy," operated in the concrete and official setting of the Jardin du Roy, the tools and institutional power of medicine, science, and anthropology at his disposal. Sexual desire and scientific duty: the relationship between these principles developed in grotesque vividness around the genitals of Sara Baartman, as her "Hottentot apron" complicated even as it initiated (as fetish of her sexual otherness) Cuvier's analysis of her body (see Maseko 1998). Analysis, the differentiation, the cutting up of a body into its constituent parts, was the bedrock of Cuvier's compara-

Figure 1. "Caucasian Race." Illustration from Cuvier's *The Animal Kingdom.* (Courtesy of the University of Florida Smathers Library Rare Book Collection.)

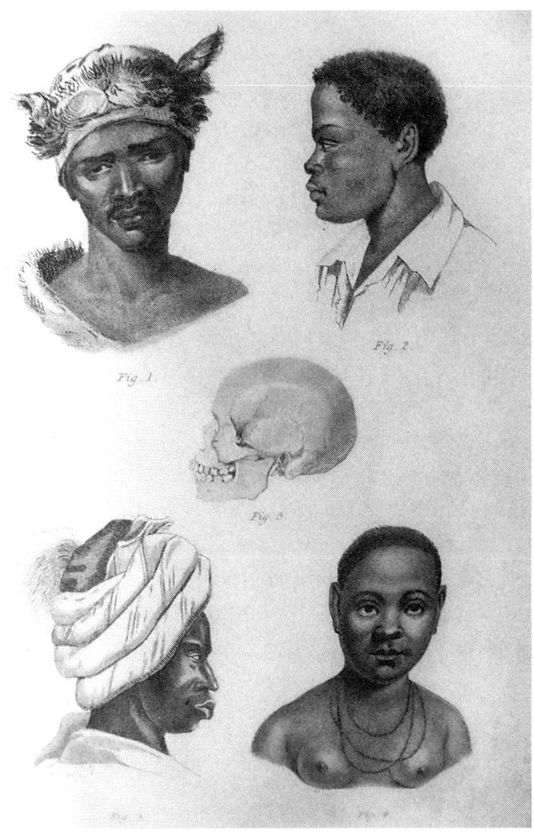

Figure 2. "Negro Race." Illustration from Cuvier's *The Animal Kingdom.* (Courtesy of the University of Florida Smathers Library Rare Book Collection.)

tive anatomy. But the literal dissection of Baartman's body had to wait until her death. With the satisfaction of visceral analysis deferred, Cuvier had first to deal with her live body, yielding his numerous complaints of her supposed shyness, stubbornness, and ignorance. His lust for knowledge was frustrated by layers of concealment: (1) the supposed tucking of Baartman's labia between her thighs; (2) the labial concealment of the vaginal interior. Baartman's body, organized genitally by her captors, existed as a knowledge problem for the medico-scientific gaze, a cover (labia) concealing a darkness (vagina) inhabiting an alterity (the black body). Cuvier was not alone in his scientific desire for Baartman's body. Upon her death, Geoffroy Saint-Hilaire "applied to the authorities on behalf of the Muséum d'histoire naturelle to retain the corpse on the grounds that it was a singular (*singulière*) specimen of humanity and therefore of special scientific interest" (Qureshi 2004, 242). Rather than receiving a proper autopsy, Baartman was dissected to satiate the scientific curiosities of Cuvier and his Muséum colleagues.[2]

In 1817, Cuvier published a report of his dissection entitled "Extrait d'observations faites sur le cadavre d'une femme connue à Paris et à Londres sous le nom de Vénus hottentotte." Much of the report concerns Cuvier's belief that Baartman's anatomy resembles that of monkeys and orangutans. Commenting on her appearance while living, Cuvier characterizes "[h]er movements" as "brusque and capricious," like "those of monkeys." Noting her mouth, Cuvier adds that "[s]he had . . . a way of pouting her lips, in the same manner as we have observed in orang utans" (quoted in Gould 1985, 296). Her buttocks and genitalia, however, assume primary significance. Cuvier reports that, upon dissection, "We could *verify* that the protuberance of her buttocks had nothing muscular about it but arose from a fatty mass of a trembling and elastic consistency situated immediately under her skin" (quoted in Gordon-Chipembere 2006, 77; emphasis mine).

Cuvier's desire to verify the true nature of Baartman's body differs little from the freak show voyeurism that brought large crowds to view her "performances" at carnivals in London and Paris. Even Cuvier himself draws a comparison between the gazes of science and the freak show, reminding his readers that "everyone was able to see her during her eighteen-month stay in our capital, and to verify the enormous protrusion of her buttocks and the brutal appearance of her face" (Gould 1985, 297). This verification serves the general needs of empire by offering a prop of inferior otherness for Europeans to define themselves against.

The Enlightenment establishes science as the most valid form of human knowledge, so radical empiricism demands Baartman's dissection—dissection alone can turn her into a scientific body of knowledge. Without the im-position of the scalpel, Baartman's inferiority remains unsubstantiated, and the one spectacle denied the freak show voyeurs—the Hottentot apron—can be seen only when her dead body reaches the dissection table. Once dissected, Cuvier prepared "the genital organs of this woman . . . in a way so as to allow one to see the nature of the labia" (quoted in Gilman 1985, 88). Upon presentation of her bottled labia to the French Academy, Cuvier declared, "There is nothing more celebrated in natural history than the Hottentot apron" (quoted in Fausto-Sterling 2002, 83). The importance of Baartman's labia resides in its ability to satiate both a collective/national desire—for scientific proof of European superiority—and a personal desire—for ultimate sexual possession of the hypersexualized female body. Science is duty bound to gratify this national, colonialist desire for white supremacy, as it meets the criteria of a *public good,* but the outright sexual desire that remains consonant with this colonial imperative masquerades behind that duty, finding its own gratification nonetheless. Cuvier asserts, "Man is at all times inclined to sexual intercourse, without ever being furiously incited" (1797, 47). Using the universal "Man" of classical rhetoric, Cuvier posits all humans, regardless of race or sex, as sexual, but the supposedly inordinate size of Hottentot genitals allows science to distinguish the civilized sexuality of Europe from the savage sexuality of Africa. As Sander Gilman has shown, the racial and sexual myths of nineteenth-century Europe drew parallels between the genitals and buttocks of prostitutes, lesbians, and black women (1985, 89). Baartman's labia signifies the most perverse and provocative female sexuality, that of primitive black women and their white counterparts, lesbians and prostitutes. Cuvier's obsession is Moreauvian in character, and where Moreau was deprived of living subjects, he created a conceptual menagerie of mixed-race specimens; Cuvier, deprived of a menagerie of living human specimens, made full use of Baartman, his exemplary black body, as soon as she was dead, analyzing her by carving out her genitals and brain. Baartman, reduced to a bottled labia and brain: Is this not the scientific equivalent of the pornographic "passion for the Real" that Žižek identifies in the use of camera-mounted dildos for extreme internal vaginal close-ups in hardcore pornography? (2002, 6). Behind the scientific duty of acquiring total knowledge for the empire lies the misogynist fantasy of a female hypersexuality reduced to a titillating and taboo labial fetish; the Sadean fantasy of reducing persons—in this case, women—into things is satiated by comparative anatomy.

These actions were authorized by and for French science. Just as reference to Moreau's political thought helps illuminate the theoretical underpinnings driving his *Description topographique,* reference to Cuvier's scientific and philosophical theories will help contextualize his dissection of Sara Baartman as a scientific endeavor. During his earlier work as a zoologist, Cuvier developed a method of comparative anatomy based on "types," in which a given specimen is compared against a preexisting type. As Edward Eigen, a historian of biological science, explains, Cuvier's use of types was indebted to the biblical exegetical method of typology: "'Types' was the term for an anticipatory figure, 'anti-type' the thing or event it betokened; for example, Abraham's sacrifice of the Paschal lamb, and the Redemption" (1997, 183). Cuvier developed this method from intense study of Buffon and Linnaeus, "whose books he once copied, committed to memory, and ultimately augmented and amended" (180). While primarily associated with his work in comparative anatomy, the influence of this approach can be seen in other writings of Cuvier's, particularly in a geological-historical piece on Egypt, Phoenicia, and the development of ancient Western civilization. Here, a form of typology more closely related to biblical exegesis than comparative anatomy appears: "The oldest colonists of Egypt or Phoenicia, who came to snatch them from a state of savagery, do not reach back more than four thousand years before the present time. . . . The Phoenicians themselves were in Syria only a short time, when they made colonies in Greece" (quoted in Rudwick 1998, 242).

Cuvier renders Western history a narrative of cyclical colonization, where one imperial power saves a lesser people from "a state of savagery"; in turn, that colonization creates a new empire, a new juggernaut of civilization that will save other peoples from their respective states of cultural underdevelopment. The typological perspective permeates Cuvier's description of the ancient West—colonization of Phoenicia prefigures colonization of Greece—and valorizes French imperialism as the ultimate prophetic fulfillment of a sacred Western history script. In this script, the old testament of the ancient West foretells the new testament of nineteenth-century Europe—what was once one of Conrad's dark places of the Earth goes forth to save the still-dark places of the Earth. In this writing, a convoluted but recognizable continuity between the political, scientific, and sexual desires of Moreau and prerevolutionary France for Haiti and those of Cuvier, Napoleon, and postrevolutionary France for Egypt becomes visible. Sara Baartman, caught in this web of colonial desires, serves as a metonym for black primitiveness, scientifically validated proof that (1) white, not black, civilization created ancient Egypt, thereby eradicating any native claims to the land and artifacts being excavated by Napoleon's scientists; and (2) the revolting slaves of Saint Domingue had no claim to Haiti, since they had no faculties for self-governance, and had thereby stolen it from France, the rightful owner. If typological comparative anatomy turned Baartman's body into a "type," she fulfilled the fabricated prophecies of black inferiority, French imperial expansion, and white cultural supremacy.

Beyond skin color, Cuvier emphasizes climate and skull shape as the determining factors of racial development. Like Moreau, Long (1977), and other eighteenth-century theorists of race, Cuvier posits climates that are too warm—torrid zones—or too cold—glacial zones—as detrimental to human development, while "[m]ild climates . . . are the natural cradle of agriculture and civilization" (1797, 49). The complexity of Cuvier's theories and methodology allowed for this scientific prophecy fulfillment to play out on individual pieces of her body—her labia proving the sexual inferiority of her race, her skull proving intellectual inferiority. In other words, the various parts of her dismembered body could fulfill various prophecies. Cuvier advocated a theory of *convenance,* in which observation of conformant traits could be used to show how "the part engendered the whole" (Eigen 1997, 187). We can see this method at work in Cuvier's 1817 comparison of Baartman's skull with that of an Egyptian mummy (Fausto-Sterling 2002, 74). "I have never seen a human head more similar to that of a monkey's," pronounced Cuvier, finding in Baartman's dissection proof of "that cruel law, which seems to have condemned to an eternal inferiority those races with small and compressed skulls" (Gould 1985, 296). Distinct from the "small and compressed" Negro skull, the Caucasian skull "is distinguished by the beauty of the oval which forms the head." Reducing the human races to their supposedly characteristic skull shapes (see figures 1 and 2), Cuvier asserts that the oval-shaped Caucasian skull "is th[e] one which has given rise to the most civilized nations,—to those which have generally held the rest in subjection" (1797, 49–50). Here, comparative anatomy serves colonialism, as the contrast in Caucasian and Negro skulls justifies the "subjection" of Africans by Europeans. Baartman's dissection, then, *verifies* this mythos. According to the law of convenance, her skull correlates to the rest of her body as well as to the rest of her "people".[3] Cuvier can then extrapolate this "evidence" to support the inferiority of all black Africans, not simply the Bushmen.

Cuvier's dissection of Sara Baartman, then, follows a process similar to Moreau's racial admixture charts—what seem to be distinct events are linked by their service to a duty (a collective national/political desire) as well as a personal desire (the sexual fantasy of the individual). The methodology and philosophy of Enlightenment science underpin both operations, authorizing them as objective contributions to the public good. Disturbingly, the authority of these figures, their racial categories, and traces of their scientific-sexual desires still persist. Just as Cuvier continues to be cited uncritically in scientific and historical journals for his contributions rather than his transgressions, Moreau has continued to appear as an authority on Haiti for over two hundred years. In 1893, nearly one hundred years into Haiti's independence, the Bureau of American Republics cited Moreau as an authority on racial admixture and its resulting mixed-race categories (*Haiti: A Handbook* 1893, 25). And one hundred years after that, the Florida Museum of Natural history cited Moreau as an authority on a myriad of Haitian geological, biological, and historical issues, such as Saint Domingue's precolonial flora and fauna, the now-extinct Amerindian population, the prosperity of Saint Domingue under French rule, and Hispaniola's exotic animal life (see Woods, Sergile, and Ottenwalder 1992, 4, 144, 145, 147, 198, 292). In the absence of a thorough critique of the methodologies that yielded eighteenth- and nineteenth-century theories of human and animal categorization like Moreau's and Cuvier's, a public desire to see those categories realized, authorized, and quantified by the sciences persists.[4] For example, Pippa Skotnes, an artist and professor, noted an unceasing obsession with the genitals of Bushmen in 1996 while researching for an installation at the South African National Gallery. The most popular "ethnic" diorama at the museum was the one devoted to Bushmen. Skotnes narrates the site as a favorite among "teachers and tour guides" alike: "'The male penis,' bellowed one German guide speaking in English to his tourist group, 'is peculiar in that it stands erect at all times when at rest. The women's labia can hang to the knees'" (2002, 255). A desire for total sexual and racial knowledge of the human, rather than disinterest and duty, propels such preoccupations with the bodies of the fabled "Hottentots," just as desire influenced the Enlightenment science of Moreau and Cuvier.

Notes

1. As a prequel to the chapters on the white, black, and mixed-race classes of Saint Domingue, "*Vaudoux*" serves as an unequivocal reminder that the slaves are inferior and thereby subject to the just rule of European domination.

2. Twentieth- and twenty-first-century black women writers such as Suzan-Lori Parks in *Venus* (1997) and Elizabeth Alexander in *The Venus Hottentot: Poems* (2004) have since interrogated this salacious medico-colonial gaze by refiguring Baartman as human rather than animal, that is, as a black woman subjected to animalized status by the pseudo-scientifically validated racism and sexism of nineteenth-century France and Britain.

3. Cuvier defines Bushmen as "beings almost entirely savage who infested certain parts of the Cape colony . . . who built a sort of nest in the tufts of the brush; they originated from a race from the interior of Africa and were equally distinct from the Kaffir and the Hottentot" (Fausto-Sterling 2002, 83).

4. A recent *New York Times* article reveals a more generalized version of this public desire for scientifically proven racial difference. Written after completion of new

DNA research that purportedly proves inequality between racial groups, the articles pits disinterested geneticists, duty bound to apolitically follow their research wherever it takes them, and their politically correct critics, duty bound to preserve and celebrate a multicultural society of racial difference and equality (Harmon 2007). If the racial categories of the colonial Enlightenment were finally dismantled, however, modern scientific debates would revolve around different issues, different avenues of research.

References

Alexander, Elizabeth. 2004. *The Venus Hottentot: Poems.* Minneapolis: Graywolf.

Cuvier, Georges. 1797. *The Animal Kingdom, Arranged after Its Organization; Forming a Natural History of Animals, and an Introduction to Comparative Anatomy by the Late Baron Cuvier.* Translated by Edward Blyth, Robert Mudie, George Johnston, and J. O. Westwood. Illus. Thomas Landseer. London: Orr, 1854.

Dayan, Joan. 1995. *Haiti, History, and the Gods.* Berkeley: University of California Press.

Deleuze, Gilles. 1967. *Coldness and Cruelty.* In *Masochism: Coldness and Cruelty and Venus in Furs.* Translated by Jean McNeil, 9–138. New York: Zone, 1989.

Eigen, Edward A. 1997. "Overcoming First Impressions: Georges Cuvier's Types." *Journal of the History of Biology* 30:179–209.

Fausto-Sterling, Anne. 2002. "Gender, Race, and Nation: The Comparative Anatomy of 'Hottentot' Women in Europe, 1815–17." In *Skin Deep, Spirit Strong: The Black Female Body in American Culture,* edited by Kimberly Wallace-Sanders, 66–95. Ann Arbor: University of Michigan Press.

Garraway, Doris. 2005. *The Libertine Colony: Creolization in the Early French Caribbean.* Durham: Duke University Press.

Gilman, Sander. 1985. *Difference and Pathology: Stereotypes of Sexuality, Race, and Madness.* Ithaca: Cornell University Press.

Gordon-Chipembere, Natasha Maria. 2006. "From Silence to Speech, from Object to Subject: The Body Politic Investigated in the Trajectory between Sara Baartman and Contemporary Circumcised African Women's Writing." PhD diss., University of South Africa.

Gould, Stephen Jay. 1985. *The Flamingo's Smile: Reflections in Natural History.* New York: Norton.

Haiti: A Handbook. 1893. Bulletin mo. 62, September. Washington, D.C.: Bureau of the American Republics

Harmon, Amy. 2007. "In DNA Era, New Worries about Racial Prejudice." *New York Times,* November 11, 2011.

Lacan, Jacques. 1963. "Kant with Sade [Kant avec Sade]." Translated by James B. Swenson Jr. *October* 51 (1989): 55–75.

Long, Edward. 1774. *The History of Jamaica: or, General Survey of the Antient and Modern State of That Island.* Vol. 2. London.

Maseko, Zola. 1998. *The Life and Times of Sara Baartman: "The Hottentot Venus."* Run/Icarus Films.

Moreau de Saint-Méry, Mederic-Louis-Elie. 1790. *The Speech of M. Moreau de St. Merry, Spoken in the Assembly of the Electors of Paris, July 29, 1789.* London: Sold by J. P. Lepards; Symonds; and L. J. Higham.

———. 1796. *A Civilization That Perished: The Last Years of White Colonial Rule in Haiti.* Edited and translated by Ivor D. Spencer. Lanham: University Press of America, 1985.

Parks, Suzan-Lori. 1997. *Venus.* Minneapolis: Consortium.

Qureshi, Sadiah. 2004. "Displaying Sara Baartman, the 'Hottentot Venus.'" *Hist. Sci.* 42:233–57.

Rudwick, Martin J. S. 1998. *George Cuvier, Fossil Bones, and Geological Catastrophes: New Translations and Interpretations of the Primary Texts.* Chicago: University Press of Chicago.

Skotnes, Pippa. 2002. "The Politics of Bushman Representations." In *Images and Empires: Visuality in Colonial and Postcolonial Africa.* Edited by Paul S.Landau and Deborah D. Kaspin, 253–74. Berkeley: University of California Press.

Stoler, Ann Laura. 2002. *Carnal Knowledge and Imperial Power: Race and the Intimate in Colonial Rule.* Berkeley: University of California Press.

Woods, Charles, Florence Sergile, and Jose Alberto Ottenwalder. 1992. *Stewardship Plan for the National Parks and Natural Areas of Haiti.* Gainesville: Florida Museum of Natural History.

Žižek, Slavoj. 1998. "Kant and Sade: The Ideal Couple." *Lacanian Ink* 13:12–25.

———. 2002. *Welcome to the Desert of the Real: Five Essays on September 11 and Related Dates.* New York: Verso.

An Oracular Swan Song?

American Literary Modernism, Modernity, and the Trope of Lynching in Jean Toomer's *Cane*

Yumi Pak

In 1921, Jean Toomer moved from Washington, D.C., to Sparta, Georgia, to serve as the principal at Sparta Agricultural and Industrial School. During this time, Toomer was introduced to "folk-songs and spirituals" that he found "very rich and sad and joyous and beautiful," yet because of the strong objection against them from African Americans who lived in the actual town of Sparta, Toomer lamented that "the spirituals, meeting ridicule, would be certain to die out." The death of the folk songs and spirituals came at the encroachment of "industry and commerce and machines," and it was this lament that Toomer put into *Cane,* published in 1923: "*Cane* was a swan-song. It was a song of an end" (Turner 1980, 123). Upon its publication, *Cane* was hailed as an exemplary American modernist text, one that took formalistically innovative risks while expounding on the themes of alienation, movement, and industrialization. The fragmented narrative form of *Cane* made it seemingly classifiable as modernist, a contortionist text that echoed the literary movement's belief that literature was "as much a rejection of the old as it [was] an advocacy of the new" (Jarab 2003, 3).

It is critical, however, to complicate Toomer's work and its standing as a modernist text, especially in light of his reliance on lynching as both the subject and narrative structure of *Cane.* Lynching has remained conspicuously absent in the discourse surrounding the novel, except when analyzing "Blood-Burning Moon" as a site of a literal lynching.[1] I argue that Toomer represents lynching through both rural and urban spaces; while he symbolizes lynching and terror through descriptions of forests and ropes, he also does so through descriptions of cities and automobiles. Toomer also focuses on lynching itself as a symbol of fragmentation; his aesthetic and formalistic representation of lynching via language and form that is fragmented and torn apart mimics a fragmented and torn-apart black physicality and subjectivity. As the text's trajectory migrates from South to North and back again (a pointed gesture toward the Great Migration, which occurs between 1910 and 1919), Toomer tracks this movement through the trope of lynching to portray fragmented black bodies in Georgia, fragmented black communities in Washington, D.C., and Chicago, and fragmented black psyches in Georgia once again. In reading *Cane* in this manner, I contend that the text disavows its own modernist positioning and, additionally, refuses to endorse America's transition into modernity as a celebratory act.

As such, it is necessary to examine the preliminary definition of what scholars, both contemporaneous as well as contemporary, are defining as "the modern" in American literary modernism. While it is generally agreed that the form of the text is crucial in literary modernism, it is imperative to think of the content as well. Werner Sollors sets forth four prototypes of modernist writers: first are authors who resent the advancement of modernity (through technology and the large-scale urbanization of cities) and express this through traditional verse; second, the authors who appreciate modernity and express this through traditional verse; third are authors who are deeply critical of modernity and express this through modern verse; and last, Sollors argues, are authors who welcome modernity and express this through modern verse (2003, 44). Toomer can be considered a modernist in that he fits into the third category, as an author who is critical of the advancement of modernity and who expresses his disapproval through the structure and content of *Cane*. Yet one must consider *why* Jean Toomer is critical of both the past and the future. Numerous American modernists viewed the past as a pastoral scene destroyed by industry and machinery, a bucolic ideal that had slipped from their collective grasp. However, Toomer refutes this notion; his text speaks as an oracle for an author who perceives communities that are, largely speaking, unable to look back at a past with fondness or nostalgia, due to the history and (to borrow from Saidiya Hartman 1997) afterlife of slavery, or to look forward to a future with optimism, due to a present that is still imbued with racist violence. What sets *Cane* apart from works being written by other modernists at this time is that it portrays urban spaces as possessing technologies that are *actively* contributing both to the metaphorical death of folk culture and the physical dismemberment and death of African Americans and their communities.

Furthermore, Toomer's text stands in opposition to the theft of black dialect and language common in the works of modernists. Michael North argues that "[l]ong before the Harlem Renaissance, Wallace Stevens signed himself 'Sambo' in a letter to his fiancée, and long after it Ezra Pound was still calling

Eliot 'de Possum' and using what he imagined was black dialect in his letters" (1994, 8). This seemingly casual practice of modernist writers hailing each other through recognizably black archetypes "is a traditional American device allowing whites to rebel against English culture and simultaneously use it to solidify their domination at home" (1994, 81). At the same time, African American authors found black dialect a constraint; many of them made the conscientious decision to abstain from it in their texts. Toomer is one notable exception, yet, as I argue, dialect in *Cane* (most significantly in "Kabnis") stands as a signifier of racialized violence perpetrated against black bodies, communities, and psyches and not as a method of rebellion or domination. Toomer's ingenuity is found in his ability to utilize a means of expression that was at once appropriated and denigrated by the majority of modernist and Harlem Renaissance writers, respectively.

This idea of lynching being intimately connected with America's development as a modern nation is further discussed in Jacqueline Goldsby's *A Spectacular Secret: Lynching in American Life and Literature*, wherein she argues that "because African Americans lacked the legal, civic, and moral authority to repel mob assaults on their collective lives—the history of those deaths could be marginalized from our conventional accounts," accounts that document this time period of the early 1900s as overflowing with a longing for either the past or the future or both (2006, 27). Instead, Toomer proposes that the symbols of modernity (and therefore civilization), including trains, electric lights, and houses, are for African Americans *active* symbols of terror, as evidenced in both the first and second sections of *Cane*. While *Cane* can be considered modernist in that it challenges notions of linearity and wholeness in the form of a literary work, it also pushes beyond the definition by archiving the brutality of lynching through the previously mentioned symbols of modernity in a narrative form that is both nonlinear and fragmented. There are several instances of a fragmented narrative voice in *Cane* and its indissoluble connection to the cut-open, dismembered, and violated African American bodies, communities, and psyches that haunt the text, but I will focus on three particular pieces—"Karintha," "Seventh Street," and "Kabnis"—in order to emphasize that in Toomer's vision, the United States exists as a continual perpetuation of, to borrow from both Hortense Spillers (1987) and Hartman (1997), the "vestibularity" of the "encumbered freedperson."[2]

The Rural South: "Karintha"

Toomer begins *Cane* with "Karintha," a piece that opens with praise for the protagonist's beauty: "Her skin is like dusk on the eastern horizon / . . . When the sun goes down."[3] Curiously, Toomer is insistent on Karintha's "carrying beauty, perfect as dusk when the sun goes down" but also "like dusk on the eastern horizon." Karintha is at once equated with the horizon upon which the sun first rises—the promise of freedom and citizenship "granted" in the 1860s—and the dusk of the sun going down—the deferment and absolute gross neglect of the very same promise (1923, 3). Because of her undeniable beauty, Karintha's sexual maturation occurs rapidly. Toomer writes that "Karintha is a woman, and she has had a child. A child fell out of her womb on to a bed of pine-needles in the forest. Pine-needles are smooth and sweet. They are elastic to the feet of rabbits" (4). Although Toomer does not specifically tell his readers if Karintha actively kills her baby or if she simply leaves it to die, it is at this precise and juxtaposing moment of birth and death that Toomer's narrative subject shifts; in contrast to the prior sentences, which took Karintha or the men who lusted after her as their subjects with their pronouns of "she" and "her," Toomer abruptly changes his focus to pine needles and rabbits, disturbing the linearity of narrative, as if to draw the readers' eyes away from the scene of death.[4] Yet Toomer immediately follows with the information that Karintha's child is born near a sawmill; the specificity indicates an importance in the location of this death, and insinuates, perhaps, that the death of Karintha's baby is not to be read as a tranquil one.[5]

In a brief sentence that trails off without conclusion—"Meanwhile the smoke curls up and hangs in odd wraiths about the trees, curls up, and spreads itself out over the valley"—Toomer utilizes the images of both smoke and trees, the former of which "hangs" about the trees and spreads out over the entirety of the valley, indicating a stealthy and pervasive symbol of violence. Toomer's analysis does not stop at the sawmill but continues to include the fire, which takes a year before it completely burns, resulting in the smoke that "hangs in odd wraiths about the trees," reminiscent of the smoke that surrounds a lynched and burned body (Toomer 1923, 4). Through the birth of Karintha's baby, *Cane* renders itself a "modernist text in that its narration is fragmented and indirect; it hides what it is finally talking about and yet makes the hidden its actual topic" (Scruggs and VanDemarr 1988, 29). This logic of revealing through hiding is concurrent with Toomer's discussion of racialized violence through the *trope* of lynching, even when an actual, physical lynching is not occurring.

Toomer subsumes the fact of lynching behind both a modernist writing style and images of what seems like a natural death, but in doing so reveals the very unnaturalness of the haunting death of Karintha's baby. While the baby is not lynched in the traditional sense, its death occurs amid the symbols and tools of lynching; thus, I argue that the specter of lynching haunts this vignette. The baby's death occurs near the sawmill, which is arguably the singular symbol of modernity in "Karintha"; as early as the first vignette in *Cane,* Toomer makes the encroachment of modernity known, thereby connecting the violence of the South with the more industrial North. Toomer relies on song to indicate the baby's death at the end of "Karintha":

> Smoke is on the hills. Rise up.
> Smoke is on the hills, O rise
> And take my soul to Jesus,

indicating at this early point in *Cane* that this kind of violence is inarguably racialized (1923, 4). The actual death of the baby ("And take my soul to Jesus") can be expressed only through folk song, a cultural formation, along with black dialect, which is too often appropriated by white writers, who eagerly anticipate the future, to signify a past that is "rural, repressive, stratified, and static," whereas for Toomer it signifies a past that is, in direct contrast, constantly present and unable to remain dead (North 1994, 97).

The Urban North: "Seventh Street"

The second section of *Cane* takes place in Washington, D.C., with the exception of one piece set in Chicago. The symbols of racialized violence and lynching, which steadily become more and more urbane in the first section of Toomer's text, culminate in the death of Tom Burwell in a factory town surrounded by a mob, and are here almost entirely industrialized. These changes are attributed to the technological advent of modernity, wherein "[c]rowded living conditions, regimented time, limited access to land, and more fluid family relationships resulted in new forms of cultural expressions," including, presumably, the creation of a new type of literature (Sanders 2005, 139). At the same time, however, any resemblance to wholeness as a community is fractured in the urban North, and Toomer expounds on the idea of communal breaking apart through the trope of lynching.

"Seventh Street," the vignette that opens the second section of *Cane,* does not focus on a particular individual woman, as do the vignettes that come prior to this section. Rather, this piece is almost an anthropomorphic description of Seventh Street, written in a form that mimics the fragmented narrative of a jazz piece, a genre of music that numerous scholars have addressed as both an indicator and a contributor to American modernism.[6] The focus here is on possessions and materialism, and in sum, there are no people, in contrast to an overflowing South. As Farah Jasmine Griffin writes, "[I]n the

South, nature is personified, on Seventh Street money is personified" (1995, 65). The piece opens with a brief poem that focuses on speed:

> Money burns the pocket,
> pocket hurts,
> Bootleggers in silken shirts,
> Ballooned, zooming Cadillacs,
> Whizzing, whizzing down the street-car tracks. (Toomer 1923, 41)

What is critical to note is that the subject of the poem continually seems to shift from line to line—the "money" burns pockets, which belongs to the "bootleggers," whose shirts "ballooned" as they went "whizzing down the street-car tracks." This constantly moving subject, along with the tempo of the poem, indicates a kind of frantic jittering down a curved street, a constant movement that is in stark contrast to the surface serenity of the forest that Karintha occupies.

Seventh Street is a "crude-boned, soft-skinned wedge of nigger life breathing its loafer air, jazz songs and love, thrusting unconscious rhythms, black reddish blood into the white and whitewashed wood of Washington" (Toomer 1923, 41). This "soft-skinned wedge" feminizes Seventh Street by alluding to the soft-skinned women in the first section of *Cane:* Fern's face is of "soft cream," Karintha's is of "dusk," and Esther's is "chalk-white" (16, 3, 22). This delicate element is quickly jarred by the intrusion of "black reddish blood." This blood can be read in two ways: first, as blood that is dark red, which is a more general reading, or second (and more likely), as reddish blood that is coming from black bodies, indicating that it is African Americans who provide the supply for this endless river of blood. The insertion of soft-skinned black bodies carrying reddish blood into Seventh Street, and specifically into the "white and whitewashed wood of Washington," serves as a reminder of both the Great Migration that occurs into the northern United States and the constant threat of lynching. African American communities have largely moved into the "whitewashed" northern United States, and they come not as a unified whole but as an ebb and flow of blood, suggesting that it is either their metaphorical corpses or their literal distancing from each other that litters Seventh Street. Whereas the individuals in the South are broken apart due to physical violence, African Americans in the North are separated from each other. The focus is less on the literal violence perpetrated and more on the communal violence instigated and exemplified through economic deprivation and racism, yet always through the language of lynching.

This "black reddish blood" moves down Seventh Street; it causes a "frenzy of dizziness" and "[w]hite and whitewash," or Washington, D.C., to disappear, liquidating and flowing into "shanties, brick office buildings, theaters, drug stores, restaurants, and cabarets" and "[e]ddying on the corners" (Toomer 1923, 41). On Seventh Street, the rising river of blood traces the path the Cadillacs have taken and swallows up the entire city, and one cannot help but note the significance that it is the nation's capital, which is to be the zenith of racial equality, that is being consumed. In a later section entitled "Box Seat," Toomer moves his audience into the Lincoln Theater, another significant move into a space that evokes liberatory politics, but which, for Toomer's characters, quickly dissolves into a place of memory and terror. For African Americans, then, both the private and public are bloodied, and this blood is invasive and knows no geographic boundaries.

In an eerie reminder of "Karintha," Toomer returns to the imagery of smoke. The earlier smoke is caused by a fire in the sawmill, whereas here the smoke is most likely the exhaust given off by automobiles. Here, too, the smoke is blood red and curls up into "where the buzzards fly in heaven," a mockery of the dream of what the North is supposed to represent. There is racialized violence and carnage in Washington, D.C., so much so that "God would not dare to suck black red blood," but would instead "duck his head in shame and call for the Judgment Day" (Toomer 1923, 41). The smoke that was to "take my soul to Jesus" in "Karintha" finally reaches God in "Seventh Street," yet there is no solace to be found here. Rather, it causes God to turn away in shame, and there is, Toomer argues, no end in sight to the river of blood. The violence that was indelibly connected to the forest and trees in the South is here represented by automobiles and well-paved streets, as Toomer analyzes modernity as a literal and metaphorical vehicle of terror and fracturing for African American communities.

The Impossible Return: "Kabnis"

The third and final section of *Cane* features a return of sorts: although Kabnis is not a migrant who had left the South prior to his entry into the narrative, he is an African American who comes to Sparta to discover his history, following the "blood-lines" that Dan Moore recognized as always being present in "Box Seat." In *Unclaimed Experience: Trauma, Narrative, and History,* Cathy Caruth argues that the history of trauma is precisely a history of a return, not in a "simple violent or original event in the individual's past, but rather in the way that its very unassimilated nature—the way it was precisely *not known* in the first instance—returns to haunt the survivor later on" (1996, 4). She writes that this event that is unable to be assimilated haunts the survivor through a "moving a sorrowful voice that cries out, a voice that is paradoxically released *through the wound*" (2). Reading Caruth in connection with Toomer allows us to see "Kabnis" as a history of trauma, wherein the wounds of those lynched and the wounds Kabnis foresees cry out together in a sorrowful voice. In "Kabnis," Toomer speaks to the difficulty of capturing that sorrowful voice; Kabnis, an almost autobiographical figure for Toomer, is speechless due to his inability to comprehend "the story of a wound that cries out, that addresses [him] in the attempt to tell [him] of a reality or truth that is not otherwise available" (Caruth 1996, 4). In other words, Kabnis is unable to understand the psychic wounds of history that manifest themselves through the physical lacerations and mutilations present in the lynched bodies.

What Kabnis is initially unable to understand is that the past remains a constant in the present, and it is this disconnect of the psyche from the current moment that Toomer locates as a site of fragmentation and violence. When Lewis, another African American, points out that Father John, the blind old man in the basement, is the "symbol, flesh, and spirit of the past," Kabnis refuses to acknowledge the connection, arrogantly stating that his "ancestors were Southern blue-bloods." When Lewis reminds him that they were black, he retorts, "Aint much difference between blue an black" (Toomer 1923, 108). Lewis comments that they are different enough to "draw a denial from you. Cant hold them, can you? Master; slave. Soil; and the overarching heavens. Dusk; dawn. They fight and bastardize you . . . tarnished, burned. Split, shredded: easily burned. No use" (108–9). Lewis connects all African Americans through the history of slavery, a history fraught with a violence that "bastardize[s]" and leaves them "tarnished, burned. Split, shredded: easily burned." The brief, one-word adjectives here mimic the pieces into which lynching victims were ripped; the double use of "burned" functions as a pointing back toward the smoke that was present in both "Karintha" and "Seventh Street." We are reminded here too of Hortense Spillers's discussion of the "lacerations, woundings, fissures, tears, scars, openings, ruptures, lesions, rendings, punctures of the flesh" that form the legibility of black flesh (1987, 67). Kabnis, in this moment, desires to forget racial difference as a means of reconciling the present moment with a brutal past, while Lewis is incapable of doing so. If the trope of lynching and the literary use of fragmentation were used in the first section of *Cane* as stand-ins for physical violence, and in the second section for alienation, here they function as a means of acknowledging the past as still thriving in the present moment vis-à-vis the continued existence of racialized violence.

"Kabnis" is perhaps the most formalistically difficult piece in *Cane*, part play and part short story. Readers gain insight into both the characters' inner thoughts and their spoken exchanges with others without a distinction being made between the two. It is also the longest piece in *Cane,* and for scholars like Barbara Foley (1998), it is the second place where lynching is explicitly addressed, the first being "Blood-Burning Moon." As "Kabnis" opens, Kabnis is sitting inside his cabin room, listening to the wind outside. He realizes that the "warm whiteness of his bed, the lamp-light" do not protect him from the "vagrant poets" that are the "winds in Georgia" and their song:

> White-man's land.
> Niggers, sing.
> Burn, bear black children
> Till poor rivers bring
> Rest, and sweet glory
> In Camp Ground. (Toomer 1923, 83)

The wind's song encapsulates the history of violence that Toomer has been expressing thus far in *Cane:* in a "white-man's land" African Americans are expected to "burn" and produce progeny to maintain this burning. Although the "rivers" are promising to bring "rest," this promised rest from the burning is only through inevitable death.

Toomer here acknowledges the difficulty in writing this history of trauma. Kabnis begins by stating the impossibility he feels in narrating this history: "If I could feel that I came to the South to face it . . . How my lips would sing for it, my songs being the lips of its soul" (Toomer 1923, 83–84). Kabnis's desire is to remember, recollect, and recount the history of the South; it is as though in this moment he, too, seeks to find the decaying idyllic pastoral that has driven a large element of literary modernism. Yet as his stay progresses, he realizes that there is no song in this history, but rather that the "form thats burned int my soul is some twisted awful thing that crept in from a dream, a godam nightmare, an wont stay unless I feed it. An it lives on words. Not beautiful words. God almighty no. Misshapen, split-gut, tortured, twisted words" (111). Toomer, through Kabnis, states that the history of blackness in the United States is one of fragmentation, of being "tortured" and "twisted" beyond recognition. The voice that cries is not only sorrowful but also broken, and the history that Toomer relates in "Kabnis" is not only present but "tortured" and "twisted." This history is a "twisted awful thing . . . a godam nightmare," a document that is always already both civilized and barbaric.[7] In the first section of *Cane,* it was the body that was "twisted," and in the second, the community; here, in the return to the South, Toomer labels history itself as being twisted, as it is something that refuses to stay dormant in Kabnis's mind and the United States itself.

This history is present in Toomer's account of Mame Lamkins's death. He writes that the night is the "soft belly of a pregnant Negress . . . Night throbs a womb-song to the South. Cane- and cotton-fields, pine forests, cypress swamps, sawmills, and factories are fecund at her touch," using the figure of the pregnant African American woman to symbolize the southern night. While the language suggests tranquility, the things that are made fertile by this night are all sites of terror that Toomer has previously addressed. The forests, the sawmills, and the factories are places where births and deaths have occurred; thus Toomer theorizes, again, that in this state of exception (to borrow from Giorgio Agamben), the African American is the figure of living death from the moment of birth.[8] This point is made explicit as Layman, at Fred Halsey's urging, recounts the murder of Mame Lamkin: "She was in th family-way . . . They killed her in th street, an some white man seein th risin in her stomach as she lay there soppy in her blood like any cow, took an ripped her belly open, and th kid fell out. It was living; but a nigger baby aint supposed t live. So he jabbed his knife in it an stuck it t a tree. And then they all went away (1923, 92)."[9] It is not that this baby dies as it is born, but rather that the sole purpose of its existence is to be killed. The baby "fell out" in much the same way Karintha's baby does, yet while Karintha's dies on a bed of pine needles, Mame Lamkin's is "ripped" out of her "belly" and pinned to a tree, indicating violence that is actively committed as opposed to passively occurring. The dual use of "belly"—first to describe the night and second to describe Mame Lamkins—points to the idea that these crimes are taking place against bodies hidden from view by their own darkness, and the darkness of night.

Specifically, even after the migration north and the return, lynching remains a reality; even as the years pass, racialized violence does not ebb. In much the same way that Kabnis feels the "split-gut" words stir within him, Mame Lamkins's baby is actually "split-gut," pinned to a tree. Mame Lamkins, too, is "split-gut," literally undergoing a vicious mockery of a Caesarean section. For Kabnis, Mame Lamkins becomes the wound that holds the sorrowful voice, and where he sees the "*crisis of death* and the correlative *crisis of life*" occurring. As such, Kabnis exists in the present moment, caught "between the story of the unbearable nature of an event and the story of the unbearable nature of its survival" (Caruth 1996, 7).

After hearing this horrific tale, Kabnis retreats even further into his immobilization; he is unable to function in his capacity as a teacher and echoes Layman's words as he thinks of his history: "I wish t God some lynchin white man ud stick is knife through it an pin it to a tree. And pin it to a tree. You hear me?" (Toomer 1923, 111). Toomer's use of black dialect here is vital; he refuses to utilize it as a means of "self-fashioning" or a representation of an exotic, ethnic literature, but as a way of presenting a history that seems to be drifting from sight. Kabnis's language has considerably lapsed into the vernacular, and the folk song itself has become embedded in the language of explicit violence, as noticeable in the rhyme scheme and the repeated "chorus" (tree/tree/me). Citing Robert Stepto, Griffin writes that the call and response is "fundamentally an act of closure performed upon a formal unit that already possesses substantial coherence. There can be no one response, no one and final closure" (1995, 147). Yet here Toomer seems to be arguing that there can only *be* one response: an acknowledgment of the past/present that makes it impossible to move into an untainted future. Kabnis' refusal—or perhaps his inability—to do so indicates that he himself is "split-gut." Borrowing from Charles Scruggs, Nathan Grant writes that Toomer is all too keenly aware of the fact that "'the demonic forces that had shaped America's past might also determine its future'" (2004, 62). In Kabnis, Toomer crafts the modern man who flees the North seeking benediction in the South and fails to find it.

The conclusion of *Cane* takes place in Halsey's basement, where Kabnis cannot help but be fixated by Father John; this is the "down" that Dan is trapped inside of in "Box Seat," the deepest point of the Deep South, a place that exists literally underground.[10] It is the presence of Father John that breaks Kabnis's prior paralysis with his words. Kabnis says viciously: "You sit there like a black hound spiked to an ivory pedestal. An all night long I heard you murmurin that devilish word . . . Mumblin, feedin that ornery thing thats livin on my insides" (Toomer 1923, 114). "Death," the devilish word that haunts Kabnis, is indelibly connected to the past, present, and future as Toomer returns to the trope of lynching: Father John is the "black hound spiked to an ivory pedestal," the stand-in for the black body lynched ("spiked") at the altar of whiteness. Avery Gordon argues that the figure of the ghost is a "social figure, and investigating can lead to that dense site where history and subjectivity make social life." Father John functions precisely as that social figure, and as a manifestation of the trope of lynching that haunts Kabnis. It is this "devilish word" that keeps Kabnis awake at night and draws him, "against [his] will and always a bit magically, into the structure of feeling of a reality [he] come[s] to experience, not as cold knowledge, but as a transformative recognition" (Gordon 1997, 8). It is through his encounter with Father John that Kabnis's brokenness is truly brought to the forefront of the text; it is the apex of Kabnis's "transformative recognition" of an undead past and his alignment with the living dead.

As Kabnis berates Father John, one cannot help but question whether his comments are addressed to the blind old man or to himself.[11] He rails out against being in the basement, which is "just like th place they used to stow away th worn-out, no-count niggers in th days of slavery. . . that was long ago;

not so long ago" before turning on Father John once more: "Do y know how many feet youre under ground? I'll tell y. Twenty . . . Do y think youre out of slavery? Huh?" (Toomer 1923, 114–15). Kabnis's claustrophobia is twofold: it is attributable both to his being physically in a cramped, clammy basement and to his entrapment in the precise history that he came to investigate. Slavery was "long ago," but immediately, with barely a pause (as indicated by the semicolon), he states that it was "not so long ago." Toomer understands that slavery itself as an institution was disbanded "long ago," but the vestiges echoing through *Cane* through the interconnected tropes of lynching and modernity suggest that it continues. Hence Kabnis returns to the South and finds not an understandable history, but rather, to paraphrase William Faulkner, a past that cannot remain dead, or even past. Kabnis is the one who truly embodies the spirit of *Cane:* he is the one who is "oracular" and "[r]edolent of fermenting syrup," the one who recognizes in the figure of Father John—and himself—the impossibility of laying claim to both the past and the future through the usage of words (Toomer 1923, iii). Kabnis is no longer what Orlando Patterson has termed a "genealogical isolate," but rather finds himself a member of a twisted, tortured family tree (Patterson 1985, 7).

In an interesting authorial strategy, Toomer ends his text, which hinges on the very idea of breaking apart the conventional narrative form, with a structurally formal method by concluding the narrative with "The end." As Kabnis leaves the basement, the omnipresent narrator states that "[o]utside, the sun arises from its cradle in the tree-tops of the forest. Shadows of pines are dreams the sun shakes from its eyes. The sun arises." Casting aside the symbol of dusk, which has pervaded the entirety of *Cane,* Toomer drenches the ending in the early morning sun. He returns to trees, but this time they are "dreams the sun shakes from its eyes," seeming to indicate the dawning of a new day. He continues, "Gold-glowing child, it steps into the sky and sends a birth-song slanting down gray dust streets and sleepy windows of the southern town. The end" (Toomer 1923, 117). It is tempting to imagine this ending as offering closure: the sun, symbolized by a "gold-glowing child," is connected to the two children who die in "Karintha" and "Becky," and instead of a death ending the narrative it is a "birth-song," indicating perhaps that the constant traumatic fragmenting of body, community, and psyche has come to an end.

What complicates this optimistic reading are, however, as mentioned above, the two words "the end" in connection to the figure of Kabnis. I read the ending of "Kabnis" and Toomer's final words not as a means of offering narrative closure but as an indication of Kabnis's ultimate fate and failure. As Kabnis leaves the basement and exits the narrative, the readers are left with the figures of Halsey's sister, Carrie, and Father John. Toomer writes that "[l]ight streaks through the iron-barred cellar window. Within its soft circle, the figures of Carrie and Father John." The sunlight touches Carrie and Father John, but it is broken by the bars on the cellar window. Thus, the light that enfolds them within "its soft circle" is not whole, but rather a circle broken into fragments, much like the crescent shapes that break the three sections of *Cane* apart. With his conclusion, Toomer offers a wholeness that is always already un-whole and mimics his fragmented writing style and subject. It is also critical to note that while Carrie and Father John are bathed in sunlight, finally free of the dusk, Kabnis is not. In his moment of departure, the narrator's gaze shifts from him to Carrie: "And then, seeing Carrie's eyes upon him . . . with eyes downcast and swollen," he "trudges upstairs to the work-shop. Carrie's gaze follows him till he is gone" (1923, 117). In much the same way that Tom's eyes burst in "Blood-Burning Moon," the narrator's eyes shift away from Kabnis; he simply disappears from the narrative as the narrative returns to Carrie's point of view. The omnipresent narrator vanishes, replaced by one whose eyes cannot track Kabnis past his exit from the basement. Thus, we are not given resolution, nor is Kabnis given absolution; he exits, but the narrative continues. Although the text ends in a stylistically structured method, I argue that Toomer's final two words actually refuse to provide closure. History, for Kabnis and for Toomer, is not a straight line, but rather a cyclical formation that is a hole, but not whole.

Conclusion: An Alternative Modernism?

Although Toomer's writing style and structure are very much in line with what we have long considered to be the project of American literary modernism, the material he writes about goes against more established definitions of the genre. Toomer utilizes and focuses on lynching to offer a critique of both the wistful dream of an idyllic past (or history as a pastoral ideal) and the dream of a progressive future (or history as a document of progress). Yet, opposed to considering Toomer and *Cane* as staunchly antimodernist, I briefly turn to Michael North in order to think of American literary modernism as not a singular project, but as American literary modernisms. In Toomer, North sees an author who seeks a "language submerged in slaughter, a language apprehensible only in the deformations of contemporary speech," and as such, sets forth American literary modernism as a project that serves to highlight a racist past, present, and potentially racist future (1994, 162).

Toomer's invocation of *Cane* as "a swan-song" and "a song of an end" is meant to indicate his wistfulness at the death of the folk culture that he experienced during his sojourn in the South (Turner 1980, 123). At the same time, however, it is also "oracular," and thus we can imagine the text as an oracular swan song. *Cane* as a swan song does not necessarily imply an end to the narrative, as exemplified in the figure of Kabnis. Rather, I propose that *Cane* points to the death of African American bodies, communities, and psyches, a marker of the living death under which African Americans lived in the post-Reconstruction era. In this way it is oracular as well: Toomer is unable to quell the possibility of a racist future at the end of "Kabnis," and despite the sunshine that floods the "southern town," it does not dispel the anxiety that prevents a full closure. In "Blood-Burning Moon," a section I did not address here, Tom, an African American man in the South, tells Louisa, the African American woman he loves, that "words is like th spots on dice: no matter how y fumbles em, there's times when they jes wont come. I dunno why. Seems like th love I feels fo you done stole m tongue" (Toomer 1923, 32). Again, it is a more urban character who "steals" the more rural character's tongue. Through Tom, as with Kabnis, Toomer notes the difficulty of writing not only the history of lynching but the concurrent documentation of it as well, as American literary modernism, or this labeling as a modernist, has, in many ways, stolen Toomer's tongue. I argue that Toomer's utilization of the symbols of lynching and the fracturing of the form in *Cane* are his attempts to capture the trauma of the past, present, and future, through torn flesh, through rivers of blood, and always as a rem(a)inder of a "language submerged in slaughter."

Notes

1. W. Fitzhugh Brundage (1993) has estimated that 3,220 African Americans were lynched between 1880 and 1930, compared to 723 white Americans.

2. Hartman (1997) compellingly argues for a reading of the Emancipation Proclamation wherein "freedom" for the slave does not mean an ascent into citizenship but an access into a law that would then be utilized in order to mete out punishment. When read together with Spillers (1987), whose definition of "vestibularity" indicates those who are close to but not completed as citizens within the structures of government, we can see in *Cane* multiple characters who expose the gap between what *should* be and what actually *is*.

3. As another method of fragmenting his text, Toomer included several places in *Cane* where the text itself would pause, as indicated by either two (". .") or three (". . .") period marks in a row. Editor Darwin T. Turner (1980) cautions the reader not to confuse the purpose of these marks, which is to bring the reading to a stop and thereby break apart the unified wholeness presupposed in a published book, with ellipses, which indicate original material either lost or edited out.

4. Compare this moment with Toomer's description of Mame Lamkins's lynching

in "Kabnis," where her death and the violently gruesome death of her baby are explicitly detailed.

5. In "'In the Land of Cotton': Economics and Violence in Jean Toomer's *Cane,*" Barbara Foley argues that while Toomer was very much aware of the "essential dynamics of Jim Crow racism," he was sorely misinformed about the economy of the South (1998, 182). She writes that the sawmill in "Karintha" was in all likelihood a "peckerwood" mill, which consisted of moveable machinery that could be set up relatively quickly near the forest and just as easily dismantled. By having Karintha's baby born near this sawmill, Toomer "has to ignore the actual material relation between man and earth—let alone between man and man," or the reality of the imbalance of power between whites and blacks (183). By making the sawmill an ominously haunted place, a place of imagination, instead of a place of "material relation between . . . man and man," Foley argues, Toomer eradicates the historical specificity of the 1921 cotton depression and the resulting violence in the South.

6. Several authors have written about the jazz form as either connected to modernity or as a language of it. See Rusch 1986; and Borshuk 2006.

7. I borrow this phrasing from Walter Benjamin's "Theses on the Philosophy of History," where he writes that "[t]here is no document of civilization which is not at the same time a document of barbarism" (1968, 256).

8. Or, to reference Orlando Patterson, the African American is the embodiment of social death.

9. Numerous scholars attest to this lynching being based on an actual case documented by Walter White in *Thirty Years of Lynching in the United States, 1889–1918* during his time as executive secretary of the NAACP. In particular, Barbara Foley (1998) looks at this case as proof that lynchings did not occur only as a means of controlling black male sexuality, but also to silence black resistance against white economic control, which complicates the nuanced discussion of lynching in American history.

10. We can think here of both the bowels of the slave ship and the deep underground of Ralph Ellison's *Invisible Man.*

11. While I myself do not do so, Kodat (2000) examines the usefulness of Lacan's mirror stage and this idea of mirroring that occurs at various moments of *Cane.* This exchange between Kabnis and Father John is one she analyzes.

References

Benjamin, Walter. 1968. "Theses on the Philosophy of History." In *Illuminations: Essays and Reflections,* edited by Hannah Arendt and translated by Harry Zohn, 253–64. New York: Harcourt Brace Jovanovich.

Borshuk, Michael. 2006. *Swinging the Vernacular: Jazz and African American Modernist Literature*. New York: Rutledge.

Brundage, W. Fitzhugh. 1993. *Lynching in the New South: Georgia and Virginia, 1880–1930.* Urbana: University of Illinois Press.

Caruth, Cathy. 1996. *Unclaimed Experience: Trauma, Narrative, and History.* Baltimore: Johns Hopkins University Press.

Foley, Barbara. 1998. "'In the Land of Cotton': Economics and Violence in Jean Toomer's *Cane.*" *African American Review* 32 (2): 181–98.

Goldsby, Jacqueline. 2006. *A Spectacular Secret: Lynching in American Life and Literature.* Chicago: University of Chicago Press.

Gordon, Avery. 1997. *Ghostly Matters: Haunting and the Sociological Imagination.* Minneapolis: University of Minnesota Press.

Grant, Nathan. 2004. *Masculinist Impulses: Toomer, Hurston, Black Writing, and Modernity.* Columbia: University of Missouri Press.

Griffin, Farah Jasmine. 1995. *"Who Set You Flowin'?" The African-American Migration Narrative.* New York: Oxford University Press.

Hartman, Saidiya V. 1997. *Scenes of Subjection: Terror, Slavery, and Self-Making in Nineteenth-Century America.* New York: Oxford University Press.

Jarab, Josef. 2003. "Modernity, Modernism, and the American Ethnic Minority Artist." In *Race and the Modern Artist,* edited by Heather Hathaway, Josef Jarab, and Jeffrey Melnick, 3–15. New York: Oxford University Press.

Kodat, Catherine Gunther. 2000. "To 'Flash White Light from Ebony': The Problem of Modernism in Jean Toomer's *Cane.*" *Twentieth Century Literature* 46 (1): 1–19.

North, Michael. 1994. *The Dialect of Modernism: Race, Language, and Twentieth-Century Literature.* New York: Oxford University Press.

Patterson, Orlando. 1985. *Slavery and Social Death.* Cambridge: Harvard University Press.

Rusch, Frederik L. 1986. "Form, Function, and Creative Tension in *Cane:* Jean Toomer and the Need for the Avant-Garde." *MELUS* 13 (Spring): 115–24.

Sanders, Mark A. 2005. "American Modernism and the New Negro Renaissance." In *The Cambridge Companion to American Modernism,* edited by Walter Kalaidjian, 129–56. Cambridge: Cambridge University Press.

Scruggs, Charles, and Lee VanDemarr. 1988. *Jean Toomer and the Terrors of American History.* Philadelphia: University of Pennsylvania Press.

Sollors, Werner. 2003. "Four Types of Writing under Modern Conditions; or, Black Writers and 'Populist Modernism.'" In *Race and the Modern Artist,* edited by Heather Hathaway, Josef Jarab, and Jeffrey Melnick, 42–53. New York: Oxford University Press.

Spillers, Hortense J. 1987. "Mama's Baby, Papa's Maybe: An American Grammar Book." *Diacritics: Culture and Countermemory; The "American" Connection* 17 (2): 64—81.

Toomer, Jean. *Cane.* 1923. New York: Norton, 1988.

Turner, Darwin T., ed. 1980. *The Wayward and the Seeking: A Collection of Writings by Jean Toomer.* Washington, D.C.: Howard University Press.

Cultural Schizophrenia and Postcolonial Identity in Derek Walcott's *Dream on Monkey Mountain* and Bernardine Evaristo's *Lara*

Kathrin Kottemann

I traveled to a distant town
I could not find my mother
I could not find my father
I could not hear the drum

whose ancestor am I?

In these lines from "The New Ships," Edward Kamau Brathwaite highlights issues that plague individuals affected by the African diaspora who strive to create their own postcolonial identities (1973, 125). The narrator of this poem has traveled away from his home to discover this identity, but he feels even more like an outsider. His parentage is not clear, although he knows he belongs in this place. The customs are not familiar, so the drumbeats do not move him. He contemplates his own existence, his own ancestry. He wonders about the past, present, and future. This type of questioning occurs in much of the literature of the African diaspora, and many characters, like Brathwaite's narrator, are left with more questions than answers. However, other characters take that journey, whether physical or mental, and end with a reformed identity. They no longer have to question their heritages or ancestries because all of their questions have been answered. Derek Walcott's *Dream on Monkey Mountain* and Bernardine Evaristo's *Lara* contain two such characters—Makak and Lara, respectively. These two characters experience an "identity crisis" because of their cultural schizophrenia:[1] Makak is a West Indian who must attempt to understand and accept his blackness in the context of a "colonized psyche" (Haney 2005, 82), and Lara is a biracial woman living in London who must accept her own "half-caste" status while being viewed as an outsider by her peers, family, and city. Both characters struggle with either imitating or reacting against the white hegemony; instead, the characters journey to Africa where they realize their status as hybrids who neither valorize nor denigrate whiteness but create an alternative space where they accept their identities and look to the future.

Both *Dream on Monkey Mountain* and *Lara,* while examining two characters from different parts of the African diaspora, have much to say about the search for a unique identity and also help readers to rethink their concepts of the diaspora. Although both main characters show the importance of embracing a newfound selfhood apart from their identifications as colonized individuals, Makak and Lara also demonstrate that this search for identity is neither easy nor outdated. In "An African Diaspora: An Ontological Project," Michael J. C. Echeruo asserts that the main issue concerning those affected by the African diaspora is one of identity. But this identity does not involve embodying disparate identities of black/white or colonized/colonizer; instead, this search for identity results in the unification of these disparate characteristics: "For the problem apparently is the striving to be 'white' *and* 'black' at the same time, to be simultaneously 'European' and 'African.' Phrased in such equal terms, the problem would become utterly insane. . . . The question arises: why should this particular plague be visited on black people? Why is it that creolisation is always an event attachable only to one of the two sources of hybridity? Or, phrased less polemically, why are Africans the ones to be 'inserted' in modernity? Why are we not the makers of modernity?" (1999, 5–6) The issues and frustrations that Echeruo discusses are reminiscent of Adetayo Alabi's (1999) discussion of the revolutionary attitudes of colonized individuals and William Haney's (2005) discussion of hybrid identities as the solution to questions of identity. Alabi asserts that by Makak beheading the white apparition who inspires him to return to Africa and claim his kingship, Walcott demonstrates the necessary revolutionary attitudes that the colonized must embody in order to transcend their prescribed identities as less-than-white. Echeruo's comments espouse the same revolutionary attitudes. He questions why Africans are the ones experiencing cultural schizophrenia when European racial categories represent the other side of the hyphen—why is the burden of identity placed solely on their black counterparts? He states that the question of identity within the diaspora "is not a matter of classification, but of being" (1999, 9). These questions of identity are precisely the "revolutions" that Makak and Lara must wrestle with in order to emerge as self-assured hybrids. They question why and how; they embody blackness while striving for whiteness; they resolve to be both and neither. Makak and

Lara, through their issues with naming, race, and location, insert themselves into the modern landscape and, through their acceptance, evaluation, and understanding of the modern world and their places within it, attempt to remake modernity to suit their own new hybrid identities.

Dream on Monkey Mountain shifts between reality and a dream state where characters die but still rise from the stage, and they can journey across oceans while still in a prison cell. The play begins with Makak, a lonely black man and seller of charcoal who lives alone on Monkey Mountain on a West Indian island, waking up in a prison cell. His guard, Corporal Lestrade, and two other prisoners, Tigre and Souris, taunt Makak because of his old age and ugliness. Makak tells the men of being visited by a white apparition who instructs him to reclaim his kingship in Africa. Makak and Moustique, his well-meaning but devious friend and business partner, set out on a journey to Africa, spreading their message and collecting money from villagers before Makak ends up in jail for disorderly conduct. Makak kills Lestrade and escapes with Tigre and Souris and continues his mental journey to Africa, where Lestrade returns from the dead and becomes his adviser. Makak is now an African king in charge of judging acts of racial oppression that have occurred throughout history. Makak beheads the white apparition who inspired his African journey, and the play's action returns to reality, in which Makak, Tigre, and Souris are still imprisoned. Lestrade, a now more benevolent jailor, releases Makak, and Makak vows to return to Monkey Mountain to become a silent prophet to his fellow West Indians.

Lara is a novel in verse that traces the heritage of a biracial woman—her father, Taiwo, is Nigerian, and her mother, Ellen, is a white Englishwoman—growing up in London in the 1960s and 1970s. The book traces both of these family histories as well as Lara's childhood in a mostly white area of London. The novel outlines Lara's grandfather's enslavement in Brazil to his freedom in Nigeria. Readers also learn of Taiwo's childhood in Lagos, Nigeria, and his decision to leave Africa for England to better his education. While there, he meets and marries Ellen, whose childhood in war-torn London is also depicted. All of these disparate strands are joined within Lara, who reconciles them when she visits Africa and Brazil and experiences a symbolic baptism in the Amazon River. She, like Makak, returns to her original home after a long journey and vows to accept a newfound identity.

Because both Walcott and Evaristo are biracial, the struggles and journeys of Makak and Lara become semiautobiographical. Walcott was born in Castries, St. Lucia, and "as a mulatto he was aware from very early of his double heritage, of black and white ancestors. . . . His was a fairly common West Indian position" (McWatt 1988, 1608). Similar to her title character, Evaristo was born to an English mother and a Nigerian father in London, the fourth of eight children (Proctor 2002, 2). Like their characters, these authors have had to struggle with whiteness and blackness and what it means to be both and neither. Makak and Lara realize their identities through similar struggles, which are more powerful because the authors themselves have also struggled with the same rejections, questions, and introspections. These texts become explorations not only of what W. E. B. Du Bois calls "double consciousness" but also of double races, double cultures, and double lives. Du Bois defines double consciousness as "this sense of always looking at one's self through the eyes of others, of measuring one's soul by the tape of a world that looks on in amused contempt and pity" (1999, 11). Walcott and Evaristo, as people of African heritage, have had to overcome this "twoness" not as African Americans, but as people possessing both races within themselves who try to establish their identities despite cultural bifurcation. Makak struggles in the same way—wanting to possess whiteness, realizing that his true identity is only seen by a white apparition, not knowing his own race or name. Lara mirrors Makak's struggles even though she does "possess" whiteness, but her struggle involves wanting to rid herself of blackness, to be part of the hegemony, to be wholly white. Both authors and both characters struggle with cultural schizophrenia and with acceptance of the white parts of themselves and society.

The struggle with identity in *Dream on Monkey Mountain* is evident in both setting and characterization. In the opening pages, Walcott lists the setting of the play as a West Indian island. This description is both specific and nonspecific; readers do not know which island, but they do know that the play being set on the island is important to the plot. This description also highlights the importance of the theme of identity because of the West Indies' relationship with both Africa and Europe. In "Cultural Reconfigurations in the African Caribbean," Maureen Warner-Lewis asserts that the cultural landscape of the Caribbean contributes to a complex and enigmatic search for identity: "The coexistence in the Caribbean of transplanted Africa and Europe led to the layering and multiplicity of identities . . . compromise and syncretism have been inevitable strategies for personal and group survival. Such transformation and readjustment necessarily involved the fracturing of customs and ritual from their African institutional hierarchies of authority and governance. . . . This has produced variations of practice, interpretation, and emphasis within the West Atlantic diaspora, all in the context of changes over time" (1999, 21–22). The West Indian natives depicted in the play live rootless existences because they are culturally African although they have never seen Africa; they speak French and have French names although they are subjects of the English crown. Because of this cultural schizophrenia, people of color in the West Indies are forced to create their own identities, just as the characters of Makak and Lestrade struggle throughout the play to define themselves. Walcott comments in his essay "What the Twilight Says: An Overture" about the West Indian psyche: "The West Indian mind historically hung-over, exhausted, prefers to take its revenge in nostalgia, to narrow its eyelids in a schizophrenic daydream of an Eden that existed before its exile. . . . The migratory West Indian feels rootless on his own earth, chafing at its beaches" (1970b, 20–21). Walcott demonstrates the powerlessness of colonized individuals, specifically West Indians, who are "slaves, the children of slaves, colonials" (20) and illustrates the importance of his own heritage and the heritages of his characters in their quest for individuality both within and apart from their homeland. The setting of the play allows the writer to experiment with the theme of identity, ascribe implied characteristics to the characters, and show them grappling with and ultimately accepting their forged and hybridized identities.

Makak's and Lara's search for identity begins with an elemental aspect—their names. Both characters' names have meanings that change throughout the texts and signify a change in the characters. Makak is French patois for "monkey," but Walcott uses an African spelling with a French translation (Uhrbach 1986, 579). This usage demonstrates the inner struggle of Makak to accept his African and European roots as a colonized West Indian. Frequently in the play, Makak is referred to as an animal. As Corporal Lestrade "holds court" in the jail with Tigre and Souris, he states: "But the animal, you observe, is tamed and obedient. Walk round the cage! *Marchez! Marchez!*" As Makak rises and marches, the chorus echoes: "I don't know what to say this monkey won't do / I don't know what to say this monkey won't do" (1970a, 222). By referring to Makak as an animal, specifically a monkey, the other characters in the play dehumanize him. Not only is he an ugly, black recluse, he is also made to seem inhuman. The white apparition who appears to Makak and is the catalyst for his journey dream is the only character who knows Makak's true identity: "Then as I start to move, she call out my name, my real name. A name I do not use" (235). The apparition, who embodies the whiteness that Makak can never obtain, does not dehumanize him; instead, she treats him as a person with a true identity. Near the end of the play, after his mental journey to Africa, Makak reveals his true name, Felix Hobain, and is finally able to return home with a clearer sense of himself as a man, not a monkey.

Lara's identity through naming is also revealed by an apparition, the Daddy People. When Lara is born, her parents name her Omilara, which means "the family are like water" (Evaristo 1997, 43). This reference to water reoccurs throughout the novel and symbolizes the ebb and flow of families that are separated by water but are eventually reunited. The Yoruba proverb that begins the novel also contains imagery of water: "However far the stream flows, it never forgets its source." While her father, Taiwo, has moved to England in search of wealth and prosperity, he eventually returns to Africa with his daughter because "the stream brings them back, at least in their recollection, to their place of origin" (Hacova 2004, 53). Lara's name represents this separation and reunion, but her full first name is rarely used throughout the novel. However, while in Africa, Lara is visited by an apparition of her ancestors, the ghosts whom she referred to as the Daddy People in her childhood. Her grandmother, Zenobia, along with a chorus of others, visits her: "My Omilara, now we take you into memory / sleep now, sleep" (Evaristo 1997, 109). In the pages that follow, Lara gains the knowledge of her ancestors that her father was so reluctant to give, and readers realize the true weight of Omilara's name. The journey across the sea to Africa has reunited her with her past, if only in dreams, and has prepared her to accept her heritage:

> I am baptized, resolved to paint slavery out of me
> the Daddy People onto canvas with colour-rich strokes
> their songs will guide me in sweaty dreams at night. (140)

Just as Makak is deprived of his true name throughout *Dream on Monkey Mountain,* Lara's true name is used by her ancestors to call her into the past and help her step into the future.

The races of the apparitions who visit Makak and Lara demonstrate what each character hopes to acquire during his or her journey toward identity. The apparition in *Dream on Monkey Mountain* is a white woman, an ideal and forbidden European embodiment: "I behold this woman, the loveliest thing I see on this earth, floating towards me, just like the moon, like the moon walking along her own road" (Walcott 1970a, 235). Later in this scene, Moustique, Makak's friend and business partner, asks: "Here? A white woman?" (236). In these lines, Walcott reveals that this beautiful white lady represents not only what Makak would like to possess but also what he must overcome in order to accept himself. Adetayo Alabi in "Recover, Not Discover: Africa in Walcott's *Dream on Monkey Mountain* and Philip's *Looking for Livingstone*" asserts that using a white apparition is problematic, but it also provides an insight into the desires and insecurities of postcolonial West Indians: "One may ask why the person to educate Makak about his self-esteem is white, what can symbolize his exploitation, and why the white goddess is beheaded in the apotheosis scene. The apparition is white because that is the color that the colonized has been taught to imitate and long for. . . . She represents what the colonized is taught to desire, the other culture that has negated theirs in many ways" (1999, 337). Makak's racialized identity has been obscured by the white racism that he has internalized. This white woman represents an identity that Makak will never possess and one that he must learn to separate himself from and no longer desire if he wishes to truly be free and reclaim his identity. According to Patrick Colm Hogan in "Mimeticism, Reactionary Nativism, and the Possibility of Postcolonial Identity in Derek Walcott's *Dream on Monkey Mountain*": "[Makak's] identity, his understanding of the world, his evaluation of himself and of others, all have been determined by white perceptions, white ideas—which is to say, by ascriptions which serve to support racial hierarchies" (1994, 108). Makak believes himself to be an ugly and useless black man, but with a few encouraging words from this white woman, he is determined to claim his kingship in Africa. This suggestion is ironic because it demonstrates the typical European viewpoint that the colonizer will be the savior of the colonized. Because Makak receives encouragement from someone who embodies his ideal self, his viewpoints change, and he resolves to follow her orders: "Makak will ride to the edge of the world, Makak will walk like he used to in Africa, when his name was lion!" (Walcott 1970a, 240). Alabi suggests that the race of the apparition is problematic because it inspires such defiance in Makak, a revolutionary spirit that he had never considered before. By gaining a new sense of self-esteem and, in the end, killing the white apparition who inspired such fervor, Makak demonstrates the dependence and independence that colonized individuals feel for their colonizers. Makak needs the apparition to inspire him; after that inspiration, he must rid himself of this woman in order to combat his internalized colonial attitudes: "Beheading her is symbolic of the resistance of the colonized to the tenets of colonialism" (1999, 337).

When he finally reaches Africa and becomes royalty, Makak realizes that he must destroy the white/European apparition in order to reclaim his roots, heritage, and identity. He must destroy this symbol of colonialism only when he feels he has the power to do so. When the apparition appears for the final time, Lestrade convinces Makak to kill her by reminding Makak of her power over him: "What you beheld, my prince, was but an image of your longing. As inaccessible as snow, as fatal as leprosy . . . if you want to discover the beautiful depth of your blackness, nigger, chop off her head! . . . She is the white light that paralyzed your mind, that led you into this confusion. It is you who created her, so kill her! kill her!" (Walcott 1970a, 318–19) Lestrade suggests that Makak created the apparition as a projection of his self-hatred; he needed that which he desired to convince him to change his life and accept his blackness. After Makak beheads the apparition, he no longer wishes to possess whiteness, which is evidenced by his refusal to keep the apparition's white mask. When Lestrade offers the mask to Makak, he shakes his head. This act demonstrates that Makak no longer sees himself through white eyes and has broken free of double consciousness to emerge as a man who belongs to himself—wholly. As he returns to the mountain, he states: "Lord, I have been washed from shore to shore, as a tree in the ocean. The branches of my fingers, the roots of my feet, could grip nothing, but now, God, they have found ground" (326). No longer wishing to possess the whiteness of his apparition and no longer feeling the rootless existence of a colonized West Indian, Felix Hobain can return home.

Unlike Makak's white phantom, the apparitions that appear to Lara are African, and they represent the racialized half of Lara's identity that she wishes to both abandon and understand. As a young, biracial girl in London, she frequently wishes to be white like her schoolmates. Unfortunately, her blackness is always physically evident, and she feels her otherness at all times:

> I saw my father in the distance,
> slid out of view, detoured, turned back, hid behind others.
> Well, it was bloody embarrassing having a black dad.
> In the showers at school I began to notice my difference.
> My skin was drier, pubies curly, titties pointy, bum perched.
> I wanted to be invisible. I wanted to be noticed. (Evaristo 1997, 70)

In this section, Lara expresses her self-hatred of being biracial, but she also hopes that she will become invisible, that her race will not matter to those who know her. By de-emphasizing her race, her personal qualities will shine through and allow her to "be noticed." Lara knows that her exterior is what defines her, and "she tries to oppose the stereotypes and prejudice by claiming that she is not as low on the social ladder as some may think since she comes from a mixed race parentage" (Hacova 2004, 53). This evolving notion of her racial identity leads her to question her African father about their shared roots. Taiwo is resistant to reveal the details she requests:

> Taiwo put his back to her, stretched his feet out onto
> his desk, said to the window, "What do you want to know?"
> "Everything! Nigeria, your childhood, family, everything!" (Evaristo 1997, 80)

When she finally visits Africa with her father, Lara still does not feel that she fits in because of the residents' reaction to her; they call her "Oyinbo," which means "whitey" (104), which is the opposite of her self-perception when she is surrounded by white schoolmates. The Africans see Lara as white, while she feels that she cannot escape her blackness. While in Africa and surrounded by this inverse racism, she thinks: "This is the land of my father . . . I wonder if I could belong" (104).

In her quest for identity, Lara moves from a desire to mimic whiteness to a desire to understand and be accepted by her African ancestors. She gets this opportunity when she is visited by the Daddy People and shown the history of her ancestors. After her dream and during her visit to Brazil, Lara says: "I become my parents, my ancestors, my gods" (Evaristo 1997, 139). The African apparitions that visit Lara embody what she wishes to accept but has not yet been able to. When she finally does accept these roots, she resolves to keep Africa as "an embryo within me" (140). This blackness has now become a part of her that will grow, with time, and allow Lara to create her own identity on her island without attempting to mimic her white counterparts. She has accepted a hybrid identity that allows her to look to the future.

Both Makak and Lara move from characters that suffer from DuBois's double consciousness to characters that accept their dual identities as hybrids. In "Hybridity and Visionary Experience: Derek Walcott's *Dream on Monkey Mountain,*" William Haney explains how Makak's journey dream helps establish a dual identity. This same principle can also be applied to Lara. Haney states that "a visionary experience is perhaps the most effective way to achieve cultural hybridity, an in-between-ness defined in terms both of an international subject as well as a conceptual void immanent within yet beyond culturally constructed identity" (2005, 81). In other words, both Makak and Lara are able to define themselves apart from the racial and cultural identities that are forced upon them by society. These characters are not concerned with white identity, black identity, black/white or African/European identity; instead, they are able to create an alternate space within themselves where their own unique identities can exist apart from mimicking or valorizing one race or heritage. They have been able to form their own postcolonial identities as hybrids that are able to both embody and analyze these disparate cultures. In Haney's opinion: "The colonized live in-between cultures, and by extension in-between different sets of conceptuality. . . . In addition to being able to identify with more than one culture, a hybrid by this definition can also distance herself from all cultures—which suggests the innate human capacity to be conscious of being conscious independently of culture" (84–85). In essence, because of their journeys and because of the help of apparitions and self-examination, both Makak and Lara are now able to accept their cultural in-between-ness and use that knowledge to scrutinize the cultures that they embody. They are in the unique position of both personifying culture and evaluating it.

This evaluation of culture and race comes at the end of each text. When Makak leaves the jail to return to Monkey Mountain, he delivers a monologue that demonstrates his acceptance and analysis of his new identity: "Let me be swallowed up in that mist again, and let me be forgotten, so that when the mist open, men can look up, at some small clearing with a hut, with a small signal of smoke, and say, 'Makak lives there. Makak lives where he has always lived, in the dream of his people'" (Walcott 1970a, 326). Although Makak has accepted his identity, he still wishes to return to the reclusive mountain and become an apparition who will inspire others. He realizes that he must not rule, as his apparition suggested, but that he must remain secluded as a silent prophet of his people. This decision shows that Makak has found what Haney calls the "home within" (2005, 97) and that, in order to accept himself, he must accept the place he lives, his home, and his roots. Makak demonstrates not only his acceptance of his heritage, but his understanding of it.

Lara also demonstrates this acceptance and evaluation at the end of the text. After her baptism in the Amazon River, Lara feels a sense of completeness:

> I savour in the living world, planet of growth, of decay
> think of my island—the "Great" Tippexed out of it—
> tiny amid massive floating continents.
> . . . .
> Back to London, across international time zones
> I step out of Heathrow and into my future. (Evaristo 1997, 140)

In these last sentiments, Lara expresses her acceptance of her home by realizing that the identity that society places upon her is not accurate and that she cannot be wholly defined by her appearance. Her feeling of otherness melts away with her possession—"*my* island." Her identity is no longer ruled by the island's inhabitants; instead, Lara will forge her identity according to her new understanding. The island may no longer be great, but Lara feels that she will be.

Echeruo also states that it is impossible for a person of color not to claim an identity without one being prescribed for him or her. "What the history of the black diaspora teaches us is that black identity must always be predicated on black experience, and to whatever additional extent possible, on the experience of those others touched enough by black blood to identify themselves with it" (1999, 11). In the opinion of Echeruo and those of many other diaspora critics, the literature of the African diaspora still struggles with this notion of identity because colonized and enslaved people must straddle the two worlds of the conqueror and the conquered. Echeruo contends that it is impossible to have an "identity-less being" (10), and African people affected by the diaspora must choose, if given the opportunity, which culture, race, and heritage to ascribe to. If they do not choose, as Makak and Lara do after their journeys to Africa, then an identity will be prescribed to them by observers who do not understand their plight. This plight is summed up in the epigraph to part 2 of *Dream on Monkey Mountain* where Walcott quotes Sartre: "That status 'native' is a nervous condition introduced and maintained by the settler among colonized people with their consent" (1970a, 277). This quotation demonstrates that native or colonized people are forced to straddle two worlds, thus obfuscating their true individual identities.

The character in *Dream on Monkey Mountain* who most poignantly embodies this concept of straddling two worlds is Makak's jailor and adviser, Corporal Lestrade. Lestrade, whose name resembles the word "straddle," is literally a cultural straddler because he is rooted in two cultures—black and white, French and English. As a mulatto, Lestrade struggles with resenting people of his own race while also being a part of them. Before Makak's dream of Africa, Lestrade comments on the black prisoners in his jail: "Animals, beasts, savages, cannibals, niggers, stop turning this place to a stinking zoo!" (Walcott 1970a, 216). He calls Makak a "being without a mind, a will, a name, a tribe of its own" (222); Lestrade tells Makak that he is "so damn ugly" that he should "walk on all fours" (226). During Makak's mental journey to Africa, Lestrade confesses his sins to Makak and asks forgiveness: "My feet grip like roots. The arteries are like rope. Was that my voice? O God, I have become what I mocked. I always was, I always was. Makak! Makak! forgive me, old father" (300). In this monologue, Lestrade finally realizes and accepts his hybrid identity, and by doing so, "grows roots" and can identify with the other black characters suffering from the same identity issues. Through his liberating confession, he recognizes his identity and is cleansed. It is important that this confession comes during the journey to Africa because this sense of home and return is also an important theme in literature of the diaspora. Echeruo states: "The members of a diaspora must have once had a home of their own, a nation, if you like, but nevertheless a convenanted forever home, a site from which they may be (for a while) excluded, but which is theirs, inalienably. This home, this land is not important only as a physical place; it is even more important as the source, root, final location for a determinable lineage" (1999, 13). Without experiencing this fantasy of home by visiting Africa in a dream, Lestrade may never have been able to reconcile his hybridity and both literally and figuratively find his roots. When Makak awakens from his dream of

Africa, the real Lestrade releases him from jail and refers collectively to himself and other black men in jail: "Our life is a prison" (Walcott 1970a, 325). His sensitive treatment of Makak after this journey dream confession shows Lestrade's transformation, his self-identification with other black men, and his acceptance of his true identity. Lestrade exemplifies Echeruo's contention that an identity will be ascribed to a person of color if that person does not choose to align himself or herself to a specific identity. Lestrade was considered a powerful white figure, although he was actually of both black and white ancestry, because of his faithfulness to English laws. However, because he had never declared his true allegiance to either side, Lestrade continued to straddle the worlds of whiteness and blackness. In the end, he is finally able to possess an individual identity that transcends race and is rooted in a specific place that is the literal and figurative home to one-half of his hybrid identity.

When Echeruo states that it is impossible to have an identity-less being, he means that living beings are prescribed identities according to their heritages, places of birth, skin colors, and so on. Makak and Lestrade both attempt to deny or forget the identities that they assume because of where they live and how they look. Makak tries to create a safe enclave for himself where his name and race do not matter, but when he is forced to confront society, he must go through a painstaking journey to reveal his true self. Lestrade, by hating and degrading one part of his race, attempts to deny his physical identity; however, he realizes that it is impossible to deny something that is an inherent part of his character and biology. Makak, Lestrade, and Lara highlight the diaspora's complex conflict with identity while also demonstrating that they are capable of divorcing themselves from the "native label" and emerging as distinctive characters who can straddle two worlds while defining themselves as unique individuals.

The journeys from their respective islands to Africa help Makak and Lara, two seemingly dissimilar characters, reach the same goal: identity through a fusion of mind, body, and spirit. Makak and Lara are able to rise above the identities that have been ascribed to them and emerge as beings who belong to themselves. These characters have freed themselves of DuBois's double consciousness. In "Of Our Spiritual Strivings," DuBois characterizes the self-educated African American as a person who strives, against all odds, for enlightenment. To DuBois, "[T]he journey at least gave leisure for reflection and self-examination, it changed the child of Emancipation to the youth with dawning self-consciousness, self-realization, self-respect. . . . He began to have a dim feeling that, to attain his place in the world, he must be himself, and not another" (1999, 14). Although this statement refers to a different group affected by the African diaspora, these words echo the sentiments expressed in both *Dream on Monkey Mountain* and *Lara*. Makak and Lara strive to create identities that can unite the disparate parts of themselves. In the end, they both realize what DuBois suggests; they understand that identity is not determined by race, culture, location, appearance, or ancestry. Instead, identity is determined by looking inward, cultivating personality and insight, and attempting to better oneself as an individual. Through these lessons, Makak and Lara forge postcolonial identities that are uniquely their own. Their journeys are echoed in Edward Kamau Brathwaite's poem "The Awakening:"

> so slowly slowly
> ever so slowly
> I will rise
> and stand on my feet
> . . . .
> I am learning
> let me succeed
> I am learning
> let me succeed . . . (1973, 156–57)

Note

1. The term *cultural schizophrenia* is borrowed from Haney (2005).

References

Alabi, Adetayo. 1999. "Recover, Not Discover: Africa in Walcott's *Dream on Monkey Mountain* and Phillip's *Looking for Livingstone*." In *The African Diaspora*, edited by Isidore Okwepho et al., 332–43. Bloomington: Indiana University Press.

Brathwaite, Edward Kamau. 1973. *The Arrivants*. New York: Oxford University Press.

DuBois, W. E. B. 1999. *The Souls of Black Folk*. Edited by Henry Louis Gates Jr. and Terry Hume Oliver. New York: Norton.

Echeruo, Michael J. C. 1999. "An African Diaspora: An Ontological Project." In *The African Diaspora*, edited by Isidore Okpewho et al., 3–18. Bloomington: Indiana University Press.

Evaristo, Bernardine. 1997. *Lara*. Guildford, U.K.: Angela Royal.

Hacova, Pavlina. 2004. "The Stream Never Forgets Its Source: Themes Explored in *Lara* by Bernadine Evaristo." *Theory and Practice in English Studies* 2: 51–56.

Haney, William. 2005. "Hybridity and Visionary Experience: Derek Walcott's *Dream on Monkey Mountain*." *Mystics Quarterly* 31:81–109.

Hogan, Patrick Colm. 1994. "Mimeticism, Reactionary Nativism, and the Possibility of Postcolonial Identity in Derek Walcott's *Dream on Monkey Mountain.*" *Research in African Literatures* 25 (2): 103–20.

McWatt, Mark. 1988. "Derek Walcott: An Island Poet and His Sea." *Third World Quarterly* 10 (4): 1607–15.

Proctor, James. 2002. "Biography: Bernadine Evaristo." *British Council.* Contemporary Writers. http://literature.britishcouncil.org/bernardine-evaristo.

Uhrbach, Jan R. 1986. "A Note on Language and Naming in *Dream on Monkey Mountain.*" *Callaloo* 29: 578–82.

Walcott, Derek. 1970a. *Dream on Monkey Mountain and Other Plays.* New York: Farrar, Straus, & Giroux.

Walcott, Derek. 1970b. "What the Twilight Says: An Overture." In *Dream on Monkey Mountain and Other Plays,* 3–40. New York: Farrar, Straus, & Giroux.

Warner-Lewis, Maureen. 1999. "Cultural Reconfigurations in the African Caribbean." In *The African Diaspora,* edited by Isidore Okpewho et al., 19–27. Bloomington: Indiana University Press.

Afterword

The Complexities of Home

Trudier Harris

"Home," Robert Frost asserts in "The Death of the Hired Man" (1915), "is the place where, when you have to go there, / They have to take you in." Frost's statement presupposes a moral obligation, one that the couple to whom the hired man Silas returns in the poem ultimately adheres by allowing him, in spite of his irregular work habits and presumptions with them, to die peacefully in his old living quarters. His frequent departures from their farm, indeed his leaving them in the lurch on many occasions, are overshadowed by his present need, a need to which they respond—Warren the husband grumpily and Mary the wife sympathetically. The voluntary departure, forced return, moral obligation, and spatial recognition of dependency that shape the poem also shape many of the ideas that the presenters offered in the "Race and Displacement" symposium held at the University of Alabama in October of 2009 and that now grace this volume. While there is no governmental obligation in Frost's poem, it is implicit by its absence. What is a society to do with its homeless persons, with those who have voluntarily or forcibly been driven from their dwellings? And what is the nature of their sojourns? Do they find solace, a home, in a different space, or must they return to their points of origins? If they return, will they be welcomed, merely tolerated, or dispatched with violence? The history of forced and voluntary movement throughout the world and internally within the United States is a history informed as much by race as it is by culture, as much by financial expediency as it is by moral obligation.

Attempts to find a new home after one is forcibly dispatched/driven from a native territory is one of the recurring threads in considering the complexities of home. Africans captured and brought to the Americas spent the better part of two hundred years waiting for the U.S. government to begin the process of allowing them to call America home. Even after they were emancipated from slavery, they still needed an additional hundred years before they could stake a claim to the moral conscience of the country during the civil rights movement. But what of the mixed race Métis, who, as nomads in Montana, Idaho, and occasionally Canada, were deliberately disfranchised and disinherited through linguistic reference? Delia Hagen notes that, to the American government, the Métis were decidedly not Native American; therefore, they had no rights to make claims on the land on which they lived. To the Canadian government, they were not Canadian, not Indian, and nonwhite, so they could make no claims to Canadian territory. They defined themselves as Native American and European, but that self-description did not earn them sufficient respect to warrant uncontested space. As the Métis were forced from their lands by the American government and in turn forced from Canada, did they ever have a chance to call either territory home? Neither the United States nor Canada was willing to admit moral responsibility in allowing the Métis to live peaceably—or even die peaceably—in their selected space. Indeed, neither government recognized the rights of these persons to claim a space. With their inability to enroll in Native American tribes, and denied the "social whiteness" that would have enabled them to change their status from outcasts to citizens, they remained nomadic, displaced at will, unable to call any place home.

Linguistic displacement also informs Sir Francis Drake's response to the Africans he encountered in Panama in April of 1573, as Cassander L. Smith explains in her essay. As he planned a robbery of gold that was intended for Spain and needed the assistance of these Africans, known as Cimarrons, he realized that they did not fit into a narrative of victimized Africans. Nor could he accept them as his equals, as is clear when he prefers to give one of the Cimarrons a sword instead of allowing him to pay for it. To Drake, the Cimarrons are a troublesome lot whose attempts to define themselves disturb him greatly. So he portrays them as Indians, sons and daughters of the land, indigenous, not like imported Africans. He therefore attempts to construct a "suffering Indian" presence in the Cimarrons under Spanish rule. While what the Cimarrons think and feel is not abundantly available to us, it is obvious that Drake would like to designate a home for them, one that does not interfere with his own notions of home and one in which they readily accept their displacement.

A comparable kind of displacement and lack of governmental moral obligation that the Métis experienced might apply to Robert Adams, on whom Melanie Fritsch focuses in her chapter. Traveling from the United States to England and on to the Barbary States, and recounting in 1816 his adventures in Timbuktu, Adams experienced voluntary displacement as a result of racial designation (enslaved person if he remained in the United States or England). Official state policy in both nations prevented him from claiming a peaceful home. In addition, with barriers of race, language, culture, and ethnicity, he could never fully be at home in any of the territories he visited and about which he wrote. He has an intense impulse to reconcile body with place, but historical circumstances perpetuated by governmental policy make that impulse impossible to achieve.

That travel of a black person outside the United States during slavery and in a historical setting is mirrored fictionally in Nella Larsen's novel *Quicksand* (1928). Helga, like Robert Adams, is put in a position where she does not feel at home. Though slavery is not the issue with her, the psychological discomfort she feels because of race and culture are nonetheless compelling. As the child of a white mother and a black father born into a society sharply segregated along racial lines, Helga has no place that she can call home on U.S. soil. She is an outcast among her white relatives in Chicago and an outsider among the blacks at Naxos, a southern Tuskegee-like college, who work so desperately to remove all negative traces of blackness from their habits and behaviors. In such an environment, the mulatto Helga has little opportunity to embrace the blackness she finds missing in her own life, for the very quality that causes her problems—her skin color—is precisely what many in that environment prefer to embrace about her. The whiteness in blackness—not the blackness in whiteness—makes it impossible for Helga to feel at home.

Uncomfortable in both black and white American settings, Helga travels to Denmark in a voluntary displacement and a desperate search for some place she can call home. The very makeup of her body, however, leads to her being considered just as exotic in Copenhagen as she is in Chicago with her white relatives and in Naxos with her black colleagues. Helga's case offers interesting opportunities for reflections upon the portability—or not—of a concept of home. For Frost's hired man, home was stationary, something he needed to return to for comfort in his last days of life. For Helga, it is uncertain where, exactly, home resides. Her lack of comfort in Chicago and Naxos suggests that neither is a place where she can put down roots and grow into her full potential as a human being of mixed-race parentage. When she arrives in Copenhagen, she relies upon features of the very culture and patterns of interactions that she has left in the States in order to shape her interactions with her aunt, uncle, and their relatives. In Denmark, Helga becomes, as Deborah Katz points out, the exotic black woman stereotype identified with many black women in the United States; she is a "'Negro' art object"—thoroughly objectified and *within* but not *of* the community in which she resides.

It might reasonably be argued that Helga is a dressed-up, modernist version of Sara Baartman, the Venus Hottentot to whom Jonathan Glover refers in his chapter. Helga, like Sara, embodies a sexual desire that whites highlight even as they paradoxically claim physical and cultural superiority to it. Does Helga's buying into the stereotype of the exotic black woman mean that she has taken that aspect of home with her, or does it mean that the people she encounters in Copenhagen are privy to international stereotypical perceptions of black women and simply impose them upon Helga? Clearly, Helga capitalizes on notions of blackness and sexuality in some of her interactions with people she meets in Copenhagen. Nonetheless, they have preconceived ideas about her as well. It finally becomes just as impossible for her to be at home in Copenhagen as it has been for her to be at home in Chicago and Naxos.

Helga's situation raises an ultimate question. Is it possible that some persons simply do not have and cannot imagine a home? When we think of people being "homeless," various ideas come to mind. They can range from Charlie Breedlove burning down his family's house in Toni Morrison's *The Bluest Eye* (1970), thereby putting his family "outdoors" and making them homeless, to notions of being without shelter that come to mind when we think of persons prematurely released from mental institutions and living on the streets or persons who have lost their jobs and have no alternative but to live on the streets, outdoors, without shelter. Helga's situation is not a matter of *not* having shelter, for she consistently has shelter at a middle-class and, in Copenhagen, upper-middle-class level. She has access to some of the finest quarters in Naxos as well as in New York, and she is a unique fashion bon vivant. Being homeless for Helga is a matter of rejection by kin on the one hand or being embraced so warmly by kin on the other that it leads to a psychological straightjacket. With Helga, homelessness is a matter of mental questing that never leads to fulfillment. It always remains in the abstract and can never be fulfilled in the empirical realm. There is no territory, space, or physical haven that can satisfy Helga, a point that is abundantly clear when she finally marries the Reverend Mr. Pleasant Green and moves from New York to Alabama. She has a house, a husband, and children, but, as one of the presenters, Ashon Crawley points out, her situation becomes a "quagmire" that probably presages her death. Unfortunately for her mental and physical condition, there is no mirror of home that can project back to Helga her notion of what such a comforting place might provide.

Helga's predicament is also unique in that it provides a glimpse of displacement that is simultaneously externally and internally imposed. Racial discrimination in the United States, both across and within racial lines, is undoubtedly responsible for Helga's not being able to find ultimate peace anywhere. However, there are equally undoubtedly thousands of mixed-race persons in America who do not experience the extreme psychological discomfort that plaques Helga. Something within her, in her personality, therefore, also makes her susceptible to displacement. Consider the fact that she could easily slide into a role in Naxos and be comfortable there. Instead, she judges herself with the eyes of one plagued by double consciousness, that is, looking at herself as she believes others do/will. On the basis of information that this process yields, she displaces herself from that environment and, later, from the United States. Nowhere is there peace for Helga, no home in spite of her many attempts to locate one.

International displacement also informs Kathrin Kottemann's discussion of Derek Walcott's *Dream on Monkey Mountain* (1970) and Bernadine Evaristo's *Lara* (1997), as well as Lauren Vedal's discussion of Dionne Brand's *In Another Place, Not Here* (1996), in which characters from the Caribbean go to Canada in attempts to find a fullness of being. Kottemann refers to the plights of Walcott's and Evaristo's characters as "cultural schizophrenia" and suggests that travel to Africa enables them to resolve desperate identity crises by accepting who they are and looking to the future. Healthy identity is accomplished through a "fusion of mind, body, and spirit." Indeed, "the home within" becomes crucial to these self-concepts. By contrast, Helga has no "home within." In addition to international displacement, Brand's characters suffer from the added dimension of same-sex desire. How can it be achieved in an island environment where persons who express such desire are routinely the objects of violence, or how can it be achieved in a foreign environment where the Caribbean body, like Helga's American body in Copenhagen, is an object of curiosity but perhaps is never truly welcomed? Where—if anywhere—can persons with same-sex preferences find home? Must they give up nationality and culture if they obviously cannot give up race? No matter its mythical conceptualization as a place of tolerance, Canada is ultimately not a haven; it is, as Vedal makes clear, "racist." Brand's characters ultimately do not have the "civilization" or "whiteness" that would make them truly welcome in a home in Canada. These women remain, as does Helga, as psychologically confounded by displacement as they are by sexuality and sexual preference.

Helga's psychological situation is not unlike that many gay black men find in churches that they attempt to call a spiritual home. African Americans routinely embrace the concept of home when it comes to discussing their churches. One might attend church in another city or state, but one tries to go to one's home church for the designated homecoming occasions. Also, the bodies of deceased members are moved throughout the United States back to some place that the deceased had considered his or her home church and burial ground. It is a paradox, therefore, to note, as Ashon T. Crawley points out in his chapter, that some portions of African American communities are not as readily welcomed into churches as are others. Church homes for persons with same-sex preferences more often than not amount to fine lines of tightrope walking in which the individuals keep to themselves the fact that they prefer lovers and partners of their own gender. In the unspoken psychological dimension of home and displacement, members of some African American churches can be just as displaced from their homes as are persons who are physically removed thousands of miles away from their churches; they, like Helga, find no mirrors to project back to them images of comfort, support, and acceptance. African American cultural scholar E. Patrick Johnson documents this pattern clearly in *Sweet Tea: Black Gay Men of the South* (2008), a volume in which he interviews and interprets the conversations of black men who navigated the treacherous waters of being gay and Christian in the American South for most of the twentieth century. Although Crawley is more optimistic than most cultural observers about the possibility of gay existence within traditional African American churches, the phenomenon remains a matter of home versus homelessness, acceptance versus toleration or downright rejection.

It is striking, therefore, that persons within a given community can be truly intolerant at times in determining who is a legitimate member of that community; they risk a form of intragroup displacement, psychologically if not physically. Consider Gloria Naylor's depiction of Willow Springs, the island off the coast of Georgia and South Carolina, in *Mama Day* (1988). It is a classic study of insider and outsider dynamics. Folks born and raised in Willow Springs are privy to the concept of "18 &23" that governs their island; those outside are simply lost. The novel makes apparent, however, how insiders can become outsiders, and the source of that alienation is education, as classically demonstrated in the case of "Reema's Boy." This young man goes away to college and comes back to the island to conduct an ethnographic study. He forgets his roots in the process and becomes the detached observer who has lost touch with his heritage. Willow Springs, therefore, is no longer home to him, and there is little indication that he would like it to be so. Importantly, it does remain home to Cocoa, one of the protagonists, in spite of her sojourn to New York and the education she has acquired beyond the island. In fact, Willow Springs is so much home to Cocoa that she easily stereotypes people—*all* people—into categories of containment that are defined by her island background. For Cocoa, Willow Springs is a place as well as a state of mind. In contrast to Helga, Cocoa easily carries home with her to New York and easily reenters island society when she returns to Willow Springs.

This comfortable insider-outsider notion of home is complicated by Matthew Dischinger's reading of the novel. Couching his critical approach in postcolonialist theory, Dischinger posits the mainland United States and Willow Springs as western space (New York) versus nonwestern space (Willow Springs). When we consider the paths of Africans from outside western space into western space, the dichotomy still designates people of African descent as more at home in the island space, as Mama Day and the majority of her relatives are, than in the citified, alien, disruptive-of-the-natural-world space that is New York. Dischinger's reading must still reconcile voluntary movement (Cocoa) with involuntary movement (Sapphira Wade and others enslaved on the island) as well as the spatial claiming of territory with authoritarian denial of that claim. No matter what laws in Georgia and South Carolina assert, Sapphira Wade and her descendents claim Willow Springs as theirs, as home. They start from the position that their claim is not to be challenged, and they hold to that stance. Of course, the text is fiction, for it is a far cry from what the historical Métis can assert or what Robert Adams could have claimed if he had remained in the United States.

These mediations on home, however, move in another fascinating direction for the essays collected here. As a point of departure, I refer to Walter Bosse's chapter on Charles Chesnutt's *The Marrow of Tradition* (1901). Ostensibly, Bosse's work is about "travel and race." I would nonetheless assert that it is also about home. Throughout American history, territories and spaces defined in the United States as being unwelcome to persons of African descent might be designated as "white" spaces. With such a line of thinking, a train during the days of segregation on public transportation might reasonably be considered "white" space. This can be extended to imply that "white" spaces are therefore home to whites and that blacks and other nonwhites who attempt to gain entry into those spaces are made to feel not at all at home. Home, in this sense, is any space designated to the exclusion of others, specifically spaces designated to exclude black people. Whites on Chesnutt's train are accordingly "at home" while blacks are made to feel that they are out of place. An extension of this argument would be to read the entire period of segregation as "home" to whites and as places where blacks could be accused of "trespassing." The ease with which Chesnutt's white characters smoke, drink, dine, and converse make these assumptions clear. When the very light-skinned but nevertheless black Dr. Miller enters into this space, he is considered the disruptive force, out of place, not at home. He may be as exotic as Helga Crane is in some settings, but not in this public accommodation, where white identity can be reinforced only by the claiming of the space as home. The whites whom Helga encounters in Copenhagen change the rules by which space can be designated as home or not home. Whites on Chesnutt's train can do so either by law or by custom, and custom is perhaps the stronger force of the two.

Designating space as "white" and "home" also applies to what happened to the Japanese during World War II—as it does to the women in Brand's *In Another Place, Not Here.* Finding its forces under attack in various parts of the world, the U.S. government determined that all continental American soil was "white" and that persons of Japanese descent residing in it, whether legally or not, were outsiders, intruders who were essentially guilty of home invasion. It could, as Abigail G. H. Manzella explores, round up the intruders and displace or deposit them into less preferable "white space," away from the immediacy of home. These spatial dynamics of home revisit the portability issue raised with Helga Crane. Could those imprisoned Japanese, many of whom had known no home other than U.S. soil, transport their notions of home as they defined it into the internment camps and come out with it intact months or years later? Or do they all end up like the young Japanese boy who looks into a mirror, takes on the role of a member of the Allies, and yells, "Kill the Japs!"? Is his split from self—and perhaps sanity—any less compelling than Helga Crane's multiple splittings of self, her mental displacement from her very body? For these characters, home can never be the place where "they" have to take "you" in if whoever "they" are change the landscape and its meaning whenever "you" set foot on it.

Changing the nature of the landscape and forcibly displacing certain groups from it or onto it might also be applicable to the lynching motif that Yumi Pak discusses in connection with Jean Toomer's *Cane* (1923). Lynching has at its base the ability of the lynchers to designate whatever space they would like as "white" space by determining when a black person has transgressed to the point of death or in deciding which spaces are appropriate to bring about that death. For example, in the sketch entitled "Blood-Burning Moon," the young white man who seduces the black woman implicitly labels his house where she works as a domestic as white space to which she must yield by giving him her body. If she refuses, then she is a trespasser who must suffer the consequences of that refusal (possible rape). Once the woman's boyfriend Tom kills the white man—it does not matter that the death occurs in a fair fight—the entire white community considers the entire black community trespassers. Space that previously may have been considered black is now white, and the lynchers pursue Tom to his inevitable death within that community. Space in *Cane* extends metaphorically from the South, with its frequent violent deaths, to the North, where black people become, as Pak argues further, an endless supply of blood—metaphorical lynchings—for whites. Any space that blacks claim can be reclaimed by whites, and blacks can be displaced from any space they purport to claim if whites need that space for their own purposes, whether those purposes result in the demise of blacks or some other objective. In such fictional worlds, no home can exist peacefully for blacks unless it is space that whites do not desire.

Displacement of peoples of African descent throughout the New World began, as Queen Quet Marquetta L. Goodwine meditates upon in her response to presentations at the conference that yielded this volume, with enslavement and forced migration. That pattern continued, historically and fictionally, in many of the works treated here. In movements that shatter a sense of home, and in which it will never be possible to retrieve fully what was lost, what option is left to the displaced person? Kathrin Kottemann's essay on Derek Walcott's *Dream on Monkey Mountain* and Bernardine Evaristo's *Lara* seeks to answer that question. Mixed-race characters who wrestle with their identities through a DuBoisian lens of double consciousness and who are dislocated from their island homes through migration travel to Africa, figuratively through the dream sequences in Walcott's novel and literally for Lara in an effort to merge conflicting identities and multiple homeplaces. Their attempts to reconcile blackness and whiteness enable them to find a sense of home within themselves and to assert new possibilities for how mixed-race persons can embrace their hybridity and move into more hopeful futures than their pasts portended.

Given the span of the several centuries the contributors cover in their essays, one cannot help but ask what has changed over the course of time. Are race and displacement different at different points in history? Is home a more valued concept at some points in time than in others? How is the involuntary displacement that slavery yielded different in its results from the voluntary displacement that so many literary characters and historical figures have undergone since slavery? Harriet Tubman, Frederick Douglass, and many others ran away from "home" in order to find *home*. Yet Helga Crane succeeded only in running into a brick wall that could barely pass for home. She failed to consider that wherever she went, there she was. She did not have the mental preparation or the spiritual desire to transform notions of home as fervently as we might imagine the Cimarrons did. Her mirror of home was always smudged and perhaps even cracked; it never yielded a clear image to her, and she never had the precisely defined fortitude to change that state.

As fictional worlds give way to the historical, we like to believe that, in the twenty-first century, displacement is more voluntary than compulsory. Of course there are striking exceptions, such as wars in various African countries that have driven people from their homes and into neighboring countries. Another noteworthy dimension to contemporary displacement is that race is not always the dominant factor in such dispersion. People who share the same racial but different ethnic or cultural groupings can be just as prone in the twenty-first century to displace their neighbors as whites were to enslave Africans hundreds of years ago. Perhaps this universal racism, this equal opportunity displacement in spite of race, culture, and ethnic affiliation, is what has led some observers to believe that the United States is now a postracial society. While race and identity politics might be shifting signifiers, there is still something visceral and salient to which they continue to refer. How far we are removed from the past in American society cannot entirely be decided by one seeming exception to all the rules of racism. The more perfect union is perhaps still generations into the future. No one will deny, however, that it is "pretty" to think that the bugaboo of race-based denial of any individual's claim to an American space is a thing of the past. Whether we are postracial or so mired in race that we cannot separate it from breathing—as Tim Tyson asserts in *Blood Done Signed My Name: A True Story* (2004)—we are still bound by spoken and unspoken rules that make home and displacement two of the most contested arenas of human existence, whether that existence is on American soil, throughout the diaspora, or throughout the world.

References

Johnson, E. Patrick. 2008. *Sweet Tea: Black Gay Men of the South.* Chapel Hill: University of North Carolina Press.

Tyson, Timothy B. 2004. *Blood Done Signed My Name: A True Story.* New York: Crown.

Selected Bibliography

Agnew, Vijay, ed. *Diaspora, Memory, and Identity: A Search for Home*. Toronto: University of Toronto Press, 2005.

Anderson, Benedict. *Imagined Communities: Reflections on the Origin and Spread of Nationalism*. London: Verso, 2006.

Anderson, Margaret L., and Patricia Hill Collins, eds. *Race, Class, and Gender: An Anthology*. Belmont, CA: Wadsworth, 2009.

Ashcroft, Bill, Gareth Griffiths, and Helen Tiffin, eds. *The Post-colonial Studies Reader*. 2nd ed. London: Routledge, 2006.

Baker, Houston A. *Turning South Again: Re-thinking Modernism / Re-reading Booker T.* Durham: Duke University Press, 2001.

Bannerji, Himani. *The Dark Side of the Nation: Essays on Multiculturalism, Nationalism and Gender*. Toronto: Canadian Scholars' Press, 2000.

Bayart, Jean-François. *Global Subjects: A Political Critique of Globalization*. Cambridge: Polity, 2007.

———. *The Illusion of Cultural Identity*. Chicago: University of Chicago Press, 2005.

Berlant, Lauren. *The Female Complaint: The Unfinished Business of Sentimentality in American Culture*. Durham: Duke University Press, 2008.

Blum, Hester. *The View from the Masthead: Maritime Imagination and Antebellum American Sea Narratives*. Chapel Hill: University of North Carolina Press, 2008.

Brah, Avtar. *Cartographies of Diaspora: Contesting Identities*. New York: Routledge, 1996.

Brand, Dionne. *Bread out of Stone: Recollections, Sex, Recognitions, Race, Dreaming, Politics*. Toronto: Coach House, 1994.

Braziel, Jana Evans, and Anita Mannur, eds. *Theorizing Diaspora: A Reader*. Malden, MA: Blackwell, 2003.

Butler, Judith. *Bodies That Matter: On the Discursive Limits of Sex*. New York: Routledge, 1993.

Campbell, James T. *Middle Passages: African American Journeys to Africa, 1787–2005.* New York: Penguin, 2006.

Cohen, Robin, and Paola Toninato, eds. *The Creolization Reader: Studies in Mixed Identities and Cultures.* New York: Routledge, 2009.

Collins, Patricia Hill. *Black Feminist Thought.* New York: Routledge, 2002.

Day, Richard J. F. *Multiculturalism and the History of Canadian Diversity.* Toronto: University of Toronto Press, 2000.

Dayan, Colin. *The Law Is a White Dog: How Legal Rituals Make and Unmake Persons.* Princeton: Princeton University Press, 2011.

DuBois, W. E. B. *The Souls of Black Folk.* Edited by Henry Louis Gates Jr. and Terri Hume Oliver. New York: Norton, 1999.

Edwards, Brent. *The Practice of Diaspora: Literature, Translation, and the Rise of Black Internationalism.* Cambridge: Harvard University Press, 2003.

Ellison, Ralph. *Invisible Man.* New York: Vintage International, 1980.

Eng, David L. *Racial Castration: Managing Masculinity in Asian America.* Durham: Duke University Press, 2001.

Gamson, Joshua. *The Fabulous Sylvester: The Legend, the Music, the Seventies in San Francisco.* New York: H. Holt, 2005.

Garraway, Doris. *The Libertine Colony: Creolization in the Early French Caribbean.* Durham: Duke University Press, 2005.

Gill, John. *Queer Noises: Male and Female Homosexuality in Twentieth Century Music.* Minneapolis: University of Minnesota Press, 1995.

Gilroy, Paul. *The Black Atlantic: Modernity and Double Consciousness.* Cambridge: Harvard University Press, 1993.

Goldsby, Jacqueline. *A Spectacular Secret: Lynching in American Life and Literature.* Chicago: University of Chicago Press, 2006.

Gomez, Michael A. *Reversing Sail: A History of the African Diaspora.* New York: Cambridge University Press, 2004.

Grant, Nathan. *Masculinist Impulses: Toomer, Hurston, Black Writing, and Modernity.* Columbia: University of Missouri Press, 2004.

Griffin, Farah Jasmine. *"Who Set You Flowin'?" The African-American Migration Narrative.* New York: Oxford University Press, 1995.

Griffin, Farah Jasmine, and Cheryl J. Fish, eds. *A Stranger in the Village: Two Centuries of African-American Travel Writing.* Boston: Beacon, 1998.

Gruesser, John Cullen. *Confluences: Postcolonialism, African American Literary Studies, and the Black Atlantic.* Athens: University of Georgia Press, 2005.

Holloway, Karla F. *Moorings and Metaphors: Figures of Culture and Gender in Black Women's Literature.* New Brunswick: Rutgers University Press, 1992.

Hubbs, Nadine. *The Queer Composition of America's Sound: Gay Modernists, American Music, and National Identity.* Berkeley: University of California Press, 2004.

Jan Rozbicki, Michal, and George O. Ndege, eds. *Cross-Cultural History and the Domestication of Otherness.* New York: Palgrave Macmillan, 2011.

Koshy, Susan. *Sexual Naturalization: Asian Americans and Miscegenation.* Palo Alto: Stanford University Press, 2004.

Kymlicka, Will. *Multicultural Odysseys: Navigating the New International Politics of Diversity.* New York: Oxford University Press, 2009.

Landau, Paul S., and Deborah D. Kaspin, eds. *In Images and Empires: Visuality in Colonial and Postcolonial Africa.* Berkeley: University of California Press, 2002.

MacManus, Sheila. *The Line Which Separates: Race, Gender, and the Making of the Alberta-Montana Borderlands.* Lincoln: University of Nebraska Press, 2005.

Manning, Patrick. *The African Diaspora: A History through Culture.* New York: Columbia University Press, 2010.

McClintock, Anne. *Imperial Leather: Race, Gender, and Sexuality in the Colonial Contest.* New York: Routledge, 1995.

Morrison, Toni. *Playing in the Dark: Whiteness and the Literary Imagination.* Cambridge: Harvard University Press, 1992.

Okepwho, Isidore, et al., eds. *The African Diaspora.* Bloomington: Indiana University Press, 2001.

Paquette, Robert L., and Mark M. Smith. *The Oxford Handbook of Slavery in the Americas.* New York: Oxford University Press, 2010.

Razack, Sherene H. *Dark Threats and White Knights: The Somalia Affair, Peacekeeping and the New Imperialism.* Toronto: University of Toronto Press, 2004.

Rice, Alan J. *Radical Narratives of the Black Atlantic.* London: Continuum, 2003.

Rivard, Ron, and Catherine Littlejohn. *History of the Metis of Willow Bunch.* Saskatchewan: n.p., 2003.

Samek, Hana. *The Blackfoot Confederacy, 1880–1920: A Comparative Study of Canadian and U.S. Indian Policy.* Albuquerque: University of New Mexico Press, 1987.

Sen, Amartya. *Identity and Violence: The Illusion of Destiny.* New York: Norton, 2006.

Smallwood, Stephanie. *Saltwater Slavery: A Middle Passage from Africa to American Diaspora.* Cambridge: Harvard University Press, 2008.

Stoler, Ann Laura. *Carnal Knowledge and Imperial Power: Race and the Intimate in Colonial Rule.* Berkeley: University of California Press, 2002.

———. *Race and the Education of Desire: Foucault's History of Sexuality and the Colonial Order of Things.* Durham: Duke University Press, 1995.

Weglyn, Michi Nishiura. *Years of Infamy: The Untold Story of America's Concentration Camps.* Seattle: University of Washington Press, 1996.

Whiteley, Sheila, and Jennifer Rycenga. *Queering the Popular Pitch.* New York: Routledge, 2006.

Young, Iris. *Justice and the Politics of Difference.* Princeton: Princeton University Press, 1990.

Young, Robert J. C. *Colonial Desire: Hybridity in Theory, Culture and Race.* New York: Routledge, 1995.

Žižek, Slavoj. *Welcome to the Desert of the Real: Five Essays on September 11 and Related Dates.* New York: Verso, 2002.

Contributors

Houston A. Baker Jr. was born in Louisville, Kentucky. He received his BA from Howard University, and his MA and PhD from the University of California at Los Angeles. He has taught at Yale, the University of Virginia, the University of Pennsylvania, and Duke. He is currently Distinguished University Professor and Professor of English at Vanderbilt University. His awards and honors include: Guggenheim and National Endowment for the Humanities fellowships, resident fellowships at the Center for Advanced Study in the Behavioral Sciences and the National Humanities Center, and honorary degrees from a number of U.S. colleges and universities. He has served as president of the Modern Language Association of America and is the author of articles, books, and essays devoted to African American literary criticism and theory. His book *Betrayal: How Black Intellectuals Have Abandoned the Ideals of the Civil Rights Era* received an American Book Award in 2009.

Philip D. Beidler is a professor of English at the University of Alabama, where he has taught American literature since receiving his PhD from the University of Virginia in 1974. His teaching interests include postcolonialism, multicultural studies, and the history of the early modern Atlantic world. He is the author of eight books, the editor of eight, and a contributor of more than fifty articles to magazines and journals. His most recent books are *Late Thoughts on an Old War: The Legacy of Vietnam*, a personal and cultural memoir of his service as an armored cavalry officer in the Vietnam War; *American Wars, American Peace: Notes from a Son of the Empire*, a collection of essays on post-9/11 American military and political culture; and *The Victory Album: Reflections on the Good Life after the Good War*, a personal and social history of growing up in post–World War II America.

Walter Bosse holds a BA in English from Xavier University, an MA in English from the University of South Carolina, and is currently a PhD candidate in the Department of English and Comparative Literature at the University of Cincinnati. He is completing his doctoral dissertation, which examines crosscurrents of aesthetic and political influence between early-twentieth century American "high modernists" and their black contemporaries.

Regina N. Bradley is a doctoral candidate in African American literature at Florida State University. Her current research is a redressing of race consciousness and agency in late-twentieth and twenty-first century African American literature and popular culture using Antonio Gramsci's organic intellectualism theory.

Ashon T. Crawley is a doctoral candidate in English at Duke University, and his research focuses on the performance of race, gender, sexuality, and religions. His dissertation project, tentatively titled "Historicity and Black Studies: The Aesthetics of Pentecost," is about the theological-ethical force of blackness, given in the historicity of practices such as the Ring Shout (dancing flesh), Testimony Service (enunciating voice, and Whooping (eclipsing breath).

Matthew Dischinger is a doctoral candidate in the English Department at Louisiana State University. He earned his MA in English literature from the University of Alabama in 2010. He studies American and postcolonial literatures, and his current projects consider the American South through both postcolonial and post-southern lenses.

Melanie Fritsch is a doctoral candidate in American studies at the University of Tübingen, Germany. She earned a master's degree in American Studies and History at Tübingen and spent many academic years at Vanderbilt and Yale. Her dissertation focuses on the radical abolitionist John Brown in African American memory. Her teaching and research interests include African American literature and culture, life writing, and cultural iconicity.

Jonathan Glover earned his PhD in English literature from the University of Florida in 2011. His research foci include postcolonial literature and theory, literature of the Americas and Caribbean, and rhetoric and composition. He is an assistant professor of English at Indian River State College in Vero Beach/Ft. Pierce, Florida, where he teaches courses in composition and American literature.

Queen Quet Marquetta L. Goodwine is a published author, computer scientist, lecturer, mathematician, historian, columnist, preservationist, film consultant, and "The Art-ivist." She is the founder of the premiere advocacy organization for the continuation of Gullah/Geechee culture, the Gullah/Geechee Sea Island Coalition. Queen Quet has not only provided "histo-musical presentations" throughout the world, but was also the first Gullah/Geechee person to speak on behalf of her people before the United Nations in Genevé, Switzerland. Queen Quet was one of the first of seven inductees to the Gullah/Geechee Nation Hall of Fame. She received the Anointed Spirit Award for her leadership and for being a visionary. In 2008 she was recorded at UNESCO Headquarters in Paris, France, at a United Nations Conference in order to have the human rights story of the Gullah/Geechee people archived for the United Nations. Queen Quet is a directorate member for the International Human Rights Association for American Minorities (IHRAAM) and for the International Commission on Human Rights.

Delia Hagen is a doctoral candidate in history at UC Berkeley, where her primary field of study is North America since 1607. Her academic work focuses on the North American West as both place and process, and she is especially interested in questions of power and social struggle in transnational western, and westering, contexts. Her essay is part of a larger project, "Northern Plains Borders and the People in Between," that analyzes the interaction of mixed, mobile indigenous communities and colonial nation-states on the northern Great Plains from 1860–1940.

Trudier Harris grew up in Tuscaloosa, Alabama. She is the author of numerous books, including *From Mammies to Militants: Domestics in Black American Literature*; *Saints, Sinners, Saviors: Strong Black Women in African American Literature*; and *Fiction and Folklore: The Novels of Toni Morrison*. She is also coeditor of a number of anthologies, including *The Oxford Companion to African American Literature*.

Deborah Katz received her MA and PhD in English from Brown University and her BA from Wellesley College. Her current research focuses on father-daughter narratives and representations of female embodiment in recent fiction by women writers of color. She teaches and writes about Asian American literature, comparative ethnic studies, and feminist theory.

Kathrin Kottemann is a PhD candidate in English at the University of Louisiana at Lafayette. She received her MA in English from the University of New Orleans and her BA in English literature from Loyola University of New Orleans. Her research interests include rhetoric, composition studies, and popular culture.

Abigail G. H. Manzella is a research associate at the National Humanities Center and has taught at Stern College for Women/Yeshiva University. Her current book project "Permanent Transients: Representations of Internal Migration and Community in U.S. Women's Writing" looks at representations of internal migration in novels by twentieth- and twenty-first-century women writers across racial categories.

Yumi Pak is a PhD Candidate in the Department of Literature at the University of California, San Diego. Her dissertation, entitled "Outside Relationality: The Politics of Antiblackness in Twentieth and Twenty-First Century African American Literature," examines four cultural modern phenomena—lynching, imprisonment, expatriation, and the blues—alongside the deformation of African American autobiographical narratives. Her research interests are mediated through the frameworks provided by Afro-pessimism, queer theory, and performance studies.

Cassander L. Smith is an assistant professor of English at the University of Alabama. Her book project, "'Not Black as Negroes': Africa, Black Africans and the English Imagination in Early American Encounters," examines representations of black Africans in early American literature, emphasizing the racial/cultural ideologies that helped shape English encounters with the early Americas and the literature produced about those encounters.

Lauren Vedal received her PhD in English from the University of Wisconsin–Madison. Her dissertation, "National Whiteness/National Witness: Traumatic Narratives by Minorities in the United States and Canada, 1980–2000," examined the mutually reinforcing relationship between national identity and white racial identity, from the perspective of marginalized writers. Her research interests include contemporary multiethnic American literature and the relationships among trauma, memory, and identity.

Index